GIBBON'S CHRISTIANITY

Gibbon's Christianity

Religion, Reason, and the Fall of Rome

HUGH LIEBERT

The Pennsylvania State University Press
University Park, Pennsylvania

Library of Congress Cataloging-in-Publication Data

Names: Liebert, Hugh, author.
Title: Gibbon's Christianity : religion, reason, and the fall of Rome / Hugh Liebert.
Description: University Park, Pennsylvania : The Pennsylvania State University Press, [2022] | Includes bibliographical references and index.
Summary: "Explores the life and work of historian Edward Gibbon, and his complex relationship with Christianity, through an examination of his correspondence, private journals, early works, and unfinished memoirs"—Provided by publisher.
Identifiers: LCCN 2021054033 | ISBN 9780271092355 (hardback) | ISBN 9780271092362 (paperback)
Subjects: LCSH: Gibbon, Edward, 1737–1794—Religion. | Gibbon, Edward, 1737–1794. History of the decline and fall of the Roman Empire. | Christianity. | Church history—Primitive and early church, ca. 30–600—Historiography. | Rome—History—Empire, 30 B.C.–476 A.D.—Historiography.
Classification: LCC DG206.G5 L54 2022 | DDC 937/.06092—dc23/eng/20220105
LC record available at https://lccn.loc.gov/2021054033

Printed in the United States of America
Published by The Pennsylvania State University Press,
University Park, PA 16802–1003

The Pennsylvania State University Press is a member of the Association of University Presses.

It is the policy of The Pennsylvania State University Press to use acid-free paper. Publications on uncoated stock satisfy the minimum requirements of American National Standard for Information Sciences—Permanence of Paper for Printed Library Material, ANSI Z39.48–1992.

CONTENTS

Contents

ACKNOWLEDGMENTS

Gibbon writes in his *Memoirs* that "few works of merit and importance have been executed either in a garret or a palace." Whatever the merits of this work, I am grateful to the institutions that facilitated its execution. First was the John Marshall International Center for the Study of Statesmanship, located in the University of Richmond's Jepson School of Leadership Studies. It was during a research fellowship in Richmond that I met Peter Kaufman, who suggested the idea of this book and proved an invaluable mentor and friend as I worked on it. Second is West Point's Department of Social Sciences. Under the leadership of Cindy Jebb, Suzanne Nielsen, Scott Silverstone, and Heidi Demarest, "SOSH" has been an ideal setting to think, write, and teach. I am grateful to the Department for a sabbatical that allowed me to complete the manuscript, and for the opportunity to teach a seminar on Gibbon's *Decline and Fall*. The cadets of that seminar, "SS490A: How Great Powers Fall," sharpened my first thoughts on Gibbon. Innumerable students, colleagues, and soldier-scholars have helped those thoughts mature, as have the intrepid auxiliaries of West Point's Jefferson Library, who secured hard-to-find sources in a babel of ancient and modern languages. Before Richmond and West Point there was the University of Chicago, where Ralph Lerner sparked my interest in Gibbon's work and my appreciation for his wit. My friends—especially John Childress, Jim Golby, Aaron Miller, Ben and Jenna Storey, and Aaron Tugendhaft—have patiently entertained my musings about the second century, the eighteenth century, and everything in between. Kathryn Yahner, my editor at Penn State University Press, has improved this work in ways small and large. Finally, I would like to thank my wife, Rana, and our children, Ava, Annabel, and Hugh, for making our home, neither a garret nor a palace, a joyous setting for scholarship and the rest of life.

ABBREVIATIONS

I use the following abbreviations in the notes.

A J. Murray, ed. *The Autobiographies of Edward Gibbon*. London: John Murray, 1896.

DF Edward Gibbon. *The History of the Decline and Fall of the Roman Empire*. Edited by D. J. Womersley. 3 vols. London: Allen Lane, 1994. [1776 (vol. 1), 1781 (vols. 2–3), 1788 (vols. 4–6)]

E Edward Gibbon. *Edward Gibbon, "Essai sur l'étude de la littérature": A Critical Edition*. Edited by R. Mankin and P. Craddock. Oxford: Voltaire Foundation, 2010.

EE Patricia Craddock, ed. *The English Essays of Edward Gibbon*. Oxford: Clarendon, 1972.

J1 Edward Gibbon. *Gibbon's Journal to January 28th, 1763: My Journal I, II, and III and Ephemerides*. Edited by D. M. Low. London: Chatto and Windus, 1929. [August 24, 1761–January 28, 1763]

J2 Edward Gibbon. *Le séjour de Gibbon à Paris*. Edited by G. A. Bonnard. In *Miscellanea Gibboniana*, edited by G. R. de Beer, G. A. Bonnard, and Louis Junod, 85–107. Lausanne: Librairie de l'Université, 1952. [January–May 1763]

J3 Edward Gibbon. *Le Journal de Gibbon à Lausanne*. Edited by G. A. Bonnard. Lausanne: Librairie de l'Université, 1945. [August 17, 1763–April 19, 1764]

J4 Edward Gibbon. *Gibbon's Journey from Geneva to Rome: His Journal from 20 April to 2 October 1764*. Edited by G. A. Bonnard. London: Thomas Nelson and Sons, 1961. [April 20–October 2, 1764]

L J. E. Norton, ed. *The Letters of Edward Gibbon*. 3 vols. London: Cassell and Company, 1956. [December 31, 1750–July 1, 1794]

Lettre Edward Gibbon. *La lettre de Gibbon sur le gouvernement de Berne*. Edited by Louis Junod. In *Miscellanea Gibboniana*, edited by G. R. de Beer, G. A. Bonnard, and Louis Junod, 109–41. Lausanne: Librairie de l'Université, 1952 [1755].

MW 1796 Edward Gibbon. *Miscellaneous Works*. Edited by Lord Sheffield. 2 vols. London: A. Strahan, T. Caddell Jun., and W. Davies, 1796.

MW 1814 Edward Gibbon. *Miscellaneous Works*. Edited by Lord Sheffield. 5 vols. London: John Murray, 1814.

Vindication Edward Gibbon. *A Vindication of Some Passages in the Fifteenth and Sixteenth Chapters of the "History of the Decline and Fall of the Roman Empire."* In *EE*, 231–313.

Voyage Edward Gibbon. *Journal de mon voyage dans quelques endroits de la Suisse*. Edited by G. R. de Beer and G. A. Bonnard. In *Miscellanea Gibboniana*, edited by G. R. de Beer, G. A. Bonnard, and Louis Junod, 5–84. Lausanne: Librairie de l'Université, 1952. [September 21, 1755–October 20, 1755]

Introduction

There has never been much doubt about the Christian faith of Edward Gibbon. As soon as the first volume of his *History of the Decline and Fall of the Roman Empire* appeared in 1776, reviewers cast Gibbon among "our modern infidels."[1] "The whole bent of his soul appears to be set against Christianity," wrote Smyth Loftus, an Irish vicar. "He sees nothing in it, but with that jaundiced eye which turns everything to its own blackness and horror."[2] Reaction to the *Decline and Fall*'s second and third volumes, published in 1781, and the concluding volumes of 1788 was perhaps more muted, but the key had not changed.[3] By the time of his death in 1794 Gibbon's reputation as "the infidel historian" seemed secure.[4]

Where Gibbon, so understood, fit among the writers of his own time seemed similarly unproblematic to his early critics. Richard Watson, then the chair of divinity at Cambridge, placed Gibbon among a "set of men . . . who having picked up in their travels, or the writings of the deists, a few flimsy objections, infect with their ignorant and irreverent ridicule, the ingenuous minds of the rising generations."[5] Both sources of these "flimsy objections" were suggestive. Gibbon had indeed traveled widely on the Continent and at one point thought more in French than in English; like Bolingbroke and David Hume (with whom he was often linked), Gibbon could be thought to have contracted a peculiarly continental strain of infidelity.[6] But he fit also among the more homegrown "deists," men like Thomas Morgan and Matthew

Tindal, who had attempted in the early part of the eighteenth century to strip Christianity of its mysteries—revelation and miracles among them—in order to expose the "natural religion" at its core.

The continental and English milieux Watson selected for Gibbon shared a psychology of religious belief rooted in fear and ignorance and a narrative of Christianity's worldly success rooted in priestly manipulation of the same. Gibbon's first critics also placed the historian in a context that reached back to the epochs described in his history. Watson considered "the Gnostics of modern times" to be "miserable copiers of their brethren of antiquity."[7] Henry Edwards Davis followed suit: "The same set of men have been alone distinguished by different names and appellations, from Porphyry, Celsus, or Julian, in the first ages of Christianity; down to Voltaire, Hume, or Gibbon in the present."[8] For all of their apparent variety, the infidels hailed from a coherent tradition. So did the defenders of the faith, in their own judgment. As the Oxford-trained cleric James Chelsum wrote in 1776, "Repeated attacks require repeated answers."[9]

What was novel in the "infidel historian" was not the infidelity but the history. The seventeenth-century forerunners of deism had suggested how sacred history might be rendered secular. Thomas Hobbes, for instance, had claimed that all religion had a "natural seed," and he had hinted that critique of pagan religion (which could be safely dissected) might apply to Christianity (which could not be).[10] Baruch Spinoza asserted more boldly that the Bible attributed actions to God not because nature had ceased to follow its course but in order to encourage devotion among the ignorant: "If Scripture related the destruction of an empire in the way political historians do, it would not appeal to the common people; but it is very appealing to them when everything is narrated poetically and all things are ascribed to God, as the Bible normally does."[11] Gibbon, however, did not attack biblical accounts of God's actions in history directly. Picking up where Acts of the Apostles left off, Gibbon insinuated that Christianity's spread, the rapidity and extent of which had long been taken to suggest supernatural intervention, could be attributed to natural causes. This was something less than a refutation of revelation. But it offered readers inclined toward skepticism an imaginative space—a narrative of their past and a conception of their present—rather different from the one offered by Christian churches.

The belief that this was no small matter united Gibbon's first readers. Gibbon intended to eradicate Christianity "out of the minds of men," they wrote. He aspired to see "the cross trampled upon, Christianity everywhere proscribed, and the religion of nature once more become the religion of Europe."[12] Much like his hero Julian, the author of the *Decline and Fall* intended "to destroy Christianity entirely."[13]

That Gibbon's early critics were right to view his personal faith as some variety of heresy—Arianism, deism, skepticism, perhaps even atheism—cannot be doubted.[14] That Voltaire and the English deists constitute the right context for Gibbon's treatment of Christianity in the *Decline and Fall* is less certain.[15]

When Gibbon wrote, personal skepticism had long been consistent with a view of Christianity considerably more nuanced than Gibbon's critics granted him. Machiavelli, whom Gibbon studied as a young man and whose work he revisited throughout his life, lamented the "weakness into which the present religion has led the world," while holding that "only [ecclesiastical principalities] are secure and happy" and adapting techniques from the Church to strengthen this-worldly states.[16] Montesquieu seemed to many of his own first critics either a Spinozist or a deist; he could write that since Julian "there has been no prince more worthy of governing men," while at the same time praising Christianity for softening mores and grounding religion not only in human fear but in hope, admiration, and love.[17] Rousseau mimicked Machiavelli's condemnation of Christian weakness—"True Christians are made to be slaves; they know it and are hardly moved by it; this brief life has too little value in their eyes"—while championing the "religion of humanity" and, especially in the *Emile*, rivaling Pascal as an analyst of religious sentiment.[18] The list could be extended, but the point is clear. Personal skepticism, to the extent we can safely assign such a view to these authors, did not require that one adopt a reductive view of the phenomenon of religion. In the eighteenth century, as before and since, one could approach Christianity from the outside without reducing it to the strictures of Epicurus and Hobbes.

For all of Gibbon's skepticism regarding the central doctrines of Christianity, he was an astute psychologist of religion. Like Machiavelli, Montesquieu, and Rousseau, he had a keen desire to understand Christianity's historical role as the conqueror of ancient paganism and the midwife of modernity.[19] Gibbon was concerned not merely to oppose Christianity but to confront it as a philosophical and historical problem.

My intent in this work is to tally the results and conditions of that confrontation. The primary result was an account of Christianity more sophisticated and sympathetic than is normally understood. Gibbon adapted explanations of the Roman Republic's rise to a new spiritual republic. Christianity's priests took the role of Rome's legions; Roman polytheism, weakened by skepticism resembling that of Voltaire and the deists, played the part of the decadent empires that enabled Rome's rapid expansion. Gibbon's account of Christianity's rise was secular and skeptical, to be sure, but it was not at bottom contemptuous. The conditions for Gibbon's confrontation with Christianity were, by the same token, more complex than is commonly thought. The pieties of Gibbon's childhood home, his conversion to Catholicism at sixteen, and his Tour of the Continent as a young man left Gibbon with something richer than the longing for revenge on Christianity that Richard Porson and other readers attributed to him.[20] What remained of these encounters was an author attentive, even in the narration of his own life, to the psychological phenomena that Christianity highlighted and deepened. We shall see, in short, that what is most compelling and least dismissive in Gibbon's treatment of religion appears when we approach the *Decline and Fall* from the historical context surrounding the conception of that great work.

The relevant context of a historian as widely and deeply read as Gibbon can be difficult to delimit, however. By the time Gibbon had completed the *Decline and Fall*, his personal library included some "six or seven thousand volumes."[21] These works stretched from remote antiquity to the latest polemics. In 1776 and again in 1789 Gibbon pestered booksellers for pamphlets just off the presses.[22] While working on the *Decline and Fall*, we find him writing his stepmother with an urgent request for his Strabo: "It is Greek, but don't be frightened."[23] Gibbon's reading extended geographically as well as chronologically, and it included works acquired during his years on the Continent and in England. If it is correct to consider a writer's library the image of his mind and his intellectual desire, Gibbon's seems to suggest an omniscience that evades efforts to confine it to any finite set of influences.[24] The nature of the intellectual desire that produced such a collection is suggested by Gibbon's description of a return to his study: "My Seraglio was ample, my choice was free, my appetite was keen."[25]

How could one hope to contextualize a mind as promiscuous as Gibbon's? Even in making the attempt, there is considerable risk of imposing one's own preferences and thereby foreclosing an opportunity to learn something new or unanticipated. One might try to mitigate the risk by replicating the author's experience: reading what he read; knowing what he knew; thinking, as much as one can, what he thought. A reader inhabiting Gibbon's mind in this way would close his eyes in his present and reopen them on May 8, 1737. Growing old alongside Gibbon, dipping in and out of the same intellectual currents, this reader attempts to chart the ocean into which Gibbon launched the *Decline and Fall.*

Even so ambitious an agenda as this, however, risks diminishing the work and the author under consideration. As the relevant context expands, the work being interpreted—the profundity and originality of which recommended the interpretive effort in the first place—can become harder to discern. Taken to the extreme, the attempt simply to replicate a writer's intellectual world resembles the pathology of Borges's Funes, who remembered all exactly as it was and found himself surrounded by an endless array of equally vivid data, not a human world always-already structured by desire, sorted into salient and nonsalient, worth remembering and properly forgotten. Far better to take an author as the best-informed (though interested, to be sure) guide to the world surrounding his work.[26]

In attempting to contextualize Gibbon without losing sight of his work's greatness and the influences Gibbon himself considered most significant, scholars are both blessed and cursed. They have an extraordinary wealth of materials from Gibbon's own hand, ancillary to the *Decline and Fall.* A rich correspondence includes Gibbon's candid exchanges with the luminaries of his age; private journals trace his path from captaincy in the Hampshire Grenadiers to epiphany on his Grand Tour to Rome; and his *Memoirs,* repeatedly drafted but never completed, amount to variations on the theme of the historian's genesis and success. All of these sources afford intimate access to Gibbon's context as he experienced it, and all will feature prominently in this study.

Readers of these seemingly candid writings must nevertheless account for Gibbon's notorious irony. Like Socrates, Gibbon was known not always to say just what he meant—that is, he presented his meaning in ways that were (and are) rather different from those one uses with confidantes.[27] Gibbon's reader had to earn his confidence. And this was particularly so on the topic that most concerned Gibbon's clerical critics, his more skeptical friends, and the readers of *Gibbon's Christianity*. Gibbon is commonly thought to have related the rise of Christianity with a "sneer" and to have blamed it, without ever quite saying so, for the decline and fall of a civilization he admired.[28] But not saying so means something different for a master of irony and indirection than it does for a more forthcoming author.

Although we cannot simply assume Gibbon dropped his mask in his diaries, letters to friends, or the drafts of the *Memoirs* he intended for posthumous publication, we can nevertheless use his speech in these discordant contexts as foils for the perhaps more guarded, because more immediately public, pronouncements in the *Decline and Fall.*

This book is divided into two parts. I begin, in the first two chapters, by considering Gibbon's context as he conceived of his great work. In the concluding three chapters I turn to Gibbon's texts.

Famously, Gibbon traced his conception of his *Decline and Fall* to a single moment in time: the evening of October 15, 1764, as he sat "musing amidst the ruins of the Capitol."[29] A historian as attuned as Gibbon was to *les plus longues durées* and the most profound "general causes" might be expected to look skeptically on the very notion of a momentary transformation.[30] Yet Gibbon chose to narrate his great work's genesis as a conversion experience. What was the significance of that choice? This book's first chapter addresses this question by tracing the trajectory of two literary genres—the travelogue and the religious autobiography—that informed Gibbon's account of his epiphany. Early literary portrayals of the Grand Tour as a confessionally charged capstone, most notably in Richard Lassels's *An Italian Voyage* of 1670, developed into more polite accounts of aesthetic formation exemplified by Addison's *Remarks on Several Parts of Italy* of 1705. By Gibbon's time, several innovative and irreverent tracts had engaged and recast that tradition. Gibbon's conversion story contributed to the history of the travelogue—and to the history of religious autobiography. The development of that genre stretched from Paul's conversion in the Acts of the Apostles, through Augustine's conversion in the *Confessions,* to John Wesley's account of his encounter with Paul (via Luther) at Aldersgate. By framing his great work's conception as a sudden transformation, we shall see, Gibbon evoked these antecedents and broke with the autobiographers he in other respects considered his "masters," Jacques-Auguste de Thou and David Hume, both of whom narrated lives unmarked by conversion.[31] In making this break, Gibbon demonstrated how one might embed conversion in a secular history without denying or dismissing the significance of the phenomenon.

Having considered Gibbon's conversion against the backdrop of some broad trends in eighteenth-century England, I turn in the second chapter to consider how Gibbon fit this experience within his own personal history. Gibbon's correspondence, journals, and *Memoirs* will allow us to set three scenes along the road to Rome: the England of Gibbon's youth; Lausanne, Switzerland, where Gibbon studied as a young man; and, finally, the Continent he encountered during his own Grand Tour. In the *Memoirs*, Gibbon presented himself as the unwitting heir to a long line of enlightening conservatives—unwitting, owing to the disruptive influence of his grandfather, a notable captain of commerce who directed the South Sea Company during the bubble. On Gibbon's telling, his grandfather allowed convention rather than family tradition to form his own son (Gibbon's father), who in turn abandoned Gibbon himself to one ill-considered tutor after another before hastily and prematurely depositing him at Oxford. Gibbon's subsequent conversion to Catholicism—the first of several conversions—amounted to a rejection of both his family and English society.[32] His father sent the young apostate to Lausanne, where Gibbon encountered a moderate strain of Enlightenment under the guidance of the minister and tutor Daniel Pavillard, returned to the faith of his father, and discovered the scholarly calling that led to his first book, *Essai sur l'étude de la littérature*. After several years in England, Gibbon disembarked for his Grand Tour of the Continent. We shall follow him through Paris, back to Lausanne, and finally to Rome. Religious influences in each of these contexts, we shall see, shaped a historian concerned to understand the central phenomena of Christian religious experience and, when possible, reappropriate them. One such reappropriation was his conversion on October 15, 1764.

Gibbon's public encounter with Christianity began in his first book, the *Essai sur l'étude de la littérature*. In this work Gibbon defended classical erudition against the attacks of the *philosophes* and proposed "philosophical history" as a science more deserving to rule than the natural philosophy favored by the Encyclopedists. In chapter 3, we shall examine the two drafts of the *Essai* that have come down to us (one from 1759, the other published in 1761) to understand how Gibbon's changing religious commitments during that time influenced his conception of history. We shall also consider two ideas that appear for the first time in the *Essai* before maturing into central themes in the *Decline and Fall*. The first is a cyclical theory of political development that Gibbon discovered in ancient authors and made his own: poor, pure peoples acquire empire by conquering rich, corrupt peoples; in doing so, the poor and pure grow rich and corrupt, until they are themselves conquered by the pure and poor. The second is a theory of religion: gods are initially personifications of nature rather than deified human beings, and worship of them reflects not only man's primal fear of the surrounding world but man's "gratitude and admiration" for it. Both theories informed Gibbon's mature approach to Roman politics and the rise of Christianity in the *Decline and Fall.*

The first of that work's eventual six volumes appeared in February 1776 and quickly became notorious for explaining the rise of Christianity with reference to "secondary" or secular causes.[33] But just as remarkable as this explanation was its placement at the very end of the first volume. Gibbon narrates the decline of Rome over a period of three centuries while barely mentioning the Christians, suggesting that the Empire was declining and indeed was primed for its fall long before Christianity made any measurable impact on its trajectory.[34] To explain the rise of Christianity, we shall see in chapter 4, Gibbon takes his readers on tour to Persia and Germany, where they study how professional priests influence the relationship between religion and politics.[35] The priests of Persia, Germany, and the nascent Christian church, Gibbon contends, stood to Rome's priest-magistrates as disciplined Roman soldiers stood to undisciplined barbarian hordes. Gibbon thus adapts the ancients' cyclical theory of political development to account for a religious transformation. In doing so, he challenges both Christian historians' claims to detect the hand of God in Christianity's rapid spread and enlightened atheists' contempt for the early church. With a peculiar blend of earnestness and irony Gibbon christens the Church a "Christian republic."[36]

In the final chapter I turn to the "General Observations on the Fall of the Roman Empire in the West," a short text that Gibbon drafted before starting to write the *Decline and Fall,* then chose to update and insert between the latter work's two halves. Here Gibbon considers what lessons his own age might learn from the history of Rome's decline. He draws a surprising conclusion: The division of Europe into independent states sharing religion, language, and manners allows modernity to escape the ancient cycle of empire.[37] Christianity contributed to this condition, "productive of the most beneficial consequence to the liberty of mankind," by enabling a form of union that transcended and tolerated political divisions.[38] In the "General Observations," as in the *Essai* and the first volume of the *Decline and Fall,* we shall recognize a historian shaped by the contexts surveyed in the opening chapters, one more eager to comprehend than to sneer at or dismiss Christianity's worldly power.

About all of these themes there is more to be said than I am able to say here. Although I draw on the entirety of the *Decline and Fall,* my close attention will be limited to the first volume that appeared in 1776 and some small sections of the second and third volumes that appeared in 1781. About the religious history of the eighteenth century the account here can hardly escape superficiality. Thankfully, other scholars have charted these vast terrains, allowing me to draw on their discoveries freely and gratefully. My goal here is merely to mark out a line of approach to Gibbon's great work by reconsidering some elements of his historical context as he conceived the project and executed its early stages. If this facilitates our learning from Gibbon about Christianity and its influence on the development of the modern world, my work will have accomplished its goal.

CHAPTER 1

Religious Controversies and Conversions in the Time of Gibbon

"It was at Rome, on the 15th of October 1764, as I sat musing amidst the ruins of the Capitol, while the bare-footed fryars were singing vespers in the temple of Jupiter, that the idea of writing the decline and fall of the city first started to my mind."[1] In the space of a sentence Gibbon evokes descent and decrepitude—ruins, vespers, the decline and fall of the city—and places in that welter and waste a sudden revelation.[2] The ancient world as readers of Gibbon's vast volumes have come to know it comes suddenly into being, along with Gibbon himself as the author of that world. Where once stood a young scholar and English heir on tour there is now "the historian of the decline and fall."[3]

It was not in fact as straightforward as this famous account suggests. Nearly a decade and several other literary projects would pass between 1764 and the moment when Gibbon wrote the *Decline and Fall*'s first words: "In the second century of the Christian Aera. . . ."[4] The epiphany may even be an invention of the memoirist, as we have no direct testimony to it before that time.[5] All the more remarkable, then, that Gibbon casts the genesis of the work as he does. He adopts, and turns to his own purposes, the structure of a conversion story.[6]

The conversion story typically turned on a point in time that divided the speaker's present from a quite different past.[7] It was, first and foremost, a religious phenomenon; the suddenness and severity of the transformation testified to the involvement of higher powers. Gibbon's contemporaries witnessed many such conversions as John Wesley and George Whitefield's

Evangelical awakening spread across the Atlantic world.[8] Although Gibbon's own life included a youthful conversion to Catholicism, as we shall see, he took little overt notice of Methodism, Pietism, or a variety of other pieties reborn in his own times. His conversion at Rome was not a religious conversion of this sort. Neither the Christian God nor Jupiter sowed the seed of the *Decline and Fall*.[9] Gibbon's conversion was, however, concerned with religion. It was the palimpsest ritual of friars praising a new god where an old god once presided, not the ruins of the Capitol alone, that struck him.[10] Gibbon traced the genesis of his great work to a vision of the world's turn from one religion to another.

As Gibbon's account of his transformation into the author of the *Decline and Fall* had something to do with the narratives of religious conversion surrounding him, so the setting of that scene on foreign soil invoked another genre familiar to readers of the mid- and late eighteenth century: the traveler's account of his Grand Tour. Since at least the seventeenth century through Gibbon's time, English travelers had returned from a year or so on the Continent to publish accounts of their adventures abroad. Often they commended the trip; occasionally they warned against it. Both the recommendations and the warnings touched on the religious significance of sending impressionable young Protestants out among the Papists. Conversions in Rome were exactly what the Tour's critics most feared.

Attending to the development of autobiography and the travelogue in the century or so preceding Gibbon's maturity will allow us to shed some new light on how the pieties of the time influenced Gibbon's work. We shall see that while the religious history of England during the mid- and late eighteenth century suggested a certain settledness, if not stagnation, this broad state of affairs hardly foreclosed novel adaptations of traditional literary forms. Indeed, if anything, there was in Gibbon's day a greater self-consciousness of the tradition and the author's place in it, evident in the most original of these literary works, from Hume's "My Own Life" to Sterne's *Sentimental Journey*. We shall see in later chapters that Gibbon's *Memoirs* and the *Decline and Fall* itself belong in that company. Like Tacitus under the Antonines, Gibbon could turn literary forms encrusted with tradition—like the conversion story—into instruments for his own purposes.

Let us now leave Gibbon (mostly) behind while we travel, first, into the religious history of his time and, second, across the terrain of eighteenth-century autobiography and travel-writing.

CATHOLICISM, DISSENT, AND DEISM

During the years of Gibbon's maturity the religious and political scene in England seemed settled and serene, at least to anyone who remembered the seventeenth century's great tumults or anticipated the revolutionary violence that would soon convulse the Continent.[11] The Church of England was firmly established. Recent analyses of surveys from the 1760s suggest that about 94 percent of Englishmen belonged to the Church of England. Only 5 percent subscribed to nonconforming sects; even fewer professed Catholicism.[12] There remained controversies and challenges, to be sure, but succession crises, uprisings of the unreformed, and attempts to establish rule by the saints there were not.

To set the broad stage onto which Gibbon stepped, it will be helpful to consider how England's mid-eighteenth-century religious establishment had silenced, or at least subdued, three sets of challengers in particular: Catholics, dissenting Protestants, and Deists.

By the middle years of the eighteenth century, Catholics offered the most historically resonant and practically impotent threat to the Church of England. In the popular imagination, at least, the sixteenth century seemed not so far off. Henry VIII's leaving the universal church; Bloody Mary's burning of Protestants in Smithfield and Lewes; Elizabeth's restoring Protestant exiles and Pope Pius VI's absolving English Catholics of allegiance to her—all of these events were preserved in the histories and apologetics read by schoolchildren, among them Foxe's venerable *Book of Martyrs* first published in 1563 and still widely read throughout the eighteenth century.[13] These distant memories had been refreshed in the late seventeenth century's succession and subsequent overthrow of the crypto-Catholic James I, and by the uprisings of his family's diehard supporters in 1715 and 1745.[14] Starting in Scotland, the Jacobite uprisings had reached as far as Preston and then Derby in the north of England. But there they stopped, and with them any serious prospect of a Catholic Restoration. On the first day of 1766 James's son, the "Old Pretender," died and was soon laid to rest in St. Peter's; the pope signaled his acceptance of the Hanoverians. Though French strategists would continue to cast the Young Pretender in Irish and Scottish plots, their designs were increasingly fanciful.[15] Any Catholic hopes that had survived the 1745 uprising had disappeared by the 1760s.

It took considerably longer for English Catholics to enjoy the privileges of Protestants, however. Since the Test Acts of the 1670s and the Popery Act of 1698, Catholics had been barred from civil and military offices, including membership in Parliament, by an oath that "there is not any transubstantiation in the sacrament of the Lord's Supper." Still in the mid-eighteenth century, English Catholics were formally barred from entering Oxford and Cambridge, practicing law, inheriting property, and openly practicing their faith; priests saying Mass and schoolmasters instructing Catholic schoolchildren in their religion could be imprisoned for life.[16] Although enforcement of these laws was sporadic, it was sufficiently common to inspire Catholic noblemen to organize a relief effort and win passage of the 1778 Papists Act, a modest relaxation of these strictures on condition of Catholics' foreswearing the pope's temporal power in England, among other items. The bill's passage touched off a mass campaign for its repeal and ultimately, in June 1780, a week of rioting in which nearly a thousand Londoners were killed. Although more substantial relief would follow in 1791, full emancipation would occur only in the next century—long after Catholics had posed any serious threat to the religious establishment that reigned securely in the middle of the eighteenth.

If eighteenth-century English Catholics had been largely excluded from English public life, members of dissenting Protestant sects, heirs to the Independents and Presbyterians who ruled the Commonwealth in the 1640s, had largely reconciled themselves to coexistence with an established church committed to toleration rather than persecution. The new policy had been set shortly after the ascension of William and Mary. The Toleration Act of 1689 allowed Congregationalists, Baptists, and other dissenting Protestants to worship privately, while still forbidding them from serving in local office or studying at Oxford or Cambridge. These strictures proved less severe in practice than they read on the page, however. A dissenter could attend an Anglican service at Christmas, attend Congregationalist services for the remainder of the year, and still serve in Parliament. The Tory parliaments under Queen Anne attempted to reinforce the letter of the law in 1711 and again three years later, but the effect was short-lived. With the ascension of George I in 1714 and the ensuing Whig dominance of national politics, toleration of dissenting Protestants was assured as a matter of law and even more so as a matter of practice.

The political shift toward toleration of Protestant dissenters reflected a profound change in religious and intellectual culture during the early eighteenth century. Writers, both pious and skeptical, began around this time to promote "politeness"—a moderate and sociable sensibility set in opposition to "enthusiasm."[17] This term had been defined and disparaged as far back as 1656, when, with the Puritans of the Commonwealth in view, Henry More traced the "misconceit of being inspired" to excessive melancholy, a condition that could be cured through temperance, humility, and reason.[18] Locke's *Essay Concerning Human Understanding* of 1689 followed More's definition and proposed a more thoroughgoing cure: a view of reason confident within its proper bounds and skeptical toward any claims to know what lay outside those bounds.[19] The case against enthusiasm would subsequently be recast by Locke's student, the third Earl of Shaftesbury, whose influential *Characteristicks of Men, Manners, Opinions, and Times* of 1711 opened with a skeptical yet sympathetic account of religious inspiration, and by David Hume's *Essays*, the first edition of which appeared in 1741 with "Of Superstition and Enthusiasm," and *Natural History of Religion* of 1757. Although leaders in the Church of England found plenty to disagree with in these writings, the works' core argument—direct revelation of God's will to inspired individuals cannot serve as a reliable source of religious authority in the present day—was by that time broadly accepted. Protestants had long held, often in polemics against Catholic sacramentalism and papal authority, that "miracles had now ceased."[20]

Nevertheless, that there had once been miracles was as essential to Protestant as Catholic belief. In some of these superficially orthodox critiques of enthusiasm, churchmen sensed an elision of miracles having ceased and miracles never having occurred. Locke himself had been careful to allow for the divinity of Christ and the reality of miracles in works like the *Reasonableness of Christianity* of 1695 and elsewhere.[21] Many of his students were less pious or prudent. Shaftesbury, for instance, implied that his own ridicule of modern enthusiasts might be extended to their ancient predecessors.[22] Anthony Collins, Locke's disciple and literary executor, urged that "free thinking"—using one's understanding to evaluate "any proposition whatsoever" according to the strength or weakness of the evidence for it—be extended to the miracles used to buttress the authority of bishops and priests and indeed to Christianity's basis in divine revelation.[23] These and many other authors held that God was better known by reason than revelation and was better understood through his creation than by miracles, which they tended to view as the inventions of priests rather than the genuine article.

Such writings were at the center of the "Deist Controversy," a literary storm stirred up by Toland's *Christianity not Mysterious* of 1696 and stretching into the 1740s and beyond.[24] The debate was notable for the boldness of the critics of revelation, but also for the suppleness and spiritedness of their respondents. Among the respondents was the Presbyterian minister John Leland, whose two-volume history of the affair, *A View of the Principal Deistical Writers*, first appeared in 1754. Leland remarked on the unprecedented nature of the "attempt to set aside revealed religion." "Never in any country where Christianity is professed," he wrote, "were there such repeated attempts to subvert the divine authority, carried on sometimes under various disguises, and at other times without any disguise at all." But the theological debates that greeted each deist thrust served to show "that the Christian religion is in no danger from a free and impartial inquiry; and that the most plausible objections which have been brought against it, though raised with great confidence, and frequently repeated, have been fairly and solidly confuted."[25] The importance of free public debate of religious doctrine had been a central tenet linking Shaftesbury, Collins, and others; to see it in the mouth of an antideist suggests the ways in which the deists won even while losing and the degree to which the Anglican clergy had taken on much of the enlightening project for its own, to be carried on in a way compatible with religious establishment.[26] Whatever the long-term impact of this controversy, the judgment of most subsequent observers has echoed that of Leland: Christianity generally, and the Church of England in particular, weathered the storm.[27]

One such observer was Edmund Burke. Looking back on this period after another storm had arisen across the channel, Burke asked, "Who, born within the last forty years, has read one word of Collins, and Toland, and Tindal, and Chubb, and Morgan, and that whole race who called themselves Freethinkers?"[28] In Burke's view, these authors had no impact on the slow and steady development of the British constitution, always "confirmed by the sanctions, of religion and piety."[29] Most Catholics and dissenting Protestants of Burke's day posed little threat to the continuation of this development. But the fact that Burke had to protest even this much against the historical significance of the deists suggests a certain anxiety that they might return from oblivion. "Polemic divines" like the dissenting minister Richard Price, whose address to London's Revolution Society in November 1789 provoked Burke's *Reflections*, seemed at once to evoke the past and the future. Price's sermon differed "only in place and time, but [agreed] perfectly with the spirit and letter of the rapture of 1648."[30] Now, however, a dissenting minister might appear "the arch-pontiff of the *rights of men*, with all the deposing power in its meridian fervor of the twelfth century."[31] Here were the traditional threats to the established Church—Catholicism and dissent—rolled into one by Burke's rhetoric and given fresh purchase by a return of the philosophical abstraction and intellectual libertinism that animated the deists, at least according to their critics. If not by Catholics and Puritans then by radical skeptics, the religiously settled setting of mid-eighteenth-century England might, after all, come undone.[32]

The arc stretching from the seventeenth century's confessional strife to the late eighteenth century's revolutionary turmoil can be traced in the development of two literary genres that, as we shall soon see, influenced Gibbon's own efforts late in life to make sense of his own spiritual formation. The travelogue was not an inherently religious genre, but when it described the Grand Tour—a long trip through the Continent's Catholic countries that was meant to conclude the education of an English gentleman—it touched inevitably on questions of confessional interest and controversy. The eighteenth-century autobiography, similarly, was not restricted to religious narratives, but religion was too central to the life stories of most men and women of the time to escape notice entirely. In autobiographies that featured religious conversions, as did many emerging from the evangelical revivals that began in the 1730s, writers adopted and revised norms of narration that reached back to the Gospels themselves. Attending to developments in travel-writing and autobiography will illuminate some of the pieties surrounding Gibbon.

THE TRAVELOGUE

By the time Gibbon left England for the Continent in 1763, the "Grand Tour" was a well-established rite of passage.[33] This term had entered into English with the publication of Richard Lassels's *An Italian Voyage* in 1670, although the idea of travel for purposes loftier than pleasure or curiosity was much older.[34] Lassels himself pointed out that "the wisest and greatest among the ancient philosophers, Plato, Pythagoras, Anaxagoras, Anacharsis, Apollonius, Architas, and Pittacus . . . were all great travelers."[35] Chaucer's Wife of Bath, who had been thrice to Jerusalem, at least once at Rome, and "koude muchel of wandrynge by the weye," was one of many English figures to set out on religious pilgrimage prior to Thomas Cromwell's restrictions of the

1530s.[36] In the reign of Elizabeth, promising young men were sent abroad "to be trained up and made fit for . . . public employments"—a practice Francis Bacon heartily endorsed.[37] Writers in the seventeenth and eighteenth centuries could draw on all of these arguments—philosophical, religious, and political—to promote travel as a worthy pursuit.

The salience of these reasons varied significantly between the time of Lassels's work and Gibbon's departure for the Continent. For Lassels and his immediate readers, an Englishman's trip toward the heart of Catholicism might be marketed as the capstone of an education in the liberal arts, but it retained some of the pilgrimage's spiritual significance. In Rome young souls might return to Catholicism, learn to tolerate rival sects, or reject papist superstition all the more forcefully for having seen it firsthand. The stakes of the Tour changed, however, as memories of the seventeenth century's sectarianism faded. In the eighteenth century, thanks largely to Addison's *Remarks on Several Parts of Italy* of 1705, the Grand Tour increasingly focused on aesthetic formation rather than faith—without, as we shall see, ever quite leaving the question of religion behind.

Lassels's *Voyage*

As Richard Lassels had more influence than any other author on how Englishmen initially conceived of the Grand Tour, it is worthwhile to consider how he understood the relationship between education and spiritual formation in his *Voyage*. The Tour's educational value came first. If the world is a great book, Lassels wrote, "they that never stir from home, read only one page of this book."[38] In addition to broadening young minds, travel improved character and prepared a nobleman for useful occupations. A few years on the Continent, away from his estates, "weans [a young man] from the dangerous fondness of his mother," exposes him to "wholesome hardship," and corrects his "self-conceit and pride."[39] If he manages to acquire some foreign languages, the young nobleman is all the better suited for "noblest employment" as an ambassador of the king.[40] At the very least the traveler is sure to impress his compatriots. The nobleman on his homecoming is like a "blessing sun," Lassels writes, "for as the sun, who hath been travelling about the world these five thousand and odd years, not only enlightens those places which he visits, but also enricheth them with all sorts of fruits and metals: so, the nobleman by long travelling, having enlightened his understanding with fine notions, comes home like a glorious sun."[41]

This pitch had the air of a high-minded brochure, for Lassels himself was something of a travel agent. The title page of the 1670 *Voyage* identified him as "Richard Lassels, Gent. who Travelled through Italy Five times, as Tutor to several of the English Nobility and Gentry." The position of "tutor"—the *Voyage* would also use the term "governor" for this role (which would later be known as "bear leader")—was crucial to Lassels's conception of the Tour.[42] Selecting a proper governor should be the parents' "greatest care," and one on which they should "spare no cost whatsoever."[43] The governor was to protect his pupil, watching over him as the Archangel Raphael watched over young Toby (says Lassels, citing the Book of Tobit).[44] Most of what goes wrong on Tour stems from a poor choice in governor. Lassels says that he himself has known many governors who were "needy bold gentlemen, whose chief parts, were their own language and some Latin, and whose chief aim was to serve themselves, not their pupils." Governors could serve themselves by accepting kickbacks from subpar foreign academies, for instance. Others have "married their pupils in France, without their parents knowing" or "locked their pupils in a chamber with a wanton woman, and taken the key away with them."[45] Lassels offered these stories to shock parents, and perhaps to entice young noblemen. They also helped to distinguish the sort of travel Lassels meant to endorse—the educational capstone—from travel for pleasure or romance. The governor's charge was not only to oversee the itinerary but to keep the traveler from losing his head or his heart.

Did the governor also watch over his pupil's soul? Perhaps most remarkable in Lassels's depiction of the benefits and dangers of travel for young Englishmen was his treatment of the religious question. In the influential "Preface" to the *Voyage* Lassels mentioned having known governors who have "led their pupil to Geneva, where they got some French language, but lost all their true English allegiance and respect to monarchy"; he also anticipated criticisms of his own work for "[hunting] too much after ceremonies, and Church antiquities."[46] He was silent, however, about the possibility of pupils losing their allegiance to Anglicanism—at least in the preliminaries of his *Voyage*.

The destination of the Tour and the centerpiece of Lassels's travelogue, however, was Rome. And Lassels made clear that it was the Rome of the popes, not of the emperors and consuls, that he intended to display for his reader: "Although Rome were anciently styled the Head, and Mistress of the world;

an Earthly Goddess; the Eternal City; the Compendium of the World; the Common Mother, and Nurse of all Virtues (while she was yet heathen); yet since her ladyship was baptized and became Christian (though she had had great elogies made of her by the Holy Fathers) I find no title so honorable to her as that of *Roma la Santa*, Rome the Holy."[47] Lassels proceeds to list eight reasons that Rome deserves this name, among them that Rome is "the seat of S. Peter and his successors," has been "washed and purged in the blood of so many thousand martyrs in the primitive times," and has conserved the apostolic traditions and creed "inviolably."[48] Here and elsewhere Lassels offers a distinctly Catholic view of Rome and the reasons for its holiness.

It is of the essence of Lassels's *Voyage*, however, that it does not address Catholics alone. In describing the catacombs beneath the Church of St. Sebastian, which "made anciently a Christian Rome under the Heathen," Lassels suggests how travel to Rome might affect members of different sects: "No man enters into the catacombs but he comes better out, than he went in. Catholics come out far more willing to die for that faith, for which so many of their ancestors have died before them. The adversaries of the Roman Church come out more staggered in their faith, and more mild toward the Catholic religion, to see what piety there is even in the bowels of Rome; atheists come out with that belief, that surely there is a God, seeing so many thousands of martyrs testified it with their blood."[49] Lassels wanted the Tour to serve purposes more serious than polishing the manners of sheltered nobles to an ambassadorial sheen. He intended to secure English Catholics in their faith and to win toleration, at least, from their adversaries.[50] Protestants cannot but be more mild after having seen for themselves the piety that persists "even in the bowels" of Rome the Holy.

Lassels himself was a Catholic priest.[51] Born in Yorkshire to a family of recusant gentry, at about the age of twenty Lassels departed for Douai College, the English seminary that had been established during Elizabeth's reign to train priests and frequently to return them covertly to England. There is some evidence that Lassels himself served in the "English mission" at Oxford in the 1620s.[52] By 1629 he had returned to the Continent, where he was ordained three years later. Some of the five trips to Rome mentioned on the title page of his great work were matters of official Church business. The first tour Lassels described in writing was a pilgrimage in the jubilee year of 1650.[53] The Tours he subsequently led for Catholic nobles retained something of that character.[54]

Nevertheless, Lassels's most enduring achievement was to make religious travel appear as something else. A papist pilgrimage became the capstone of a classical education for Catholics and Protestants alike. This act of transubstantiation might seem a late-born refinement in England's century-plus of spiritual warfare, a weapon forged by and for the Catholic side. Or perhaps Lassels's project arose out of the confident ecumenism that followed the Restoration of 1660, even while expressing some of the struggles that would spark the Revolution of 1688.[55] Perhaps Lassels's *Voyage* escaped these contexts altogether and harkened further backward and forward—back to the Renaissance ideal of an elevated and ambivalently Christian classicism, forward to an era of postsectarian politeness. If this last possibility seems best to describe what the Grand Tour had become by the middle of the eighteenth century, this fact might also raise an important question: Did any remnant of Lassels's seventeenth century—a scene of sectarian strife, in which a tour of Rome could not but be freighted with confessional significance—survive into the eighteenth?

Addison's *Remarks*

Lassels's conception of the Grand Tour certainly seemed to undergo a substantial revision. An avowedly Protestant vision of the Tour rose up to challenge Lassels's covertly Catholic one. In 1687 Gilbert Burnet, then in exile in the Netherlands and soon to return to England as William of Orange's chaplain, published a popular epistolary travelogue intended to "lay open the misery of those who lived under an absolute government and a devouring superstition."[56] Four years later came Francis Misson's *Nouveau voyage d'Italie,* which recounted a Tour occasioned by the revocation of the Edict of Nantes. Misson condemned Lassels's *Voyage* for "[abounding] in unexactnesses, puerilities, gross ignorances, and false relations" and for taking advantage of "all occasions to magnify those things that flatter the Roman Religion . . . as there are many Catholics in England who may be dazzled by those places, not knowing the other faults of the book."[57] By the time Joseph Addison's *Remarks on Several Parts of Italy* appeared in 1705, the Tour's Roman culmination could represent a compelling confirmation of a young traveler's Protestantism. "There is not a more miserable People in Europe than the Pope's Subjects," Addison wrote. "His Subjects are wretchedly poor and idle. . . . These ill Effects may arise, in a great measure, out of the Arbitrariness of the Government, but I think they are chiefly to be ascrib'd to the very Genius of the Roman Catholick Religion, which here shews itself in its Perfection."[58] This Rome was no longer Lassels's *Roma la Santa* but a residue that testified to both the glory of antiquity and the prosperity and power of modern Britain.[59]

Addison's Rome remained, however, a city of beauty, a fact that presented challenges for the young Englishman on Tour. Although Addison's traveler was inclined toward antiquity, kicking up clouds of Latin poetry with every step on "classic ground," he had still to adjudicate the quarrel between the ancients and moderns impartially.[60] And this task required some measure of aesthetic openness, at least, toward objects that reflected a theology on which the traveler's mind was to remain closed.[61] Addison modeled the ideal in judging St. Peter's superior to the Parthenon. "After having seen these Two Masterpieces of Modern and Ancient Architecture," he wrote, "I have often consider'd with myself whether the ordinary Figure of the Heathen, or that of the Christian Temples be the most beautiful, and the most capable of Magnificence, and can't forbear thinking the Cross Figure more proper for such spacious Buildings than the Rotund."[62] This judgment does not arise from a merely Christian ecumenism. It is a question instead of how shapes affect "the Eye."[63]

Addison's description of the Holy House of Loreto shows just how close theology and aesthetics can come without intersecting. The riches of the site are "suprizingly great," which seems an appreciation until Addison plots an operation to seize them. "It would indeed be an easie thing for a Christian Prince to surprize it, who has Ships still passing to and fro without Suspicion, especially if he had a Party in the Town, disguis'd like Pilgrims, to secure a Gate for him."[64] Venetian ships guarding the Adriatic are an addressable concern. The horror and resentment that such a raid would elicit from the Catholic princes of Europe are a more daunting challenge—these are in fact "as great a Security to the Place as the strongest Fortification."[65] But they are risks perhaps worth taking. "For I can't but look on those vast Heaps of Wealth, that are amass'd together in so many Religious Places of Italy, as the hidden Reserves and Magazines of the Church, that she would open on any pressing Occasion for her last Defence and Preservation."[66] Just as orders are being drafted, Beauty bursts into Addison's war room:

> The Case of the Holy House is nobly design'd, and executed by the great Masters of Italy, that flourish'd about a hundred Years ago. The

> Statues of the Sibyls are very finely wrought, each of 'em in a different Air and Posture, as are likewise those of the Prophets underneath 'em. The Roof of the Treasury is painted with the same kind of Device. There stands at the upper End of it a large Crucifix very much esteem'd, the Figure of our Saviour represents him in his last Agonies of Death, and amidst all the Ghastliness of the Visage has something in it very amiable.

Ancient and modern are delicately balanced (the sibyls and the prophets are both finely wrought); the author awards a palm to the modern ungrudgingly (the House's case is nobly designed); and the beauty in a work that might offend Protestant sensibilities is admitted (the visage of the crucified Christ is amiable even in its agony). If the Last Judgment requires that a crucifix be desacralized into a sculpture, that an object of appreciation replace an occasion for devotion, aesthetic rapture redeems the distortion. Addison liberates "the Eye" from the soul. Or rather, he traces the path from the eye to a new kind of soul, one that takes pleasure in art and classical learning rather than theological dispute and religious war.

If Addison's aesthetics were meant to dampen the longings that sent young men marching as to war, the passions that he roused in their stead carried their own set of burdens and dangers.[67] It was increasingly insufficient just to go to Rome, to visit this shrine or that ruin—one had also to *feel* a certain way. Addison himself wrestles constantly with his predecessors and the "expectations" that haunt his trip. At the outset he assures the reader that "there are still several of these Topicks that are far from being exhausted, as there are many new Subjects that a Traveler may find to employ himself upon."[68] Where his predecessors go wrong, there is indeed something new for Addison to say. In entering the Cathedral of Naples, for instance, he can record that having heard so much of it, he "was never more deceived in [his] expectation"; Loreto's Holy House "as much surpass'd [his] Expectation as other Sights have generally fallen short of it."[69] In Florence, Addison passes curiosities "which all voyage-writers are full of" to reach "the celebrated Venus of Medicis."[70]

What could be left to say about Venus? For Addison her nudity and outsized company diminish her stature, but he confirms she is "as big as the ordinary size of a woman" by measuring her wrist. It might go without saying—it has been said so many times before—that "the Softness of the

Flesh, the Delicacy of the Shape, Air and Posture, and the Correctness of Design in this Statue are inexpressible." Addison does not make much of an effort to express them. He allows us to glimpse how a set of expectations can simultaneously direct one's gaze and deaden the response. After leaving this ambivalent tryst with Venus—measuring her wrists, expressing her beauty so flaccidly as to call that beauty into question—Addison admits he "saw nothing that has not been observed by several others in the Argenteria, the Tabernacle of St. Laurence's Chapel, and the Chamber of Painters."[71] The regimen of appreciative works Lassels had laid out was in its own way less taxing than the aesthetics emerging in Addison. What was one to do when the rapture of beauty did not come?

This was not an experience Addison had often, thanks to predecessors more ancient than Lassels and Misson. Before beginning his voyage, Addison writes, "I took care to refresh my Memory among the Classic Authors, and to make such Collections out of them as I might afterwards have Occasion for." He proceeds to examine these descriptions "upon the spot, and to compare the natural face of the country with the landscapes that the poets have given us of it"; his *Remarks* translate the relevant passages into English couplets. The geography of Italy—the fact that "heaven, sun, and elements had not varied" (as one of Addison's modern predecessors put it)—was the constant against which one could measure the distance separating ancient and modern and collapse that distance in the work of translation.[72] Addison meant to see Italy as Vergil saw it. He would not parrot Lassels's impressions of the Argenteria, but to repeat and perhaps to rival the Roman bard's *Lago di Garda* was a worthier challenge:

> *Oh could the Muse my ravish'd Breast inspire*
> *With Warmth like yours, and raise an equal Fire,*
> *Unnumber'd Beauties in my Verse shou'd shine,*
> *And Virgil's Italy shou'd yield to mine!*[73]

It was because Vergil was sufficiently old and the human world so changed that the recovery of this constant—Italian landscapes as an object of quasi-pagan poetics—seemed sufficiently new.

And yet after Addison this recovery, too, had been achieved. The literature of travel induced a desire to see and feel for oneself. In direct proportion to that desire came anxiety over its frustration. By the first decades of the eighteenth century, a Tour of the Continent, and Italy in particular, had become the capstone of the classical education of Britain's elite. The reformation of this practice under Burnet, Misson, and Addison made it more widely available because it was less politically and religiously objectionable. But it had raised, too, the bar of expectations in a way rather like the Protestant change to Catholic doctrine on salvation. Works were insufficient. One had not only to travel but to experience and express a certain set of interior transformations.

The Grand Tour After the Seven Years' War

Gibbon's narration of his famous epiphany placed him among a group of writers pioneering paths to Rome quite different from those Addison had left behind. The conclusion of the Seven Years' War in 1763 released a backlog of British Tourists onto the Continent.[74] They made the Tour for much the same reasons that Addison, adapting and recasting Lassels, had recommended. The Tour represented a classical education's culmination: one was to see firsthand all of the ancient scenes that had previously been imagined, and one was to reenact the ancients' refined, polite judgment over men, art, and nature. But because these Tourists were latecomers in a by then firmly established tradition, the most reflective among them could wonder whether they were seeing things for themselves or by the book. What they felt always had something to do with what they were supposed to feel.

Addison, too, had felt the need to say something of Venus, and he wrote obligingly of her inexpressible delicacy. Tobias Smollett, visiting the "celebrated Venus" some sixty years later, could not bring himself to reenact Addison. "I believe I ought to be intirely silent, or at least conceal my real sentiments, which will otherwise appear equally absurd and presumptuous," Smollett wrote. "It must be want of taste that prevents my feeling that enthusiastic admiration with which others are inspired at sight of this statue. . . . I cannot help thinking that there is no beauty in the features of Venus; and that the attitude is awkward and out of character."[75] Smollett's philistinism provoked his portrayal in Laurence Sterne's *Sentimental Journey* as "Smelfungus," a dyspeptic traveler who "had fallen foul upon the goddess, and used her worse than a common strumpet, without the least provocation in nature."[76] But Smollett was in his own way a pioneer. Rather than revel in Addison's staid classicism, he recorded aesthetic impressions with a novelist's candor, logged financial transactions with a miser's precision, and charted his own vital signs (including a nasty "pulmonic disorder") with a physician's scrupulousness—all of which he was.[77] The travelogue that resulted may have been mistaken in particular judgments, but these judgments were unmistakably Smollett's.[78] Here was a new way for British travelers to conceive of the Continent.

Sterne's Yorick, for his part, was concerned to contrast himself to Smollett—and indeed every other travel writer in the tradition. He represented a new type, "altogether of a different cast from any of my fore-runners": the "Sentimental Traveler."[79] Yorick traveled for the sake of self-knowledge, which implied openness to a wider range of experiences than those Addison related. "I pity the man," says Yorick, "who can travel from Dan to Beersheba, and cry, 'Tis all barren;—and so it is: and so is all the world to him who will not cultivate the fruits it offers. I declare, said I, clapping my hands cheerily together, that were I in a desert, I would find out wherewith in it to call forth my affections." To such a traveler every inch of the world offered its fruits. But if the experiences that sparked sentiments and reflection upon them were as likely to occur in a Calais inn as on the steps of the Ara Coeli, why must one travel to Rome? By extending so far what was to be experienced on Tour, one could begin to question the necessity of the Tour itself.

This Sterne did not hesitate to do, and by the time his *Sentimental Journey* appeared in 1768 he had good company. Locke (commonly taken for Sterne's master) had lodged influential objections to the timing of travel. Before sixteen was preferable for languages; after twenty-one, for improving in "wisdom and prudence."[80] Locke's approach echoed in the pages of Addison and Steele's *Spectator*, and it influenced as well the discussion of travel in Rousseau's *Emile*.[81] The tutor Jean-Jacques agreed with *le sage Locke* on the timing and purpose of travel: Emile was to set out at twenty-two to study "government, morals, and public order."[82] Rousseau departed from Locke in stressing the practical question that travel helps one to answer—where ought I to live?—and in his conception of what one ought to do on Tour. Locke would have his young man speak to "the best and most knowing persons"; Rousseau sends him to the countryside to comprehend "the genius and morals of the nation."[83] Cities, Rousseau has his tutor insist, are all alike and all to be avoided, Rome no less than London.[84] In Rousseau's unfinished sequel to the *Emile*, an overlong stay in Paris undoes the tutor's education and destroys Emile's marriage.[85]

As the tradition of the Tour was being established in the seventeenth century, critics had worried that British nobility might convert to Catholicism. Even before Lassels's *Voyage*, James Howell had warned that only the most settled Anglicans should go abroad: "It is very requisite that he who exposeth himself to the hazard of foreign travel should be well grounded and settled in his religion."[86] After the failed Jacobite rebellion in 1745 and Britain's victory over Catholic France in 1763, these sectarian concerns had faded. Critics of the Tour were more likely to worry about moral corruption and atheism than Catholicism per se.[87] These concerns featured prominently in Richard Hurd's 1763 reprisal of Locke's earlier critiques and in Adam Smith's criticisms of the Tour for making young men "more conceited, more unprincipled, more dissipated, and more incapable of serious application either to study or business" than they would otherwise be.[88] Although religious conversion on Tour was rare when Hurd and Smith wrote, and was if anything growing rarer, the moral freedom of the Tour could still scramble confessional commitments. As late as 1785 we find a British envoy's report on one Mr. Fox Lane, "a man of fashion and great fortune having, from an infatuated complaisance to the lady he was in love with, changed his religion, or rather for the first time adopted one, which unluckily for him, is the Roman Catholic."[89]

The surge in British travel to the Continent lasted a generation.[90] This period, from 1763 to about 1792, was, however, the Indian summer of the Tour. The tradition of the Tour and the debates surrounding it had been well established. One could relate to the Tour with a bit of dismissive distance as a convention that even participants were not capable of endorsing or owning completely. Samuel Johnson (who did not go on Tour) struck this tone when he said in 1776 that "a man who has not been in Italy, is always conscious of an inferiority, from his not having seen what it is expected a man should see."[91] He had been preceded by Sterne, and he would be followed by Gibbon. "According to the law of custom and perhaps of reason," Gibbon wrote in his *Memoirs*, "foreign travel completes the education of an English gentleman."[92] The "perhaps" suggested derision but allowed for potential.

When Gibbon set out, Addison's Tour was being reappropriated and reinvented. The Tour was not altogether stale—there were still the dangers of corruption, atheism, or even Catholicism, and there was still the prospect of discovery. It depended in good measure on the gentleman in question whether foreign travel would complete his education or perhaps spark some more profound transformation.

THE CONVERSION STORY

For Christians the fundamental such transformation had long been the moment of conversion. Elements of the convert's experience had preceded Christianity, to be sure. Greek philosophers wrote of the wonder and "turning-around" that commenced the philosopher's education; the authors of the Hebrew Bible recorded the patriarchs' and prophets' visions. Nevertheless, the conversion experience was most proper to Christianity, and its prototype occurred in Paul's epiphany on the road to Damascus: "And suddenly there shined round about him a light from heaven: And he fell to the earth, and heard a voice saying unto him, Saul, Saul, why persecutest thou me."[93] Paul is shortly transformed from a persecutor "breathing out threatenings and slaughter against the disciples of the Lord" into the apostle to the Gentiles. The story originates and justifies Paul's unique calling. Acts has God declare Paul his "chosen instrument" and notes that Paul alone can "see" (*theôrein*) the source of the voice he and his companions hear.[94] The story also deprives Paul of any personal credit for his election. Indeed, the narrative turns on Paul having done everything one can do *not* to deserve forgiveness, *not* to merit a vision of God. The less the desert, the greater the credit to God and the greater, too, the justification of Paul's mission. Acts shows this experience entering immediately into autobiography as Paul recounts his conversion in Jerusalem and again in Caesarea.[95]

Paul's conversion story turned on the immediate experience of God through blinding light and the voice of Jesus. In the tradition of writing about conversion that Paul inaugurated, Paul's texts often augmented or even replaced direct revelation. Most influential was Augustine's recasting of Paul's conversion scene in the *Confessions*.

Augustine, more than any author, is responsible for eliding the conversion story and the ancient *Life* (or biography) to produce Christian autobiography. Pagan *Lives* had traditionally centered on public achievements. The structure of the *Life* reflected this third-person, public perspective, beginning with birth and ending in death, with character mostly fixed and resistant to sudden transformation. What we have of ancient autobiography resembles biography.[96] Augustine maintained the frame of the pagan life but greatly increased its depth by erasing the distinction between private and public actions. Since an omniscient God rather than the eyes of one's fellow citizens served as the source of significance, the author's own memory became more significant than the memory of the text's audience. Christian life-writing was more essentially autobiographical than pagan. Augustus and the Romans had witnessed the events recounted in the *Res Gestae,* but the Christian convert was uniquely suited to narrate his or her own life.[97]

We can appreciate Augustine's innovation by comparing his conversion story to that of Paul. Augustine's, like Paul's, begins when a voice is heard. In Augustine's case, however, the speaker does not identify himself, and Augustine does not understand him to be Jesus. It is a "voice from some neighbor's house, as it had been of a boy or girl."[98] The voice Paul heard sent him into Damascus to confer with Ananias, who himself had received instructions directly from God. Augustine's voice directs him to Paul's epistles: "I snatched [the book] up and in silence I read that chapter which I had first cast mine eyes upon . . . instantly even with the end of this sentence, as if a light of confidence infused my heart, all the darkness of doubting vanished away."[99] Paul had seen a light so bright that he was blinded for three days. In Augustine's conversion, light appears instead as metaphor: As light dispels darkness, so confidence dispels doubt. What was external and supernatural in the original is interior and familiar in the reprise. It is crucial that Augustine no more doubts these experiences to have issued from God than Paul does. In fact, Augustine expands considerably the instruments available to perform the work of conversion.[100] Not only the blinding light and the thundering voice but the light of confidence and the voices of the neighbors' children become providential.

Just as Augustine expands the range of experiences that reflect the will of God in the moment of conversion, so he expands the temporal frame of the conversion story. Paul's story had turned on essentially three moments: he lived one way, God intervened, and then he lived an entirely new life. Augustine's narrative, however, lingers on not only the climactic experience itself but all that leads up to and follows that moment. Expanding the conversion narrative in this way carried some risk. Since the suddenness and starkness of the convert's transformation testified to God's intervention, an autobiography that allowed the narrator and his reader to anticipate the conversion might make it seem a less miraculous event. It would take a bold skeptic, for instance, to read against the grain of Acts to attribute Paul's transformation to prolonged exposure to Christians rather than divine intervention. Augustine's narrative makes it considerably easier to trace conversion to his having "devoutly imbibed that name of [his] Savior . . . along with [his] mother's milk."[101] But for Augustine this too is the work of the Lord. Just as the voice of the neighbor's child could be understood as an instrument of providence, so could every experience in the Christian's life. Augustine's form of autobiography makes God the author of a narrative of a particular sort, derived from Paul's story and yet distinct from it. Augustine's conversion story peaks in a stark transformation that could be understood, in retrospect, to have been foreshadowed. At the center of Paul's self-portrait was a conversion that divided the light from darkness; at the center of Augustine's, conversion divides light from a dim but dappled terrain. The task of Christian autobiography after Augustine involved gathering up the crumbs of light God had strewn along the path to conversion.

It was also owing to Augustine's influence that texts would feature so prominently among these crumbs. Paul's works, as in Augustine's case, were perhaps most prominent. The closest thing we have to a conversion story by Luther's hand—his testimony to the moment he "was altogether born again and had entered paradise itself through open gates"—arose from an encounter with Paul's Letter to the Romans.[102] In Pascal's impressionistic account of a mystical experience on the night of November 23, 1654, we find the single word *feu*—fire—written in the center of the page without further context.[103] Is this meant to memorialize a vision of God that Pascal received, just as Paul had seen a "light from heaven"? Commentators have pointed out that Pascal's *feu* recalls Paul's Letter to the Hebrews: "Our God is a consuming fire."[104]

Augustine's *Confessions* commonly stood in for Paul in conversion narratives. In a letter from 1336, Petrarch describes taking with him on a hike the *Confessions*, a "handy little work very small but of infinite sweetness," to which he applies the same methods of reading that Augustine had applied to Paul. "I opened [the *Confessions*] and started to read at random," Petrarch says, and the results are as remarkable as Augustine's had been.[105] The sixteenth-century mystic Teresa of Ávila records a similar encounter with the *Confessions*: "When I got as far as his conversion and read how he heard that voice in the garden, it seemed exactly as if the Lord were speaking in that way to me, or so my heart felt."[106] In all of these reenactments and variations, a tradition not only of experience but of reflecting on and writing about that experience was taking shape.

By the seventeenth and eighteenth centuries, the tradition of Christian autobiography was well established, even familiar—so much so that it imposed certain burdens on authors writing in the genre. The seventeenth-century

Puritan Richard Baxter, for instance, narrated his life in tropes borrowed from *Confessions*. He told of "robbing an orchard or two with rude boys" and then realizing the gravity of his sin thanks to a copy of *Bunny's Resolution*: "In the reading of this book (when I was about fifteen years of age) it pleased God to awaken my soul."[107] But Baxter went on to doubt that this experience and others lived up to the standards his predecessors had set. "I could not distinctly trace the workings of the Spirit upon my heart in the method which Mr. Bolton, Mr. Hooker, and Mr. Rogers and other divines describe; nor knew the time of my conversion, being wrought on by the forementioned degrees."[108] John Wesley's journals contained a similar account of faith lapsing and surging, particularly in response to devotional texts like Kempis's *Christian Pattern* and William Law's *Christian Perfection* and *Serious Call*. But for Wesley, as opposed to Baxter, these ebbs and flows culminated in the definitive conversion of May 24, 1738. The day began with Wesley opening to an auspicious passage from Paul's letters, continuing with Psalms at St. Paul's, and concluding with study at Aldersgate of Luther's preface to *Romans*: "While he was describing the change which God works in the heart through faith in Christ, I felt my heart strangely warmed. I felt I did trust in Christ, Christ alone for salvation; and an assurance was given me that He had taken away *my* sins, even *mine*, and saved *me* from the law of sin and death."[109] Here was the tradition wrestled with and a reenactment achieved, almost as if in ritual or sacrament.

LIVES WITHOUT CONVERSION: JACQUES-AUGUSTE DE THOU AND DAVID HUME

The personal narratives left behind by Wesley and his contemporaries in the evangelical revival of the mid-eighteenth century ensured the ongoing centrality of conversion experiences in eighteenth-century Christian autobiography. But there was by that time a parallel and contrasting tradition of philosophical or scholarly autobiography that did not turn on a single moment in time after which nothing was the same. In his own *Memoirs* Gibbon pledged allegiance to two members of this alternate tradition whom he called his "masters": Jacques-Auguste de Thou and David Hume.[110]

Perhaps the first thing to note about Gibbon's "masters" in autobiography is how odd a couple they make. Both de Thou ("Thuanus" in Latin) and

Hume were historians turned autobiographers;[111] both indeed had chronicled periods of religious controversy, de Thou having written on the French wars of religion in the sixteenth century, Hume the English civil wars in the seventeenth.[112] But one was a sage and a skeptic, the other at least a pious Catholic *politique,* if not a saint. Gibbon's philosophical commitments seemed to favor the skeptic; so did his affections. Gibbon knew Hume personally, and his admiration for the man—"one of the greatest men our island has ever produced"[113]—and his work, which Gibbon cited frequently if sometimes critically in the *Decline and Fall,* was profound and enduring.[114] De Thou was hardly as prominent in Gibbon's work as Hume. Indeed, based on Gibbon's published works one might wonder whether he had read de Thou prior to composing the three concluding volumes of the *Decline and Fall* that appeared in 1788.[115] Although in those volumes Gibbon twice mentions "the great Thuanus," the *Decline and Fall* hardly justifies the epithet. Citations of de Thou's works serve mostly to support minor points of fact, one of which, Gibbon notes, de Thou gets inexcusably wrong.[116]

De Thou's *Commentaries*

The work that Gibbon cites in these notes is de Thou's *Historiarum sui temporis,* or *History of His Own Times,* a monumental study of France's religious wars in the second half of the sixteenth century. The first installment of de Thou's *History,* covering the years 1546 to 1560 in eighteen books, appeared late in 1603 with a dedicatory letter to Henry IV.[117] Amid praise of the king and testimony to his own benign motives, de Thou included an impassioned defense of religious toleration that, centuries later, would stir the souls of French *philosophes* like Voltaire.[118] In its own time, however, the *History* offended the papal nuncio and soon landed on the Vatican's Index of Prohibited Books.[119] Follow-on attacks from Catholic polemicists culminated in the French Jesuit Jean de Machault's *Notationes* of 1614, which questioned Thuanus's scholarly accuracy, challenged his faith, and insulted his deceased wife.[120]

De Thou's counterattack, the *Commentariorum de vita sua libri sex,* has come to be known as his *Memoirs.*[121] But the original title, so unconventional for a work of autobiography, indicates the distinctive features of de Thou's self-portrait.[122] The object of the seventeenth-century commentary was not normally a person but an ancient book; the commentator explicated and emended his source text, stripping away accretions and revealing the author's intent.[123] Any originality on the part of the commentator might be amplified and obscured by the text's authority. To write commentaries on one's own life as if it were a text was to make the autobiographical subject (the writer) entirely into an object and to suggest that the object that has been received is a distorted version of the original, in need of emendation and explication.

This is in fact how de Thou constructs his autobiography. Rather than write in the first person, de Thou assumes the persona of a narrator—a close friend who has conversed with "Thuanus" on even the most intimate and sensitive matters, religion very much included.[124] The narrator finds Thuanus a thoroughly Catholic author. The third son in a noble family, Thuanus receives holy orders and lives for some time with his uncle in the cloister of Notre-Dame.[125] Following the death of his older brothers and his father, Thuanus leaves the priesthood, marries, and pursues a literary career that blends deep learning and profound faith. He sets the Book of Job, Ecclesiastes, and the Hebrew prophets into Latin verse.[126] To express "his sense of God's mercy towards him" upon recovering from an illness, Thuanus writes the *Parabata Vinctus, sive Triumphus Christi, tragoedia*, an imitation of the *Prometheus Bound* that, as the title suggests, turns the myth to ends unknown to Aeschylus. The Thuanus depicted in the *Commentaries* feels little tension between his Christianity and his classicism.[127]

De Thou's adoption of the third person allowed him to dwell on the details of his life, even to engage in the self-examination of Augustinian autobiography, without worry of appearing vain. The Thuanus of the *Commentaries* is elaborately drawn indeed; at one point the narrator calls the work a narrative of "private events."[128] It includes amusing trivia—encounters with a "gluttonous boy" who eats a hundred oysters and another who though "otherwise sober" drinks fifty glasses of sulfur water daily—and poignant scenes of mourning.[129] When Thuanus's father dies unexpectedly, he is "pierced with grief" and "hurled into sadness."[130] But for all of that, the protagonist's character is curiously lacking in development. Thuanus is at the beginning what he is at the end of his *Life*.

Even Thuanus's great work, the *History of His Own Times*, seems to have never quite begun. When the autobiography reaches 1593, we are told that Thuanus's "historical work was commenced," having been planned some fifteen years before.[131] The narrative of 1578 concludes the first book of the *Commentaries*, but we search in vain for some dramatic act of authorial resolve; it is as if the genesis of Thuanus's great work fell into the gap separating the first and second books. The first mention of the *History* comes earlier in 1572, and it is strikingly *en passant*: Thuanus records an event in his journal, "having already begun the design of writing his *Annals*."[132] A decade later we find him continuing "his studies, and, wherever he went, earnestly courted the friendship of those persons, whose conversation and acquaintance he stood in need of for the historical work, which he now had in his thoughts."[133] At this point Thuanus's historical project has fused with his political action. Wherever he goes as a diplomat he encounters statesmen and scholars who can be of service for his *History of His Own Times*.[134] Thuanus's life and work are so much of a piece that one could hardly have preceded the other. An epiphany like Gibbon's of October 15, 1764, could not have been the genesis of Thuanus's *History*.

De Thou treats the phenomenon of religious conversion in the same spirit. As an admirer and counselor of Henry IV, de Thou might have made much of the king's conversion from Calvinism to Catholicism on July 25, 1593.[135] The 107th book of his *History* describes the scene in detail.[136] But as he had done with Thuanus's decision to write his *History*, the narrator of the *Commentaries* relates Henry's conversion after the fact: "In the next year [1594] the counsels turned upon the consecration of the king, who by this time had reconciled himself to the Church."[137] Nothing more is said; it is a *fait accompli*. The only indication of what this silence is meant to signify comes in a remarkable paean to religious toleration de Thou gives to Henry in 1589, after the assassination of Henry III but before the new king has secured the throne. The soon-to-be Henry IV insists (as de Thou also did in his own voice) that faith cannot be compelled. Toleration, he suggests, does not entail the mutual recognition of immovable obstinacy so much as it requires a certain gentleness on both sides, a willingness to follow what is best, where "best" is not defined in sectarian terms. As king, Henry IV promises to promote the safety of the whole realm, Catholics and Huguenots alike; as author, Thuanus sends Protestants, like his friend and fellow classicist Joseph Scaliger, to "a better place" whether or not the Vatican approves.[138] Even to discuss the conversion of Henry IV, it seems, would grant too much to those who staked everything on confessional identification. The point, for de Thou, was rather what lay beyond the confessions. One of the ways he expressed that point was by conspicuously demoting the very phenomenon of conversion.

Hume's *Life*

Hume's "My Own Life" does much the same. Religion does not figure nearly as prominently in Hume's self-portrait as it did in his life. Hume's heterodoxy had denied him the chair of moral philosophy at Edinburgh, and he had nearly been convicted of infidelity in the mid-1750s.[139] But these troubles are absent from the *Life*, or nearly so. Hume says that as a boy he secretly read Cicero and Vergil rather than the jurist Vinnius and the theologian Gisbertus Voetius. In recounting the reception of his books Hume notes the praise of two "dignified prelates," the "odd exceptions" to his *History*'s early neglect, and the criticisms of "Reverends and Right Reverends," including Warburton and Hurd.[140] But these are fleeting notices, the insignificance of which Hume seems to explain in his peroration: "Not but that the zealots, we may well suppose, would have been glad to invent and propagate any story to my disadvantage, but they could never find any which they thought would wear the face of probability."[141] Hume has passed through life unscathed and survived to compose an autobiography of seamless serenity, he says, owing to the constancy of his character.

Hume attributes his unstinting mildness and moderation not, of course, to reason's conquest of passion but to the unchallenged power of a "ruling passion," the love of literature and "literary fame."[142] Hume discovered this passion as a boy. In his early twenties while studying in rural France, he laid a "plan of life, which [he has] steadily and successfully pursued."[143] The autobiographer is not concerned to chart changes in opinion or belief. We know about the flash of insight Hume experienced at eighteen—"there seemed to open up to me a new scene of thought, which transported me beyond measure, and made me, with an ardour natural to young men, throw up every other pleasure or business to apply entirely to it"—from a letter of 1734, not his *Life*.[144] The only "confession" Hume makes touches on the moment after the first volume of his *History* had sunk into oblivion, and he considers renouncing his ruling passion: "I was, however, I confess, discouraged."[145] But he picks up courage, perseveres, and ultimately succeeds, such that he can die with "hope"—not for salvation but that his life has justified whatever vanity an autobiography necessarily entails. The momentary lapse of faith in himself is the most psychological anguish Hume allows us to witness.

Hume's is a *Life* without conversion, almost without development. It approximates a précis of achievements, a literary *Res Gestae*. Indeed, but for the fleeting hints at sectarian strife, Hume's *Life* might be mistaken for an ancient rather than a modern text. It is as if, in a parting shot of impiety, Hume had amputated Augustine's lasting influence on the genre of autobiography, which became again an organ of worldly glory rather than a confession to God. Hume himself compared his self-portrait, written as he was ill and approaching death, to a "funeral oration."[146]

Both de Thou and Hume were great historians who turned to autobiography late in life, and both offered self-portraits centered on devotion to truth above the confessional or philosophical tumults of their times. For all of their similarities, Gibbon's masters differed in their orientation toward religion. De Thou was a Catholic, Hume a skeptic. By pairing them Gibbon suggested that the historian's self-reflection might be approached by reason or by faith, by the saint or the sage.[147] Gibbon's models also differed over the literary form most appropriate to autobiography. Indeed, they might be taken to have marked the outer boundaries of the genre. Hume offered an Olympian, first-person view of literary achievements with very little by way of personal history; de Thou, an exquisitely detailed, third-person account of a life of action that was simultaneously a life of contemplation.

Most importantly for our present purposes, however, neither de Thou nor Hume left behind a *Life* marked by conversion. Indeed, both seemed to have consciously diminished the significance of development in the characters they depicted. Hume cast himself as an unflappable philosopher; de Thou made Thuanus a steady scholar of faith, transcending all the confusion of confessional allegiance. Both testified, and their testimonies might be multiplied, to the vitality in Gibbon's day of a pre-Christian mode of autobiography applicable even, perhaps especially, to the philosophical historian of Christianity. In following masters like these rather than "fanatics" like Baxter or Wesley, Gibbon could act as an Addison of autobiography, reaching past the discontents and narrative tropes of the recent past to resurrect the beauty and serenity of pagan antiquity.[148]

This was not, however, the path Gibbon chose to follow. Gibbon's conversion story marked his departure from his "masters" in autobiography, while placing him among an innovative group of travel writers. Attending to Gibbon's religious and literary context helps us not only to tally his debts but to appreciate his originality. We also learn something about the world into which his works were launched.

The very fact that so many English gentlemen could venture into Catholic Europe and return home spiritually unscathed suggests the religious stability of Gibbon's age. As we have seen, the Church of England during Gibbon's maturity had largely overcome its main confessional rival as well as the dissenting sects. The steadily expanding laws of toleration that embraced the dissenters in 1689 and culminated in Catholic Emancipation in 1829 were signs of Anglican strength and magnanimity rather than grudging concessions to rivals. Even the Deist controversy, so redolent of the secularizing trends that would stretch from Emancipation into the present day, had largely subsided by the time Gibbon reached Oxford. The Church of England was so firmly established that Burke (and, indeed, Gibbon) could portray the Continent's politicized atheism and revolutionary violence as inimical to England's national character.

The remarkable stability at the highest levels of the English Church and State did not forestall significant changes in literary culture, however. We have seen the crypto-Catholic travelogues of the late seventeenth century give way to more orthodox Protestant accounts of the Grand Tour, until Addison's pioneering work left classically informed aesthetes holding the ground formerly occupied by warring Christians. Even this more polite Tour, however, generated anxieties of influence that led innovative travel-writers, like Smollet and Sterne, to strike out on their own.

In autobiography, as in travel-writing, there were significant, if not quite revolutionary, developments during Gibbon's time. Religious autobiographies of the eighteenth century had to contend with a tradition reaching back to Paul's conversion on the Damascus road and Augustine's in the Milanese garden. Near-contemporaries of Gibbon, like John Wesley, made this tradition their own. Others, like Hume, departed from this tradition to reinvigorate a classical model in which character was relatively fixed and the phenomenon of conversion was implicitly called into question. As the alternative traditions of travel-writing—the confessionally fraught and the aesthetically above-the-fray—left latecomers like Sterne to develop their own forms, so the alternative models of autobiography—one centered around the conversion story, the other on a classical account that ruled out conversion—left Gibbon's contemporaries room to innovate.

Gibbon's conversion story in Rome was one such innovation. The staging of this epiphany on the steps of a Catholic Church at the peak of his Grand Tour suggested the potential for novelty contained within long-standing traditions of travel-writing and autobiography alike. Gibbon the autobiographer attempted to embed conversion in a secular personal history while preserving the phenomenon—not denying its power or otherwise explaining it away. We will soon see that the *Decline and Fall*, for all of its skepticism, constituted an analogous attempt by Gibbon the historian.

Religiously settled conditions facilitated such innovations and experiments. A religious establishment with little to fear from Anglican gentlemen traversing Catholic Europe could allow gentlemen historians wide latitude to explore the pagan and Christian past. In a time of revolution, however, these conditions changed. Gibbon wrote his *Memoirs*, our surest guide to the religion immediately surrounding the author, in the late 1780s and early 1790s. The work was complicated by the tumultuous events surrounding it. The world seemed to be undergoing a conversion experience comparable—Gibbon drew the comparison—to the one Gibbon described in the *Decline and Fall*.[149]

CHAPTER 2

Gibbon's Autobiographies

Edward Gibbon was a consistent counterrevolutionary. Both as an engaged member of London society and then as a Member of Parliament, he supported Lord North's efforts to put down the American rebellion. Gibbon also opposed the revolution in France. "I am as high an Aristocrat as Burke himself," he wrote to his friend Lord Sheffield in 1791, and in the penultimate draft of his *Memoirs* Gibbon would formally "subscribe [his] assent to Mr. Burke's creed."[1] Gibbon's enthusiasm for Burke was such that he presented his own great work, even at its most controversial, as an essentially conservative endeavor. "The primitive Church, which I have treated with some freedom, was itself at that time, an innovation, and *I* was attached to the old Pagan establishment."[2] Readers have largely considered Gibbon's retrospective a rather last-ditch attempt to resist the "French disease" by recasting his great work's subversive account of religious belief into a bulwark of the Old Regime.[3]

We have already seen that Gibbon's approach to his own past differed in some significant respects from that of his "masters," de Thou and Hume, each of whom wrote lives without conversion. Something similar might be said of Gibbon's relation to Burke. Where Burke's conservative historiography stressed continuity rather than rupture, sanding away the sharp joints and rough edges of a ramshackle structure until it resembled a "stolid British oak," Gibbon's was more concerned than Burke's to confront—indeed, on many occasions, to construct—discontinuities.

Conversions figured prominently in Gibbon's life. There was the famous epiphany at Rome, of course. But Gibbon also wandered as a young man into Catholicism, only to return a year later to the Protestant fold.[4] His *Memoirs* described each of these twists and turns in rich detail and for that reason constitute an invaluable guide to the religions immediately surrounding Gibbon. But they are not an infallible guide. Composed in fits and starts between 1788 and 1793, the *Memoirs* were left in six incomplete drafts at the time of Gibbon's death.[5] The drafts suggest changes in Gibbon's vision of the work, perhaps in response to contemporary developments in France.[6] As David Womersley has noted, five of the drafts seem intended for posthumous publication; one (the least critical of English institutions), for publication during Gibbon's life.[7] It is also possible that Gibbon died not wanting any of the drafts to see the light of day.[8] Although the *Memoirs* have a privileged place in our attempt to understand Gibbon's immediate context, the decades separating Gibbon's composition of them from the events he depicts and the incompleteness of the work require that we supplement them with other sources.

In this chapter we will use Gibbon's *Memoirs*, correspondence, and journals to set three scenes along Gibbon's long road to Rome. We shall visit the England of Gibbon's youth, the setting of the historian's first, failed attempts at education and his conversion to Catholicism. Then to Lausanne, Switzerland, where Gibbon returned to his father's faith and received instruction and independence more suited to his nascent talents. Finally, we shall follow Gibbon's own Grand Tour with its culmination amid the ruins of the Capitol. Our "bear leader" on this journey, Gibbon's *Memoirs*, will emerge as not, or not only, an old man's attempt to cast a conservative veneer over a revolutionary youth but a meditation on the challenge of conserving an enlightened—that is to say, no longer traditional—society, one that could not be made to resemble (at least not by an author committed to truth rather than beauty) a steady growth but was shot through with changes, ruptures, and conversions.

ENGLAND: THE ROAD TO ROMAN CATHOLICISM

It is not certain when the idea of writing *Memoirs* first started to Gibbon's mind. The genesis seems to have had something to do with Gibbon's reading, in late 1786 or early 1787, of a volume on heraldry by one John Gibbon, whom Edward Gibbon took (mistakenly, as it turned out) to be "not only my namesake, but my kinsman."[9] This volume included John Gibbon's notes on his ancestry, reaching back into the fourteenth century. Edward Gibbon the historian may have been excited by the length and dignity of the lineage; Edward Gibbon the memoirist seems to have been stirred by the fact that this lineage was a chance discovery rather than a familiar inheritance.

Having celebrated the publication of the *Decline and Fall*'s final volumes in May 1788, Gibbon returned to Lausanne and opened the first draft of the *Memoirs* by constructing a Burkean utopia of ancestral custom and unproblematic transmission of virtue. Among Gibbon's distant ancestors, as he described them, religious faith, largely presumed, had power perhaps to support but not to disrupt tradition. Then Gibbon proceeded to deconstruct this world. The pieties more immediately surrounding Gibbon were not mute auxiliaries to a powerful tradition. Indeed, what there was of tradition (including the history of Gibbon's family) had itself been fragmented by the forces of commerce, political revolution, and religious dissent—leaving the young Gibbon to seek security and solace in the arms of the Roman Church. As a memoirist, Gibbon presented his first conversion as an indictment of the religious commitments that surrounded the young man.

Genealogy

Gibbon started from his ancestors—or rather, by considering why an autobiographer might start in this way. The desire to know something about our ancestors is so prevalent, Gibbon says, "that it must depend on the influence of some common principle in the minds of men"—namely, the desire to "enlarge the narrow circle in which Nature has confined us."[10] Both religion and philosophy express this desire by offering hope for some form of life beyond death; genealogy extends the same desire in the opposite direction by "[filling] up the silent vacancy that precedes our birth."[11] Genealogy also expresses our longing for something more than mere life, for few would prefer "the longest series of peasants and mechanics" to ancestors "possessed of ample fortunes, adorned with honorable titles, and holding an eminent rank in the class of hereditary nobles."[12] What initially seems a rather straightforward matter—Gibbon starting an account for himself by first discussing his ancestors—in fact reflects the heart's deepest longings.[13] One starts from family history because humans long to project noble images of themselves onto eternity.

Is this a reasonable desire? Gibbon immediately introduced "a philosopher" to critique it.[14] "Parts and virtue cannot be transmitted with the inheritance of estates and titles," says the philosopher, and even the assumption that estates and titles trace natural lines belies the naïve belief in "the unspotted chastity of *all* our female progenitors."[15] Gibbon's philosopher values virtue more highly than wealth; he also holds that wealth and virtue do not coincide, and that virtue is not transmitted by heredity. He resembles a republican critic of hereditary aristocracy. The philosopher's critique also suggests a certain view of virtue itself, one that is jaundiced or at least skeptical of appearances. Our female progenitors might *seem* chaste, the philosopher winks, but we know how rarely this virtue, if such it is, is observed in fact.[16]

Responding to his "philosopher's" critique of ancestral pride, Gibbon concedes that virtue is transmitted with greater difficulty than property, and that all who appear virtuous are not necessarily so. But Gibbon nevertheless opposes to philosophy, so understood, a different sort of "reason" that respects "the prejudices and habits which have been consecrated by the experience of mankind."[17] Accordingly, Gibbon says, one should not mock the urge "to respect the son of a respectable father" or the desire to search one's past for great lives and writings to peruse "with the diligence of filial love."[18] The great men and women we consider our own shape our characters because they inspire a "warmer curiosity" than mere historical facts, considered objectively. "Where the distinction of birth is allowed to form a superior order in the state," Gibbon writes, "education and example should always, and will often, produce among them a dignity of sentiment and propriety of conduct which is guarded from dishonor by their own and the public esteem."[19] Gibbon's defense of hereditary aristocracy against the philosopher's critique turns on this pedagogical power—the power of familiar examples to shape character—rather than on the transmission of virtuous natures.[20]

This use of reason, however respectful of prejudice and habit, is compatible with reform of a sort. Gibbon recommends that we "esteem in our ancestors the qualities that best promote the interest of society"—the qualities not of a king or a general but of a philosopher or an author. Gibbon ranks Fielding over Marlborough, Cicero over Marius, Chaucer over the Companions of the Garter. He praises Confucius most highly of all.[21] Within his own line, Gibbon selects for attention John Gibbon, architect to Edward III; James Fiennes, whose career as Henry VI's treasurer came to an end when, accused of treason for speaking "French, the language of our enemies," he died "a patron and martyr of learning"; and Blue-mantle Poursuivant, a domestic tutor and an author of a study of heraldry that he expected to secure his "immortal fame."[22] It is from this last work that Gibbon derived his knowledge of the Gibbons back to 1326, when the family was given lands. If Gibbon's link to the Gibbons described therein was (and was eventually suspected by Gibbon himself to be[23]) historically untenable, this seems rather beside the point. Gibbon selected from among his ancestors the best models for himself and his readers: a team of "high [Tories] in Church and State," whose royalism in no way compromised their commitment to broad education.[24] By choosing for himself a heritage of enlightening conservatives, Gibbon indicated how "reason" might respect and elevate prejudice, rather than attempting to eliminate or replace prejudice with something more rational.

Gibbon considered the power of noble examples to form their successors "natural," but it was not automatic.[25] Family memory required active curation. Gibbon acknowledged that had he not "by a strange accident discovered [Blue-mantle's] book, the memory of John Gibbon would have been obliterated in his own family."[26] Gibbon was not raised with that book in view, nor with tales of James Fiennes's martyrdom, nor with any of the other legends he rehearsed for his readers. The chain of family memory, embossed in ancestral piety and a seemingly unproblematic (because unmentioned) Christianity, might have lifted the son and grandson toward their callings, but it had been broken—long before the revolution in France. The reason, as Gibbon described, had to do with a grandfather who presented himself as "a son of the Earth, who by his industry—his honest industry perhaps—had raised himself from the Work-house to the Cottage."[27]

Edward Gibbon I (1666–1736)

A director of the South Sea Company and a central player in the bubble of 1720, Edward Gibbon I was a great, or at least a consequential, man. Gibbon's readers might expect a figure cut to the significance of the controversies he shared in. Gibbon gives them instead a petty merchant, the iron residue of the golden line Gibbon had traced or invented:

> According to the mercantile creed that the best book is a profitable ledger, the writings of John the herald would be much less precious than those of his nephew Edward: but an author professes, at least, to write for the public benefit; and the slow balance of trade can only be pleasing to those persons to whom it is advantageous. The successful industry of my grandfather raised him above the level of his immediate ancestors; he appears to have launched into various and extensive dealings: even his opinions were subordinate to his interest, and I find him in Flanders clothing King William's troops; while he would have contracted with more pleasure, though not perhaps at a cheaper rate, for the service of King James.[28]

Gibbon considered his grandfather to have habitually put profit over principle, but his grandfather's principle was sufficiently problematic unto itself. The restoration of King James was the project of the English Jacobites, who attempted in 1715 and again in 1745 to reverse the Revolution of 1688. These were not the enlightened, reform-minded conservatives that Gibbon discovered among his ancestors. Even by the first and certainly by the second uprising, the Jacobites aimed to replace a recent but well-established fusion of Church and State, even at the risk of undermining traditionalism and restoring something so ancient as to seem new. They resembled revolutionary conservatives.[29]

In his grandfather's generation, not only Jacobitism but all moral principle seems to have been replaced by profit and popular opinion. In tracing the ancestors who preceded his grandfather, Gibbon notes that "before our army and navy, our Civil establishments and Indian Empire, had opened so many paths of fortune, the mercantile profession was more frequently chosen by youths of a liberal race and education who aspired to create their own independence."[30] The aspiration to create one's own independence, however compatible with a liberal education, stood in some tension with the spirit of veneration that Gibbon identifies with a defensible hereditary aristocracy. So too did the epochal changes encapsulated in Gibbon's succinct defense of commercial nobility: Had the rise of British military, civil establishments, and empire—the opening of "so many paths to fortune"—altered the conditions that made commerce and nobility compatible?[31] By the time of Gibbon's grandfather, even the prosecution of the corrupt bore the taint of corruption. The fleecing of the South Sea directors Gibbon considered a "pernicious violation of liberty and law," in which the House of Commons bowed to a popular clamor by ruining men of means for "offences which did not exist at the time they were committed."[32] Men like Gibbon's grandfather in societies like Britain, however, were not easily ruined. Using the seed money of a fellow Jacobite and "the skill and credit of which Parliament had not been able to despoil him," he restored his fortune.[33] He was a self-made man twice over, a new prince whom we might expect Gibbon to admire. Instead, Gibbon leaves him "the oracle and tyrant of a petty kingdom."[34] The name of this kingdom was Putney; its king, either Gibbon's grandfather or the exiled James III, whom the grandfather would honor in toasts and prayers. "In the daily devotions of the family," Gibbon says, "the name of the king for whom they prayed was prudently omitted."[35]

Presiding over these daily devotions, alongside the "oracle and tyrant" himself, was the Gibbon family's spiritual director, "the celebrated Mr. William Law." Law had joined the Gibbon household in 1723, seven years after refusing to abjure the Old Pretender and swear allegiance to George I, six years before publishing his most famous book, *A Serious Call*. This work urged Christians to live their everyday lives entirely according to God's will and to reject "worldly pleasures, sensual pleasures, and the pride of life."[36] A practical and exacting manual of devout Christianity, it would have a profound impact on John Wesley and other English evangelicals. It also featured the Gibbon family prominently—and not altogether favorably.

Law cast Gibbon's paternal aunt Catherine, veiled as "Flavia" (Latinate pseudonyms being a hallmark of Law's style), as a worldly pagan who "has no grounds from Scripture to think she is in the way of salvation."[37] Her sister, Hester or "Miranda," however, was Law's heroine. "There is nothing that is whimsical, trifling, or unreasonable in her character," Law writes, "but everything there described is a right and proper instance of a solid and real piety."[38] Miranda's salvation is secure: "When she dies, [she] must shine amongst Apostles, and saints, and martyrs."[39] The ultimate fate of "Flatus," Gibbon's father, was less certain. His was a "ridiculous, restless life" spent in passionate pursuit of a series of hobbies that seem to promise happiness. After exhausting a gamut of options—from hunting to mastering Italian opera—Law has Flatus pause for several days of reasoning and reflection, which seems promising until "a new project comes in to his relief" and he begins to live only on herbs.[40]

Law knew Flatus both as a member of the Gibbon family and, more intimately, as his pupil. Gibbon's grandfather, a man of prudence but not of liberal education, had attempted "to supply in his children the deficiencies of which he is conscious in himself" by selecting as their tutor a man famous for learning and piety.[41] Whereas Gibbon's justification of hereditary aristocracy turned on the power of a long line of family examples to shape younger generations, his grandfather's conception of education appealed to other sources: the ultimate purpose of education was to know and serve God, and this purpose was best served by retaining the most famous specialists in that field. Where legends of Blue-mantle and James Fiennes might have stood, there was William Law.

On Gibbon's understanding, Law failed as an educator. Having dutifully accompanied the family's heir to Cambridge, Law remained at Putney when Gibbon's father toured the Continent. Gibbon considered Law's absence a breach in the tutor's responsibility, and he attributed that failing to Law's piety: "The mind of a saint is above or below the present world."[42]

Gibbon's assessment of Law as an author, however, is less straightforward. Gibbon praises Law's style and capacity for satire, the latter skill springing from "the strange contradiction between the faith and practice of the Christian World."[43] Law's "enthusiasm" and "religious frenzy," in Gibbon's view, led him to side with faith against practice. Gibbon's account of Law in the *Memoirs,* by contrast, sides with practice against faith. Gibbon pardons the aunt Law had damned. Flavia's "sins . . . may not appear to our carnal apprehension of so black a dye," says Gibbon. "Her temper was gay and lively; she followed the fashion in her dress, and indulged her taste for company and public amusements; but her expense was regulated by economy: she practiced the decencies of Religion, nor is she accused of neglecting the essential duties of a wife or a mother."[44] The same pen also saves the pious Miranda, but on grounds quite different from Law's. First Gibbon hints that Miranda's virtues were not as otherworldly as they seemed: the interests of "this world" alienated her from her brother, he says, and he proceeds to cast doubt on her ultimate salvation, speaking of "the psalms and hymns of thanksgiving, which she now, perhaps, may chant in a full chorus of saints and angels."[45] Does Gibbon raise in his reader's mind the thought that the "pious virgin" was something else when he says that "Mr. Law died in the house, I may not say in the arms, of his beloved Miranda"?[46] But Miranda is ultimately redeemed when Gibbon considers the worldly joys her otherworldly virtues afforded her. "Of the pains and pleasures of a spiritual life I," Gibbon stresses, "am ill-qualified to speak; yet I am inclined to believe that her lot, even on earth has not been unhappy. Her penance was voluntary, and, in her own eyes, meritorious; her time was filled by regular occupations; and instead of the insignificance of an old maid, she was surrounded by dependents, poor and abject as they were, who implored her bounty and imbibed her lessons."[47] There is irony here, to be sure. Is the company of "poor and abject" dependents meant to recommend a life? But there is earnestness as well. Gibbon here offers, we might say, the view of a generous pagan onto a Christian life. To die proud of the busy and sociable life that one has lived is indeed a good thing. If the good of this life is not ultimately so different from the good of the pagan's life, the harsh judgments of the pagan and the Christian on one other are perhaps blunted. Or perhaps it is better to say that a charitable paganism reveals the good of the two.[48] This reconciliation is Gibbon's, not Law's. And in making it, Gibbon shows himself more humane—perhaps more Christian?—than the "wit and scholar" who presided over Putney alongside his grandfather.

Gibbon's grandfather, recall, broke the chain of family memory that might have shaped his son and grandson to the mold of Blue-mantle Poursuivant and James Fiennes. On that older theory of education, noble lines were justified in wielding authority not because virtue was genetically heritable but because the noble examples we consider our own have a peculiar power to shape our characters, making us nobler. This education entailed a certain humility—a spirit of deference to those who came before. Gibbon's grandfather, however, understood himself to be a self-made man. The grounds for this pride had nothing to do with French philosophy. They were implied in the commercial and imperial revolution of the British, which gave second and third sons the ability to make something of themselves, something far greater in fact than their older brothers had inherited. But Gibbon thought that Christianity, at least as represented by Law, could hardly repair this breach for the simple reason that those concerned with the next world care insufficiently for their obligations in this one. If there was an ideal mean between the worldliness of the grandfather and the mysticism of the tutor, Gibbon did not find it in fact.

Edward Gibbon II (1707–1770)

Gibbon certainly did not find anything ideal or deserving of imitation in his father. On the son's understanding, Law left Edward Gibbon II to be shaped by the world around him. But his was not a world of challenge and opportunity like that which engaged the grandfather. It was instead a world of convention and comfort, the milieu of "a scholar and a gentleman" of means.

Some of the fault for the steady mediocrity of Gibbon's father rested with him rather than his times. When Gibbon's father made an abbreviated Tour of the Continent in the 1730s, for instance, Richard Lassels's world of high-stakes confessional politics had not entirely disappeared. Had Gibbon's father made it to Rome he might have called on the Stuart Court at the Palazzo del Re, already at that time an important stop for traveling Englishmen.[49] His conversations there might have been noted by British agents or by cardinals sympathetic to Hanoverian interests.[50] While at Rome or in his travels to or from the city Gibbon's father might have encountered his near-contemporary, the diplomat-cum-spymaster Horace Mann, then making his own introductions on the peninsula.[51] But Gibbon's father was not one to seek out education, much less adventure. On Tour he passed time in Paris pleasantly but profitlessly, imbibing much French wine but little French (says a son who would for some time consider himself more French than English).[52] After his return and election to Parliament, Gibbon's father was surrounded by men of similar station making names for themselves as statesmen. "With them, he gave many a vote," wrote the son, "with them he drank many a bottle."[53] In the son's eyes, the father was sociable but unserious, a man capable of great love (as he felt for Gibbon's mother) but not of great action.

Was there anything to be said of the religious experience of such a man? In England he passed time with High-Church Jacobites but joined the Tory opposition to the rebellion of 1745.[54] He socialized with the family of David Mallet, the freethinking playwright, but seems himself only to have dabbled in radicalism. Law imparted neither his own religious enthusiasm nor the liberal education Gibbon's grandfather had desired. To the mind of the son, the father was mild to the point of absence. Gibbon's grandfather had been wrong, in Gibbon's eyes, to entrust his son to a private tutor and to England's institutions of liberal education, but his mistake was motivated by a defensible desire to give his son advantages he had not known. The result was an idle, pleasure-seeking gentleman, capable of romantic love but ill-suited for statesmanship, the merchant's life, and—as it happened—the sort of wrong-headed-but-right-hearted concern for a son's education that his own father had displayed.

Edward Gibbon III (1737–1794)

If Gibbon's father was abandoned by the grandfather to William Law who then abandoned him to the world, Gibbon himself was abandoned by his father to no one in particular. First, John Kirkby, an "indigent curate," served as Gibbon's private tutor for eighteen months. Kirkby stood to Gibbon as Law had stood to his father; in the final draft of the *Memoirs*, Gibbon structures his account of the two episodes—narrative followed by analysis of their writings—so as to make the parallel clear. It does not favor Kirkby. Law arrives at Putney a celebrated author; Kirkby's "learning and virtue" introduce him to Gibbon's father (whose judgment of such qualities Gibbon has already primed us to suspect), but he is otherwise unpublished and unknown.[55] Law dies having lived exactly as he wished—"in the house, I may not say in the arms, of his beloved Miranda"; of Kirkby, Gibbon says, "*How* the poor man ended his days I have never been able to learn." Law was a nonjuror supported by a man of means who omitted the "name of the king for whom they prayed" from the family prayers; Kirkby, a clergyman in the Church of England, was dismissed by the spendthrift son for omitting the name of King George while preaching in the parish church. The triad of Father/Kirkby/Gibbon marks a steep decline from Grandfather/Law/Father.

Gibbon's education declined further still. After Kirkby's tutorship, Gibbon passed two years at a school in Kingston, a year of solitude in his maternal grandfather's library (the "most propitious" year, says Gibbon, "for the growth of my intellectual stature"), some time in a public school in Westminster, and a year in Bath—all the while tormented by illnesses and largely unguided. Suddenly healthy, Gibbon was sent on the Mallets' recommendation to the home of Mr. Phillip Francis, an author and translator of some reputation. But Francis "indulged himself in the pleasures of London," leaving his pupils "idle at Esher in the custody of a Dutch usher, of low manners and contemptible learning."[56] Gibbon's father rescued him, only to embrace a "singular and desperate measure": the fourteen-year-old Gibbon was sent to Oxford.

Gibbon's education had so far consisted of a series of abandonments, repaired only partially by his own aimless initiative (and the kind encouragement of an *alma mater* in the person of his maternal aunt). His father's hasty deposit of Gibbon at Oxford might accordingly seem a hopeful emancipation. Gibbon recorded his youthful "surprise and satisfaction" upon arriving at the university. But these impressions did not last. Instead, Gibbon's Oxford years marked the final nadir in a descending narrative: from an invented tradition of architects, treasurers, and scholars to a worldly grandfather who entrusted his firstborn to a tutor made neglectful by concerns for the world to come; from that grandfather to a father serious only about society and romance and content to cast *his* sickly son from one ill-considered tutor to the next and then, in desperation and disregard, to Oxford. The university was the last stop in the world of Gibbon's youth. It came to represent for him the corruption and unseriousness—about education, learning, and religion—of the world into which he was born. It was the scene of his first conversion.

The trouble at Oxford was not merely poor tutors, dissolute colleagues, and an outmoded curriculum, though Gibbon cites these and other shortcomings. The core of the issue was deeper, more historically evocative and suggestive of Gibbon's approach to religion as a teenager and as a fifty-something memoirist. "Founded in a dark age of false and barbarous science," Gibbon writes, Oxford and Cambridge "are still tainted with the vices of their origin."[57] "Their primitive discipline was adapted to the education of priests and monks; and the government still remains in the hands of the Clergy, an order of men whose manners are remote from the present World, and whose eyes are dazzled by the light of Philosophy."[58] In Oxford Gibbon discovers not only a university ill-suited to his needs but an institution of a particular sort: a monastery.[59] Gibbon develops the analogy at length. "The stated hours of the hall and chapel," Gibbon says, represent the discipline of "a regular, and, as it were, a religious community";[60] England's academic corporations "may be compared to the Benedictine abbeys of Catholic countries" as the library shelves "groan under the weight of the Benedictine folios";[61] and the faculty of Gibbon's college, "the monks of Magdalen," live in a "cloister" with other "fellows or monks," all of them "addicted to a life of celibacy."[62] At Oxford Gibbon confronts for the first time the vices, as he would come to understand them, of medieval Catholicism.

Both the student and the memoirist rejected all of this violently, but the forms their rejections took differed significantly. The memoirist of the early 1790s explained the vices of the cloister using economic arguments adapted from his friend Adam Smith's *Wealth of Nations*, a work published nearly simultaneously with the first volume of *Decline and Fall* and unavailable to the student of 1752.[63] The young Gibbon, on the other hand, converted to Catholicism. This was indeed a momentous rupture with Gibbon's world. It amounted to a rejection of not only his university ("the gates of Magdalen

College were forever shut against my return") but his father and his country. As we have seen, in the England of Gibbon's youth conversion to Catholicism could still be considered high treason, resulting in imprisonment or the forfeiture of one's inheritance.[64] It was not a decision to be taken, or a calling to be heeded, lightly. What was it, then, this conversion?

Gibbon's accounts of it across the six drafts of his *Memoirs* vary widely. In his first attempt at describing the conversion, Gibbon's longstanding interest in religious questions and the unguided freedom to pursue his curiosity leads him "to the study of the disputes between the Protestants and the Papists."[65] He "persuaded himself" that the Papists had the better case and yielded to the argument (judged "specious" in hindsight) that "a wise legislator would provide a supreme and visible Judge for the interpretation of his laws."[66] This was a conversion of the intellect rather than the heart, initiated by books rather than individuals of exemplary piety (or as Gibbon puts it, there were to his knowledge no "Romish Wolves" amid the Oxonian flock). "The sincere change of my speculative opinions was not inflamed by any lively sense of devotion or enthusiasm," Gibbon says.[67] In subsequent drafts, Gibbon would allow himself "the ardor of a youth, and the zeal of a proselyte," while calling the sincerity of his own conviction into question.[68] "Without a master or a guide," Gibbon writes, "I unfortunately stumbled on some books of Popish controversy; nor is it a matter of reproach that a boy should have believed that he believed, etc."[69] Having devolved from an intellectual transformation into a youthful indiscretion, the conversion can be filed away alongside similar episodes in others' lives: "I was seduced like Chillingworth and Bayle, and, like them, my growing reason soon broke through the toils of sophistry and superstition."[70] This is the least that can be said of the matter.[71]

In the last draft of his *Memoirs*, Gibbon returns to the generosity that characterized the first narrative to touch on the conversion. The scene expands considerably, and the emotional register in which Gibbon narrates the scene develops as well. "Youth is sincere and impetuous," he writes in this final draft, "and a momentary glow of Enthusiasm had raised me above all temporal considerations." Gibbon declares himself "proud of an honest sacrifice of interest to conscience."[72] Here Gibbon's conversion is every bit as literary as it was before. "I never conversed with a priest, or even with a papist, till my resolution from books was absolutely fixed."[73] But the spiritual significance of an intellectual conversion is more clearly on display. Books occasion a change of not only mind but heart.

Which books? In earlier drafts Gibbon hadn't said, but in this final draft he cites two sources in particular.[74] The second, Jacques-Bénigne Bossuet, whom Gibbon credits with having "achieved his conversion," is the more conventional of the two. Gibbon cites the French bishop's "Exposition of the Catholic Doctrine," originally written in 1670 to return Huguenots to the Catholic faith, and the *History of the Protestant Variations*, published in 1688, which argued that the incessant sectarianism and schism afflicting Protestants indicated the need for an authoritative judge like the Catholic pope. The young Gibbon found the theology of these works persuasive; looking back, the later Gibbon appreciated them as works of rhetoric. Bossuet was a "master of all the weapons of controversy" who used "consummate art" to transform "the ten-horned Monster . . . into the milk-white hind."[75] "I surely fell," Gibbon says, "by a noble hand."

But Gibbon fell, on his telling, because Bossuet's treatises came on the heels of another, unexpected, intellectual transformation occasioned by Conyers Middleton's *Free Inquiry*.[76] This work attempted to answer an important and potentially explosive question within Protestant sacred history: If "miracles had ceased," at what point had they ceased? As we have seen in the previous chapter, this question was important insofar as Catholic claims to sacred and sacramental authority rested on the continuance of miracles into the present; it was potentially explosive insofar as techniques used to expose fraudulent miracles in one era might be turned on even earlier eras, including the time of Christ and the apostles. Conventionally, Protestant historians respected a three-century fence around that period and held that genuine miracles had ceased when Christianity became the established religion of the Roman Empire.[77] Middleton moved the fence closer to sacred territory. On the basis of careful and critical reading of the Church fathers—figures whom Gibbon would himself go on to scrutinize in the *Decline and Fall*—Middleton claimed that genuine miracles had ceased with the death of the last apostle toward the end of the first century.[78] To Middleton's mind, this approach to sacred history offered the only sure way for Protestants to resist papal authority, since the same fathers who attested to miracles after the apostles also established the power of the Roman Church. Many attacked Middleton's argument as a gateway to the denial of miracles altogether, but it could not plausibly be taken as a road to Rome.[79] Indeed, it was precisely to close such roads that Middleton claimed to have written. "I found myself particularly excited to [search into the origin and evidences of our religion], by what I had occasionally observed and heard, of the late growth of Popery in this Kingdom, and the great number of Popish books, which have been printed and dispersed amongst us, within these past few years," Middleton wrote. "The most powerful of all their arguments, and what gains them the most proselytes," he continued, "is, their confident attestation of miracles, as subsisting still in their Church, and the clear succession of them, which they deduce through all history, from the Apostolic times, down to our own."[80] Gibbon read against the grain. Revering the names Middleton cited and "unable to resist the weight of historical evidence," Gibbon rejected Middleton's exposure of these miracles' fraudulence and accepted that they were inextricably bound with the authority of the Catholic Church.[81] Based on this unusual response to Middleton, Gibbon was "more than half a convert" when he encountered Bossuet.

The ironies of Gibbon's conversion were many. He rejected Oxford by enacting its medieval and monastic essence, as he would come to understand it. Gibbon also broke with his father by carrying to its extreme a principle that generations of Gibbons had lacked the courage to pursue. Though hardly all English Catholics were Jacobites, and an even smaller portion of Jacobites were Catholic, there was still something bracingly reactionary and ancestrally appropriate in the particular sort of rupture that Gibbon settled on.[82] Most remarkable of all was Gibbon's ambivalence—to call it irony would suggest perhaps too much control over the effect—about what his conversion amounted to. In one draft, the conversion was a fleeting swoon, a quick switchback on the path from superstition to reason; in another, it was merely a change of opinion, all head and no heart. In neither of these retellings was Gibbon, whose dalliance with Catholicism was a welcome point of attack for Protestant critics of the *Decline and Fall*, particularly proud of the episode.

In the fullest and last account, however, his conversion ran along the nerve joining head and heart: an encounter with books kindled new opinions and "a momentary glow of enthusiasm," issuing in action so resolute and courageous that the memoirist could only admire his younger self. The first two accounts of conversion were stages in the education of a skeptic and infidel. The last account suggested an author with sufficient range to appreciate both the virtues and the vices of religious faith.[83] This later Gibbon could put on or take off his "sneer" at will.

What, then, were the pieties surrounding Gibbon as a young man? In the *Memoirs* Gibbon recognized the potential for education through familial veneration that had little to do with Christianity. By the time of his grandfather, however, the links to this sort of education had been lost. In its place were his grandfather's worldly interests and Law's disinterest in the matters of this world. Neither had any lasting impact on Gibbon's father, according to his son, and England's religious and educational institutions were inadequate to repair the failures of the family. As a young man, therefore, Gibbon encountered a gamut of religious options—from Law's uncompromising devotion to the Mallets' freethinking—none of which had any particular hold on him. His desire to find the authority, elevation, and education his world lacked left him prey to the "Romish wolves." His first conversion was a farewell to all of that.

SWITZERLAND: GIBBON'S RETURN TO THE "RELIGION OF [HIS] COUNTRY"

Gibbon's father did not take the news well. In a panic, he informed the university of his son's transgression.[84] He then lodged his son briefly with a friend in Putney, the Scottish playwright David Mallet, who had himself been raised a Catholic before converting to "freethinking." Gibbon would record being "rather scandalized than reclaimed" by Mallet's philosophy, which it seems the playwright attempted to impart.[85] Days later, on the advice of another friend, Gibbon's father settled on exiling his son to the house of Daniel Pavillard, a Calvinist minister in Lausanne, Switzerland. Not two weeks after becoming a Catholic, Gibbon had been sent to the Continent to be returned to Protestantism.

The reconversion occurred more quickly than his father could have hoped. On Christmas Day 1754, having been a Catholic for eighteen months, Gibbon "sincerely confessed that the doctrine and worship of the Protestants are most agreeable to sense and scripture, and . . . received the sacrament in the Cathedral of Lausanne."[86] This account of the reconversion, set clearly in Switzerland and leaving Gibbon an unambiguous Protestant, occurs in the third of Gibbon's six drafts of the *Memoirs*; in later drafts, Gibbon would circumscribe the scene considerably. In the fourth draft, the reconversion occurs early in the section on Switzerland: "The first use of my reason was to reject the dreams of superstition, and my father rejoiced in the intelligence that I had again professed myself a member of the Protestant Church."[87] In the fifth, the reconversion is extracted from Switzerland altogether and collapsed into the conversion scene: "I was seduced like Chillingworth and Bayle, and, like them, my growing reason soon broke through the toils of sophistry and superstition."[88] In each of these accounts, the source of the conversion, Gibbon's "reason," remains constant: the more reason, the less Catholicism. But just what Gibbon is converting to shifts subtly, from the firm avowal of the "doctrine and worship of the Protestants," to rejection of superstition joined to 'profession' of Protestantism, to rejection of "sophistry and superstition" with at least some ambiguity regarding what is being affirmed. Is it possible to break through "sophistry and superstition" and emerge into something other than Protestantism?

The fullest account of Gibbon's reconversion appears in the second draft of the *Memoirs*, which anticipates his subsequent gestures at the ambivalence of the religious position he arrived at in 1754. In this draft, Gibbon narrates his time in Switzerland as the inversion of his time in Oxford. At Oxford, Gibbon had an initial impression of "surprise and satisfaction" at his own freedom and the beauty of his surroundings; at Lausanne, Gibbon discovers the "strange and melancholy prospect" of life *chez Pavillard*, a household located on "a narrow, gloomy street, the most unfrequented of an unhandsome town," maintained by an "ugly, dirty, proud, ill-tempered and covetous" woman (that is, Madame Pavillard), and in which Gibbon was "degraded to the dependence of a schoolboy."[89] But Gibbon's first-sight love of Oxford gave way, as we have seen, to his condemnation of an antiquated and corrupt institution. His loathing for Lausanne (but not Madame Pavillard) would also transform, and he would go on to describe the city as "a place where I spent near five years with pleasure and profit, which I afterwards revisited without compulsion, and which I have finally selected as the most grateful retreat for the decline of my life."[90] Gibbon could "disclaim [Oxford] for my mother" because the true site of his education—he goes so far as to say his "creation"—was Lausanne.[91]

For Gibbon, Lausanne represented a new model of education. In place of the series of ill-suited and untalented tutors and schoolmasters who punctuated his early education there was now Daniel Pavillard. Gibbon describes him as far from brilliant but nonetheless clearheaded, kind, and "rational because he was moderate." Above all, Pavillard was "skilled in the arts of teaching."[92] Aware of his own intellectual limits and eager to know the character of his pupil, Pavillard devised a pedagogy that suited the respective strengths and weaknesses of teacher and student. Pavillard focused more on the form than the content of Gibbon's curriculum: he did not prescribe a syllabus of books, for the most part, but did insist on a schedule and a broad designation of subjects, within which he allowed his pupil freedom to pursue his own interests. Gibbon responded marvelously. Whereas Gibbon's reading as a young man had been voracious and indiscriminate with a pronounced taste for the exotic, under Pavillard he pursued a plan and developed "habits of application and method," including the "salutary habit of early rising."[93] Pavillard provided enough structure to direct his pupil's prodigious intellectual energy but not so much as to stifle it. Gibbon found the result invigorating.[94]

There was one notable exception to Pavillard's general rule, and it touched on the purpose of Gibbon's stay in Lausanne. To facilitate Gibbon's reentry into the Protestant fold, Pavillard assigned the *Logic* by Jean Pierre de Crousaz, the master of Pavillard himself as well as many other Swiss clergymen.[95] Crousaz had been the apostle of Enlightenment to the Swiss. From an appointment at the Academy of Lausanne, where he had been born and would die not long before Gibbon's arrival, Crousaz spread a moderate strain of reform—the Enlightenment of Locke, Limbroch, and Le Clerc[96]—which he turned by equal measures against "Calvinistic prejudice" and the skepticism of Bayle. The mature Gibbon would find much to criticize in Crousaz's *Logic*, but at the age of sixteen Gibbon had seen nothing like it.[97] He found in Crousaz's "art of reasoning" a weapon of power that he could master and turn to his own purposes.[98] "I studied, and meditated, and abstracted" Crousaz's work, Gibbon writes, "till I have obtained the free command of an universal instrument, which I soon presumed to exercise on my catholic opinions."[99] In a subsequent draft of the *Memoirs*, Gibbon would describe the impact of Bossuet's insistence on the plain meaning of "Hoc est corpus meum!" against the "figurative half-meanings of the Protestant sects."[100] Here in the second draft he deploys Crousaz's empiricism on just this point: the text of scripture attesting to the real presence appeals to our sight but is disproved by sight, touch, and taste.[101] Demonstrating the intellectual pride that Pavillard had evidently detected, Gibbon reminisces about the "solitary transport" that this discovery afforded.[102] While allowing Pavillard "an handsome share of the honor of my conversion," Gibbon reserves the larger share for himself on the basis of his "private reflections" in response to the reading Pavillard had recommended and supervised.[103] However teacher and pupil apportioned the credit, their relationship—remote guidance but for the inculcation of scholarly habits and with the exception of the study of Crousaz and the discussions it produced—had the intended effect. Gibbon returned to the faith of his father.

Gibbon's father was hardly a saint, however. His own pious tutor William Law had dubbed him "Flatus." The son was more kind, at least in depicting his father's reaction to the initial conversion: "He was neither a bigot nor a philosopher; but his affection deplored the loss of a son, and his good-sense could not understand or excuse my strange departure from the Religion of my Country."[104] His was not, or was not necessarily, a burning faith of the heart but a more conventional form of devotion mediated by commitments to family and fatherland. It was not Christianity per se but the "Religion of [one's] Country" that the father meant to defend. And it was to something like this attitude toward religion that the son would return.

In the fullest account of his reconversion, Gibbon notes the time (Christmas Day 1754) and the place (Church of Lausanne) before closing the scene with a remarkable coda. "It was here that I suspended my religious enquiries," Gibbon writes, "acquiescing with implicit belief in the tenets and mysteries which are adopted by the general consent of Catholics and Protestants."[105] This Gibbon, who could acquiesce (not assent) to implicit belief (rather than genuine faith) in the doctrines shared by Catholics and Protestants (not those that distinguished a particular sect), was a young man quite different from the Oxford student willing to stake his inheritance on a point of conviction. In Lausanne, Gibbon converted not to any particular religion but to a new view of the phenomenon of religion. He would now be largely indifferent to religion as a matter of salvation or personal devotion. Gibbon was willing to acquiesce and follow the "general consent" in his outward actions because his true energies—the calling that he now began to feel in earnest—directed his attention elsewhere.[106]

In the years following his reconversion Gibbon became not a saint but a scholar. He consciously rejected the *topoi* of conversion in accounting for this development: "Every man who rises above the common level has received two educations: the first from his teachers; the second, more personal and important, from himself. He will not, like the fanatics of the last age, define the moment of grace; but he cannot forget the aera of his life in which his mind has expanded to its proper form and dimensions."[107] The language of conversion appears inappropriate because it attenuates Gibbon's personal responsibility for his education, and because it attributes to a single moment what in fact occurred over an era. But it is not only as a form of historical explanation that conversion seems ill-suited to Gibbon at this point. The content of his intellectual interests had also changed. He was no longer the young man whose soul stirred at Bossuet but not yet the historian who would follow Middleton's path into early church history. Instead, he devoted himself to becoming a "man of letters," a humanist as concerned with pagan antiquity as with what followed it.

Gibbon pursued his education assiduously in the years following his return to Protestantism, especially during an eight-month stretch from April to December 1755 that he considered "the period of the most extraordinary diligence and rapid progress."[108] Gibbon immersed himself in the literary culture not only of ancient skepticism but of medieval and modern Catholicism. It was during this time, for instance, that he first read Pascal.[109] Gibbon also had the opportunity to travel outside Lausanne. These travels included some exposure—carefully chaperoned, of course—to Catholicism as practiced outside of England.

It was on his initial minor tour of Switzerland that an eighteen-year-old Gibbon visited the Einsiedeln Abbey and recorded in his journal the powerful impression it made. "It takes a mind well prepared by good philosophy not to feel a certain trembling (*tremoussement*), a certain—in English I would say Awe—easier to feel than to define. Such is the force of prejudice, so great is the power of our imagination."[110] Gibbon gives the impression here of a soul not yet entirely reformed. His reconversion was carefully guarded by Pavillard, who accompanied Gibbon on the trip, and by the tools his spiritual guide had imparted: "good philosophy" (Locke, de Crousaz, et al.) and an account of Catholicism as a superstition rooted in prejudice and imagination.[111]

It was also during this time that Gibbon mastered both Latin and French. By the end of 1755 he had read much of Cicero; by 1756 he maintained Latin correspondences with European scholars.[112] His reading notes dropped his mother tongue for French, which he would continue to prefer until service in the Hampshire militia and careful study of Addison and Swift repatriated him.[113] But that was almost a decade in the future. In the fall of 1756 Gibbon proudly used his French to report his progress in the Latin classics to his *tres cher Pere*.[114] He reported starting Greek as well. In *Memoirs* we learn that on Pavillard's suggestion Gibbon began with John's Gospel; then "at my earnest request we presumed to open the Iliad."[115] The "trembling" of his heart notwithstanding, Gibbon's interests were now more classical than Christian.[116]

Gibbon's Swiss education culminated in his first book, *Essai sur l'étude de la littérature*, which we shall consider in the following chapter. This period also had something to do with an episode toward the end of 1759 when Gibbon, having returned to England from Lausanne a year earlier, made "a regular trial of the evidence of Christianity" and, finding the evidence wanting, abandoned Christianity as a matter of personal faith. Gibbon did not, however, abandon Christianity as a matter of social practice; he continued to attend services at the parish church at Buriton.[117] As a matter of scholarly inquiry, Christianity became increasingly central to Gibbon's concerns. Partly this growth in interest had to do with Gibbon's voracious reading. But it had also to do with his reflections on the religions surrounding him—never so much as during his Grand Tour of Catholic France and Italy.

EUROPE: GIBBON'S PILGRIMAGE TO ROME

A few months short of twenty-six when he disembarked, Gibbon was older than the average Tourist. He was also more experienced, having already encountered at close range many of the foreign and potentially dangerous ideas that critics of the Tour traditionally feared. Thanks to the Oxford conversion he was familiar with Catholicism—much more so, at any rate, than his father would have preferred. And he had known other forms of heterodoxy as well. Recall that Gibbon was thrust into the arms of the freethinker David Mallet just before his Swiss exile. On Tour, Gibbon encountered Catholics more beguiling than Bossuet and atheist *philosophes* more aggressive than Mallet. The *Memoirs* affect a rather dismissive stance toward both.[118] Gibbon's writings of the period, by contrast, reveal him to have engaged regularly and sympathetically with atheists *and* pious Catholics. Some of the "trembling" the eighteen-year-old felt and explained away at Einsiedeln remained. The explanation matured, however. Gibbon no longer attributed his sentiments in those moments to lingering faith. It was now beauty, not belief, that stirred his soul. Without rediscovering personal faith Gibbon began in this period to part company from the more extreme anti-Christian *philosophes* on the question of how to account for Christianity's worldly power. Indeed, the line between aesthetics and apologetics blurred to the point where Gibbon could pose as a "pilgrim" and undergo a second Roman conversion, different and more enduring than the one he experienced at Oxford.

Paris

When Gibbon reached Paris in January 1763, on the first leg of a European Tour that would subsequently take him back to Lausanne and then to Rome, he was very much in the wake of his *Essai*. An enthusiastic review had stretched across three issues of the *Journal étranger* between August and October 1761.[119] A "man of spirit and taste" has produced "one of the best works of literature to appear in our time," announced Jean-Baptiste Suard.[120] Suard found much to praise in Gibbon's work, but he paid particular attention to the *Essai*'s treatment of paganism and the origins of monotheism. "We cannot resist transcribing here a very wise and ingenious passage on the origin and progress of polytheism," Suard wrote.[121] Large extracts followed in full, and a litany of praise concluded with Suard's call for the republication of Gibbon's *Essai* in France. As the third and final installment of Suard's review appeared, the *Journal de sçavans* published a summary of the *Essai*. Glowing reviews in the *Journal encylopédique* and the *Bibliothèque des sciences* would soon follow.[122] In 1762 a new edition of the *Essai* was printed in Paris.[123]

Gibbon was hardly insensitive to this praise of his first book; the journal he kept during his stay in Paris noted six publications that had reviewed the *Essai*.[124] He was equally thrilled at his reception in the French salons. A month after his arrival he would report on his literary reputation to his father: "My book has been of great service to me, and the compliments I have received upon it would make [me] insufferably vain, if I laid any stress on them."[125] The modesty is touching and evidently insincere.[126] Gibbon's journal recorded more candidly the pride he felt at having arrived: *J'etois homme de lettres reconnû*.[127]

Among the *philosophes* receiving Gibbon in Paris in 1763 were the Encyclopedists d'Alembert and Diderot and the radical materialists d'Holbach and Helvetius.[128] The memoirist of 1789 and 1790 would strike a critical tone in narrating these particular encounters. In one draft, d'Alembert and Diderot hold "the foremost rank in merit, or at least in fame"; in the next, Gibbon listened "to the oracles . . . who reigned at the head of the *Encyclopedie* and the philosophic sect."[129] Gibbon first insinuates the *philosophes* were overrated, then revises to suggest that these critics of religion had adopted religious vices. ("Sect" is never a term of praise for Gibbon.) The *philosophes* "laughed at the skepticism of Hume, preached the tenets of Atheism with the bigotry of dogmatists, and damned all believers with ridicule and contempt."[130] They are zealots every bit as intolerant as those they mock. Their critic, by contrast, appears a moderated Tory and friend to Burke, the young man "rather scandalized than reclaimed" by Mallet's deism, grown now into a sensible, religiously settled Englishman.[131]

Gibbon's contemporary accounts are rather different. Two weeks into his stay, Gibbon reports in a letter to his stepmother that he has "seen more men of letters amongst the people of fashion, than I had in two or three winters in London." Gibbon continues: "Among my acquaintance I cannot help mentioning M. Helvetius, the author of the famous book *de l'Esprit*. I met him at dinner at Madame Geoffrin's, where he took great notice of me, made me a visit next day, & has ever since treated me not in a polite but a friendly manner. Besides being a sensible man an agreeable companion, & the worthiest creature in the world He has a very pretty wife, a hundred thousand Livres a year and one of the best tables in Paris."[132] Two weeks later Gibbon would write to his father: "I have connected myself with M. Helvetius who from his heart his head and his fortune is a most valuable man. At his house I was introduced to the Baron d'Olbach who is a man of parts & fortune and has two dinners every week."[133] Gibbon's journal has him dining with Helvetius on a Monday (February 21), meeting the Baron d'Holbach, "a friend of Helvetius," at his *fort bonne maison* two days later, then receiving d'Holbach on Friday at the third-floor, two-bedroom walk-up Gibbon rented in the Faubourg Saint-Germain.[134] Although these contemporary sources are hardly exhaustive, we find little in them to suggest the shock and scandal that Gibbon would discover for his *Memoirs*.

As Gibbon appears more skeptical toward religious faith than he would later present himself, so he seems more generous toward French Catholicism.[135] Here too we must read past the defensive patriotism of the *Memoirs*. In early 1789 Gibbon could attribute the opulence of Paris to "the defects of the government and Religion" and acknowledge only fleeting glances at the ornaments of the Church.[136] "As an Englishman," Gibbon writes later that year, "I beheld without envy the rich ornaments of Paris, which has devoured a kingdom; I darted a contemptuous look on the stately monuments of superstition, and I viewed with horror the prodigies of Versailles and Marly, which have been cemented with the blood of the people."[137] Here is Gibbon at his most Protestant and republican, refusing to liberate the beautiful from the just. Monuments of superstition, no matter how stately, deserve contempt.

But there is little contempt, much less horror, in Gibbon's letters home from this period. He remarks to his stepmother that people of fashion are "incomparably better lodged" in Paris than in London. He judges the Parisians' "vast Hotels, courts, stables, gardens . . . very magnificent, as well as convenient."[138] Years later, as he nears the end of his Tour, Gibbon will report to his stepmother, "I am become a better Englishman . . . without adopting the honest prejudices of a Hampshire farmer, I am reconciled to my own country."[139] But it will take the "pride, vice, slavery and poverty" of Naples to evoke that sentiment.[140] The vast hotels of Paris only impress.

Even more telling are Gibbon's reactions to Paris's "monuments of superstition." The same day he dines with Helvetius, Gibbon visits the Church of Saint-Sulpice and a "charming little Carmelite church" nearby.[141] Gibbon records his admiration for a painting of Joseph visited by an angel and a statue of a cardinal. But he is particularly struck by "the portrait of Madame de la Valiere," Louis XIV's mistress, who, having fallen from favor, fled to the Carmelites in 1674:[142] "She is painted as Magdaline, in the moment of her conversion. She casts away her ornaments with disdain, she tears her clothes; her hair is disheveled, a stream of tears flows from her eyes. But the painter knew to preserve all of the beauty of her features and the gentleness of her bearing. It was a difficult task. If sadness and tears only embellish her charms, shame and remorse are their opposites."[143] Gibbon appreciates the composition of the painting and the craft of the painter; he considers *Madeleine repentante* one of le Brun's "masterpieces." We find Gibbon less concerned than he had been at Einsiedeln to account defensively for the way in which the painting moved him. His reaction to the painting indeed reflects some sense of the mixture of disdain, shame, and remorse the convert feels for the life left behind and the beauty and calm that hope for a better life can bring forth. Personally less pious than at Einsiedeln, Gibbon is all the more curious to understand, on secular but sympathetic terms, the power that religious belief exercises over others.

The next day Gibbon accompanies a close friend,[144] Madame Bontems, to Mass at the "large and beautiful" Church of Saint-Roch, where he takes in a homily given by a Carmelite priest. The theme, again, is conversion; specifically, the "incertitude and uselessness" of deathbed conversions. As with his recollections of Saint-Sulpice, Gibbon's reflection on the homily touches on technique and the religious theme itself. Gibbon's judgment of the priest's rhetorical style is mixed—"he frightens more than he hits home (*touchoit*)," though his voice is "distinct and very beautiful"—but his evaluation of Father Elisée's message is not. A god unreceptive to deathbed conversions is a "harsh judge, or rather a pitiless master," rather than a "common father of all nature."[145] If this last phrase recalls the bland deism with which Gibbon is frequently associated, the subtle rhetorical analysis, and the psychology of religion it suggests, reflects Gibbon's interest in how religion exercises its hold over men.

Gibbon's judgments of the Catholics he met in Paris are similarly and beguilingly mixed. Closest to him was Madame Bontems, a "devotee untainted by religious gall" in Gibbon's *Memoirs*.[146] In his journals she is a character of striking complexity: "A good Catholic, she believes firmly in the most contradictory mysteries, and she humbly practices the most popular superstitions. Fortunately the sensitivity of her character, which could have led her toward devotion, prevailed. It did not allow the goodness of her soul, nor the gaiety of her humor, to vanish. Madame Bontems could love God like a fanatic, but she could not hate her enemies. She said to me a hundred times that the damnation of the heretics challenged her faith very much. Her heart corrected her mind."[147] To be a "good Catholic" entails firm belief in contradictions and humble practice of popular superstitions. Gibbon does not think that fanatical love of the God who enjoins us to love our enemies can explain Madame Bontems's inability to hate hers. Her virtues stem instead from her character, soul, and humor—her nature rather than her faith. Still, Gibbon does not dismiss Madame Bontems for her faith—quite the contrary. As with his admiration for the beauty of "monuments of superstition," so with the superstitious themselves.

Lausanne

In May 1763 Gibbon left Paris for a homecoming of sorts in Lausanne, where he passed eleven months reconnecting with old friends and anticipating the culmination of his European Tour. The religious life of his foster fatherland had changed little in the five years he had been away. There were no new churches to visit, no strange rituals to observe. Gibbon himself, however, had matured. While serving in the Hampshire militia he had made a trial of his faith and found it wanting. In Paris he discovered and practiced the capacity to appreciate the beauty of Catholic art—indeed, of Catholics, if not Catholicism—free of the confessional distortions that had interposed at Einsiedeln. The twenty-six-year-old returning to Lausanne was not the twenty-one-year-old who had departed, nor was he the young man who, on Christmas Day 1754 in the Church of Lausanne, had acquiesced "with implicit belief in the tenets and mysteries which are adopted by the general consent of Catholics and Protestants."[148] Gibbon was now less concerned with religion as a matter of personal faith and considerably more concerned to understand how religion influenced worldly politics.

It was during this second stay in Lausanne that Gibbon wrote his most extensive reflection on contemporary Swiss politics, the "Letter on the Government of Berne."[149] This remarkable letter is the closest approximation to a republican, if not revolutionary, tract that we have from Gibbon's hand.[150] But for the hand we might not guess the letter to be Gibbon's. The anonymous author of the letter identifies himself as a Swede banished from his homeland as a young man to a Swiss exile. Like Gibbon, the author of the letter passed formative years of his youth in the Pays de Vaud.[151] He has since returned home, to a country that is "tranquil under the protection of its laws," and seems to have reflected on the differences between the two countries that formed him. The Swede writes to persuade his "dear friend" that he is wrong to think the Pays de Vaud free. Borrowing language from Montesquieu and Rousseau, and anticipating the slogans of the French (and, as it happens, the Vaudois) Revolutionaries, the Swede portrays the Bernese aristocrats who have ruled the Pays de Vaud more or less peaceably for two centuries as "masters"; their bailiffs, tyrants; and the Vaudois, slaves. "If freedom consists in submitting only to those laws that aim at the common good of the society," writes the Swede, "you are not free."[152]

The religious politics of the Pays de Vaud figure prominently in both the Swede's analysis of tyranny and his friend's misperception of freedom. The Swede first acknowledges that in countries surrounding the Pays de Vaud "reason is stupefied by superstition," while the Vaudois "profess a Christianity restored to the divine purity of its founding, taught by worthy pastors who can be loved and respected without being feared."[153] The Reformation, with its reconception of the priesthood, constitutes a form of liberation. The Swede then proceeds to subvert this pleasing picture, first with a sweeping claim about the internal dynamics of empire. "The citizens of a capital city look with a jealous eye on the improvement of the provinces. If the provinces ascend, they say, we fall."[154] It is for this reason that the aristocrats of Bern chose not to welcome the wealthiest and most industrious Huguenot refugees after 1685; it is for the same reason that those Huguenots who did manage to settle in the Pays de Vaud—those "lacking the means and the will to travel further"—were subject to religious persecution. "The state's governing party had imbibed with its mothers' milk all the hardness of the system of Calvin, that splenetic theologian (*théologien atrabilaire*), who loved liberty too much to allow Christians to wear any chains but his own."[155] The Bernese probed into "theological minutia." Pastors who had grown old in their ministry and wanted only to avoid controversy were given the "choice between perjury or poverty."[156] The Swede suggests, then, that the same forces that impoverish the provinces—namely, the capital city's fear of nascent rivals—also militate for religious uniformity.[157] Although the public persecution of the Huguenot refugees ended long ago, a "muted inquisition" remains. A private letter branding a Vaudois an Armenian or a Socinian prevents him from holding office.

For all of that, and though he expects remonstrance to fall on deaf ears, the Swede does not recommend revolution. "I will never, like a seditious tribune, seek to have the people shake off the yoke of authority, to lead them from murmur to sedition, from sedition to anarchy, and from anarchy perhaps to despotism."[158] What, then, is to be done? The Swede exhorts his Vaudois friend not to fear "fictional monsters" (*quelques monstres de romans*) and to follow reason rather than prejudice. "The Bernois have rights to your obedience; you fear to do them injustice in withdrawing it."[159] There the manuscript breaks off.

To what conclusion was the Swede building? Perhaps to a recommendation of passive resistance or civil disobedience.[160] The Swede seems at the very least to want his friend to deny the Bernois' *rights* to obedience and not to see the act of disobedience as *injustice*. In short, if the Pays de Vaud is to remain under the government of Bern, the Vaudois ought at least to acknowledge that government for what it is—a tyranny—and to agitate for laws that more nearly reflect the common good, not just the narrow interests of Bern. It is possible, too, to read the letter more expansively as an articulation, through the specific politics of Swiss cantons, of a much broader project of enlightenment. In the Swede's crucial recommendation not to let the fear of fictional monsters blind one to the dynamics of empire, we might discern the early stirrings of an account of Christianity's rise rooted in secondary or secular causes. To open sacred history to rational examination would mitigate imaginary fears and constitute a sort of liberation—one even more thoroughgoing than that of the Reformation.

However compelling each of those interpretations may be, the text of the letter offers yet another way to conceive of the Swede's practical advice. In the course of considering what the Vaudois should do, the Swede rejects the way of William Tell—that is, revolution—but comes close to endorsing the way of Abraham Davel. The onetime commander of the Vaud militia, Davel initiated in 1723 an unarmed uprising against Bern's imposition of the "Helvetic Consensus," the creed hostile to the Huguenot refugees then living in the Pays de Vaud. Davel claimed at the time and maintained under torture that his advocacy for Vaud's autonomy from Bern was inspired directly by God. "What stopped the persecution?" the Swede asks. It was not the Bernois' shame, nor the Vaudois' arms, but "the fear inspired by the enterprise of Davel—an enthusiast, it is true, but an enthusiast for the public good."[161] An unarmed prophet trained in the art of war had preserved or recovered the liberty the Vaudois had enjoyed. If the Swede allows that Davel's grander ambitions were thwarted—he did not achieve his goal of regaining the Vaud's autonomy nor in precluding a "muted inquisition"—his mode of opposition to foreign tyranny still seemed exemplary. At the very least, the example of Davel required one to acknowledge that religion might inspire resistance to tyranny as well as tyrannical persecution.

This line of argument may have been suggested to Gibbon by a sermon he took in on December 1, 1763, in the Church of Lausanne—the same where he had entered into communion not quite nine years before. The occasion was a ceremony enacting Bern's sovereignty over the Vaud. The bailiff—one of the magistrates whose tyranny the Swede decried—would be presented to the congregation, the citizens of Lausanne were to swear an oath of allegiance, and the minister would preach a sermon. Gibbon had so far attended Church only infrequently since returning to Lausanne, but he knew enough of this minister to have low expectations. "His compositions, lacking passion and ideas, do not often qualify for the name of 'sermons,'" Gibbon recorded in his diary. But the minister cleared this low bar. "Today he showed the talents of an orator and the sentiments of a citizen," Gibbon wrote of the minister. "He knew to speak to the Sovereign about his duties, and to the people about their rights, both of which were founded on the will of free men to give themselves a prince, and in no way a tyrant. He praised only a little—with justice, and without blandness."[162] Here was a latter-day Davel, superior in moderation and probably in prudence. His advice to the citizens of the Pays de Vaud was essentially that of the Swede to his friend: do not revolt and do not merely remonstrate but conceive of your relationship in a manner that dignifies the ruler and the ruled. It is not incidental that the speech is spoken by a minister inside a cathedral to congregants anticipating a sermon undeserving of the name. Gibbon at this point, if not before, discovered that religion—even a religion that opened the way to persecutions and inquisitions—could facilitate worldly strength and political liberty.[163]

If this seemed a lesson particularly suited to Switzerland, Gibbon did not allow it to confine his attention to his immediate surroundings. Throughout his stay in Lausanne he kept an eye on the roads leading south. "My studies were mostly preparations for my Classic tour," he would write of his reading during this time. "Perhaps I might boast that few travelers more completely armed and instructed have ever followed the footsteps of Hannibal."[164] Gibbon's journals suggest that his preparations proceeded along three tracks.

Most prominent were readings and drafts for *Recueil Geographique*, a study of Italian topography that Gibbon envisioned as a fusion of erudition and philosophy along the lines suggested by his *Essai*.[165] "I would place myself with Romulus on the Palatine Mount, and thus proceed to the different quarters of Rome, from the cradle of the nation to the first pomoerium of the city," before following the progress of the Roman legions and then surveying the whole as divided by Augustus. Simultaneously, Gibbon intended to examine "with the eye of a philosopher the interior of the country and the manners of its inhabitants."[166] Gibbon expected that the public would receive such a book favorably—"it might enrich a bookseller"—but he never completed it.[167]

A second line of reading, sometimes intersecting with the first, consisted in Gibbon's ongoing survey of ancient literature. He read the *Satires* by Juvenal, "who, in future, will be one of my favorite authors." Juvenal's "inconstancy of opinion" regarding the gods struck Gibbon. At times Juvenal was pious and submissive, but elsewhere "wisdom suffices, and prudence usurps the throne of all the divinities"; a few days later Gibbon considers Juvenal "an old Roman . . . who sincerely venerated the divinity though he was inclined to laugh at the polytheism of his fellow-citizens."[168] Gibbon returns to Strabo and Vergil and passes Christmas Day with Horace, who inspires an essay on Roman roads. Alongside Claudius Rutilius, Gibbon travels through the Roman Empire of the fifth century, a time when "the springs of government were worn out; the national character, religion, laws, military discipline, even the seat of empire, and the language itself, had been altered or destroyed, under the impression of time and accident."[169] Gibbon criticizes Rutilius's poetry but considers his character on the whole amiable, if vain. In a remarkable passage Gibbon even excuses Rutilius's sectarianism:

> Rutilius detested the Jews, and despised the monks. Was this in *him* a crime? I could wish indeed that his feelings had been expressed with more philosophical moderation, and rested on a better principle. But he was a Pagan, who beheld his religion sinking under the weight of years, and involving the empire in its fall. The Christians insulted the decline of his sect, which they endeavored to hasten by persecution. A little bad humor was excusable. Nothing can be more animated than his description of the monks in the isle of Capraria, or more judicious than the reflections with which it is accompanied. The folly of these monks is extreme, in thinking that God took pleasure in the sufferings of his creatures; but their conduct was conformable with their principles. Had Rutilius lived in the twelfth century, what would he have said of their successors, who availed themselves of their voluntary poverty and humility, to acquire the esteem of the multitude, and of that esteem, to appropriate to themselves temporal power, and half the riches of Europe?[170]

In his reading of Rutilius, as with Juvenal, Gibbon begins to adopt the persona of a philosophical pagan. Although he condemns Juvenal's "hatred of mankind" Gibbon sympathizes with his (and his contemporary Tacitus's) caustic irony toward Rome's tyrants; although he considers Rutilius immoderate and ill-humored, Gibbon can adopt his detestation of Jews and monks. Most remarkable in these passages is the way in which Gibbon expands the purview of the personae he adopts. While conversing as a contemporary with Strabo and Horace on Roman roads, Gibbon has Rutilius peer past his own time into the twelfth century. The question he presents Rutilius appears rhetorical but is not. How could a philosophical pagan, a persona Gibbon was beginning to inhabit with ease, account for the acquisition of temporal power by means of poverty and humility?

Gibbon's third line of study during this time consisted in reading some fifty volumes of the *Bibliothèque Raisonnée*, a learned journal "containing easy and interesting productions, that . . . may be read by snatches, at moments which would otherwise be lost."[171] Gibbon's reactions to these productions in his journal offer a relatively unfiltered record of how he placed himself among the authors of the day. Gibbon criticizes a *Letter concerning the Food of the First Men* for hurrying men out of their vegetarianism, since "nothing short of urgent danger could overcome [man's] natural repugnance to the shedding of blood."[172] We find him endorsing the intent of Voltaire's *Treatise on Toleration*—"to awaken the soul the feelings of humanity, and display the dreadful consequences of superstition"—but criticizing its execution.[173] In response to a review of Heinrich von Allwoerden's *Historia Michaelis Serveti*, Gibbon offers a psychology of religious persecution: "Calvin was not actuated by worldly motives, but by a mistaken religious zeal, and a respect for maxims which, though cruel and sanguinary, were acknowledged and avowed by all Christian churches."[174] He continues, "Men's actions are never less guided by their principles, than when those principles run counter to the natural sentiments of humanity. The heart here corrects the errors of the understanding. A man of a humane character, under the influence of a false zeal, will in his closet condemn a heretic to death; but will he drag him to the stake? Not to shudder at the shedding of innocent blood, requires a heart totally insensible to pity."[175] Even under the sway of "false zeal and an erroneous conscience," pity makes itself heard. "Will not the unhappy theologian feel a combat in his own breast between religion and humanity?"[176] How then to explain Calvin's "abominable cruelty"? Perhaps worldly motives matter after all. "[Calvin] was the legislator of a new republic, and experienced the difficulties incident to innovators," Gibbon writes. "It was necessary that the throne of the reformer should be cemented with the blood of Servetus."[177] Gibbon here measures the psychological forces capable of overturning pity or humanity; though initially inclined to credit religious zeal with this power, he is more comfortable with an account rooted in political ambition. Calvin's cruelty is at bottom a political passion animating and instrumentalizing theological maxims. That recognition does not prevent Gibbon from endorsing Voltaire's verdict: "Calvin had an atrocious soul and an enlightened mind."[178]

In the "Letter on the Government of Bern" Gibbon had said in the voice of a Swede that Calvin "loved liberty too much to allow Christians to wear any chains but his own." It is a delightfully ambivalent statement that ties up the political and the religious so tightly as to make them indistinguishable. Calvin is legislator and liberator, and he is zealot and theologian. His kingdom is and is not of this world. Gibbon's Swede could see that the subjection of the Pays de Vaud had something to do with the intractable problem posed by theological politics of the sort that enthused Calvin. If Gibbon himself seemed at times to fly from this problem into antiquarianism—as when placing himself alongside Romulus on the Palatine mount, surveying the provinces with Augustus, or charting Rome's roads with Strabo and Horace—he increasingly put to his ancients a question derived from his experience of modern things. It was the same question he posed to Rutilius. What would you, could you, make of *this*?

Italy

In April 1764 Gibbon left Switzerland for fourteen months in Italy. He traveled from Turin as far south as Naples with William Guise, a fellow Englishman Gibbon befriended in Lausanne the year before. Gibbon considered Guise "a prudent worthy young man" who "has seen much of the world . . . without being a profound scholar."[179] As this suggests, the two friends were hardly identical. Gibbon had first traveled to Lausanne to repair a conversion occasioned by books; Guise, to learn some French while recovering from a heartbreak.[180] Guise, like Gibbon, recorded his impressions of the trip in a journal, which at times serves as a useful control, allowing one to appreciate how Gibbon's reactions diverged from those we might expect of his countrymen. After an uneventful day in Florence, for instance, Guise records, "We drove about the town to see some ridiculous ceremonies of the ridiculous religion of this bigoted people."[181]

Gibbon sometimes approaches this tone. An audience with the king of Sardinia, for instance, stirs his love of English liberty: "For me a court is an object both of curiosity and disgust. . . . I view with horror the magnificence of palaces built with the blood of the people."[182] And Gibbon's doctrinal skepticism sometimes influences his aesthetic judgments. He praises Guido Reni's painting of Saint Francis for "converting a madman canonized by superstition into a great man, without completely losing the resemblance"; at the same artist's *Holy Trinity* Gibbon snickers, "What a satire of the doctrine is a picture of it."[183] But these sorts of dismissals and critiques are surprisingly scarce in Gibbon's journal. As at Paris, so on his journey to Rome Gibbon could acknowledge that "the Catholic superstition, which is always the enemy of reason, is often the parent of taste."[184]

Gibbon's reactions to the art he encountered in Italy reveal his taste to have been liberated from his condemnation of superstition. In Genoa Gibbon visits the Church of the Jesuits, where he sees Rubens's *Circumcision* and *St. Ignatius Healing a Possessed Woman,* the themes of which readers of the *Decline and Fall* might expect to elicit at least a passing sneer.[185] Instead, Gibbon praises the "nobility and ease of [Rubens's] brush," and he admires the figure and bearing of Ignatius. If only the crowds of the faithful would allow him to come closer to the paintings: "I am disappointed because I love Rubens so much."[186] A week later in Parma Gibbon encounters Correggio's *Madonna del S. Girolamo*. "I had never before known the power of painting," he writes. "I would admire the art of the imitation without being touched by its truth. [But] here the character of peace and tenderness that breathes on the canvas communicates itself to the soul of the Spectator. Forced at last to tear himself away, he experiences the sad feeling of losing what he loves."[187] How far Gibbon has come from the young Protestant traveling in Switzerland, indignant at the very idea of "the mother of God."[188]

Gibbon responds in a similar way to artistic renderings of pagan themes. Venus figures prominently in his entries after visits to Florence's Uffizi Gallery. Of the *Venus de' Medici* Gibbon writes, "To know it one must see it. I have seen it: but will the most faithful, the most vivid imagination preserve the image that my senses have given me? It is the most voluptuous sensation that my eye has ever received."[189] On his final visit he describe Titian's *Venus of Urbino* similarly: "Can one forget the Venus of Titian, an admirable and voluptuous piece?"[190] In the *Memoirs* Gibbon would relate these aesthetic experiences in Florence in the tones of a conversion story: "In the gallery, and especially in the Tribune, I first acknowledged, at the feet of the Venus of Medicis, that the chisel may dispute the pre-eminence with the pencil—a truth in the fine arts which cannot, on this side of the Alps, be felt or understood."[191]

If Gibbon had previously reenacted the Christian conversion as modeled by Paul and Augustine, by the time he reached Florence he was fully in the midst of the sort of transformation that latter-day advocates of the Tour had envisioned. One was meant to experience nature in its beauty, through immediate exposure to ancient and modern works of art. Gibbon's experience indeed elided the pagan and Christian worlds. He was moved by both the "peace and tenderness" of Correggio's Mary and the "voluptuous sensation" aroused by the *Venus de' Medici.*

On the morning of July 14 Gibbon and Guise had planned their eighth visit to the Uffizi, but their usual guide was unavailable owing to the visit of a distinguished guest. Henry Benedict Stuart, the younger brother of the

Young Pretender, had been made a cardinal in 1747 (much to his brother's chagrin) and ordained a year later. Although in 1764 there was little prospect of another Jacobite rising, Cardinal York was nevertheless a living reminder of how recent those turmoils were.[192] Gibbon and Guise lingered near the Uffizi to catch a glimpse of him. Guise thought the thirty-nine-year-old "very thin, unhealthy, and decay'd";[193] Gibbon thought he seemed sickly and had the air of one much older than he in fact was. "They say he is a good man but excessively bigoted and under the Jesuits' control," Gibbon recorded.[194]

It was thanks to this coincidence—"a pause or more precisely a singular chance"—that Gibbon passed several days in Florence reading the *Introduction à l'Histoire de Dannemarc* by Paul Henri Mallet.[195]

Born in Geneva in 1730, Mallet at the age of twenty-two had been appointed Royal Professor in French Literature at the University of Copenhagen. This was a new position created only two years earlier, and when Mallet arrived it had yet to earn much of a following. "The professor often found himself without students," explains his biographer, "but he made the most of his leisure."[196] He set out to write a modern and French-language history of his new home. The work that resulted bore some striking similarities to the "philosophical history" Gibbon had conceived in his *Essai*.[197] Mallet, like Gibbon, considered the discernment of "true causes" the proper work of the historian, and like Gibbon he conceived these causes not as material facts or outstanding individuals but as elements of culture: ways of thinking, spirit, manners, and genius.[198] These phenomena were more enduring than princes and legislators, but they were not unchanging. Indeed, Mallet showed particular interest in two epochal shifts: Odin's "great changes in government, manners and religion," and the subsequent introduction of "new arts, manners and opinions" with Christianity.[199]

Gibbon's notes on *l'Histoire de Dannemarc* praise the author (whom he would soon have occasion to meet in person) as a "man of sense and candor," commend the "great principle" of his work—"that the religion of Odin formed the character of the northern nations, whose effects are still perceptible among ourselves"—and take especial, and critical, notice of Mallet's accounts of conversion.[200] Gibbon dates Odin's religious innovations considerably later than Mallet, and he questions how innovative they in fact were. "This era tends to show the poverty of the human invention," Gibbon records, "as well as the policy of prophets, always obliges them to enrich new religions at the expense of the old, and to mold them conformably to the national character."[201] Odin's "conversion" of the Danes resembled at most a reformation.[202]

There followed a day of social visits and sightseeing in Florence before Gibbon was drawn back to Denmark. "I did not wish to proceed with Mr. Mallet's large history . . . [since] this would have diverted me too much from my present pursuits," Gibbon writes, "but I could not deny myself the pleasure of reading a detached part, relative to the conversion of Scandinavia, in order to see the downfall of Odin's superstition."[203] Gibbon poses himself the following question: Why did Odin's devotees in the North reject Christianity, while those in the Roman Empire embraced it "with the utmost readiness"? Gibbon rejects on historical grounds Mallet's psychologically plausible claim that these converts were largely unformed young men (in fact, Gibbon says, whole communities migrated south). Gibbon rejects as well the more cynical notion "that the leaders of the Barbarians embraced Christianity through policy . . . in order to ingratiate themselves with the conquerors."[204] Why would leaders risk alienating their followers by adopting the religion of a people they despised?[205]

Gibbon then proceeds to offer the most developed theory of conversion that we have from him prior to the *Decline and Fall.* Conversion, Gibbon acknowledges, can be achieved through fear of corporal punishment, as when the Saxons grudgingly adopted the religion of their conquerors; it can also be achieved through persuasion or conviction, when either reading and reflection or "a natural warmth of fancy" lends objects a "mental existence" so powerful as to stand for their "real presence."[206] But what most interests Gibbon at this moment, and what he considers most helpful in understanding the conversion of the Danes, is the way in which physical sensations other than fear can be bound up with a change in religious faith.

The reason some Danes retained the faith of their fathers while others converted to Christianity, he writes, "arose merely from this circumstance, that the one class left their country, whereas the other remained at home."[207] "All religions depend in some degree on local circumstances," he continues. "The least superstitious Christian would feel more devotion on Mount Cavalry than in London."[208] Surrounded by the temples and runes of their native land the Danes would massacre missionaries or spare them out of contempt. But when they moved south things changed. "Temples, altars, tombs, and consecrated places were all on the side of a new religion, which naturally insinuated itself into the void of credulity left craving in their minds. They first wondered, and then believed."[209] The northerners' encounter with the people of the south tended in the same direction. "[A barbarian's] understanding would be improved, and his heart softened, in his perpetual intercourse with the vanquished," Gibbon wrote. "Every cause would concur to make him quit a mode of worship founded on ignorance and barbarism, and to substitute in its stead a religion connected with a science which he began to relish, and inculcating the virtues of humanity which he began to value."[210] Particularly effective were "women, who mingled caresses with controversy" to win over "princes and great men." "Such means of conversion are far more efficacious than those with which a few Benedictines are furnished, who travel into the woods of Sweden to preach patience, humility, and faith to numerous bands of pirates."[211]

Gibbon's account of conversion in these passages is that of a pilgrim, or a Tourist. A pious Englishman might travel to Calvary expecting to be moved more profoundly by the firsthand experience of the place than he or she could possibly be moved by its representation. The pilgrim might expect to buttress belief with wonder. There was in any event something new that one traveled to encounter. With this novelty came excitement—and risk.

Advocates and opponents of the Grand Tour agreed that travel could transform as well as reinforce. Indeed, Richard Lassels's founding vision of the Tour had turned these alternatives into one another by packaging as an educational capstone what he very likely intended as an occasion for spiritual transformation. Traveling north from Naples Gibbon claimed to have reinforced his prior commitments: he would return home "a better Englishman . . . reconciled to my own country."[212] But on his journey south, while reading Mallet's *Introduction*, Gibbon articulated travel's alternative purpose. "The least superstitious Christian would feel more devotion on Mount Calvary than in London"; the Danes' icy recalcitrance had melted as they descended into the heart of Italy.[213] The traveler might change radically and suddenly. He might convert.

Gibbon's Tour, too, would culminate in a conversion of sorts. On September 22, 1764, Gibbon and Guise left Florence. Ten days later they reached Rome.

"We arrived at Rome at five in the evening. Since the Milvian Bridge I have been in a dream of antiquity."[214] So Gibbon's journal describes his entry into the city. The image would recur a week later in a letter to his father: "I am really almost in a dream."[215] Accustomed for more than a decade now to imagining himself "with Romulus on the Palatine Mount" surveying the city's quarter's, he was now there in person—actually walking inside of what he had to that point seen only in his mind's eye.

But if Gibbon in Rome was a classicist transported into an ecstatic reverie, he was also a gentleman on Tour, confronted with inconveniences that did not easily lend themselves to fantasy. Like Addison, Gibbon was struck by the desolate countryside surrounding the eternal city. "It seems that in this country, the more nature does for men, the more they neglect her gifts."[216] He could also descend into a Smollettian register to relate the indignities of travel. His "dream of antiquity" was "interrupted only by the customs clerks—very modern people who forced us to go on foot to search for lodging, for there are no inns, while they drove our post-chaise to the custom house. The approach to Rome is not graceful."[217] Gibbon's departure for Naples a few months later was little better. "The journey from Rome has satisfied at least one species of a disagreeable curiosity," he wrote his stepmother, "that of being acquainted with the very worst roads in the universe. You are sometimes sunk in sloughs and sometimes racked and battered on the broken remains of the Old Appian way, and when after a tedious day you at last arrive at the long desired inn, you soon wish for the moment of setting out again."[218] For all of Gibbon's grumpiness, there was, even in these candid complaints, something more than appeared in Smollett. Gibbon's mind was alive to the contrast between ancient and modern, and he was eager to generalize from his experiences, however petty, of what Rome had become.

What Gibbon witnessed, after all, was not the *laetae segetes* nor the *via Appia* but their remains. In the same letter to his father in which Gibbon claimed to be "really almost in a dream," he touched on the stuff these dreams were made on: "Whatever ideas books may have given of the greatness of that people, their accounts of the most flourishing state of Rome fall infinitely short of the picture of its ruins."[219] This last phrase is evocative and ambivalent. It is possible that Gibbon refers here to the picture one can conceive on the basis of the ruins, but it is more likely that he means to refer to the ruins themselves. Perhaps the textual descriptions of the flourishing state are not equal *even* to the ruins. Or does Gibbon suggest that the ruins are more instructive than the flourishing state—that they have more to teach us, insofar as they evoke not only the Romans' greatness but their decline? That ruins instruct in the vicissitudes of fortune, the flimsiness of glory, the danger of *hubris*—these were all important and well-worn lessons, but they were not the only lessons that Gibbon could draw. His letter home continues, "I am convinced there never existed such a nation and I hope for the happiness of mankind that there never will again."[220] Here was ancient Rome as the pinnacle of human achievement but not of human flourishing. Its ruins were not, or not only, an occasion to lament.

Rome had, after all, succumbed to a new power, the edifices and monuments of which were very much in evidence. St. Peter's did not impose the same imaginative burdens on the Tourist as did the Forum. This living Rome was the city that Richard Lassels had wanted Englishmen to see firsthand, in hopes that the sight would bring them into communion with the ancient history of the Roman Church. For Lassels, the ruins of pagan Rome—the "Head, and Mistress of the World . . . the Common Mother, the Nurse of all Virtues (while she was yet heathen)"—functioned mainly as apologetics for Rome the Holy.[221]

Lassels's process of appropriating ancient sites for Christian history included the Colosseum, the Circus of Maxentius, and temples to ancient gods. His visit to the onetime Temple of Jupiter on the Capitoline Hill was particularly noteworthy: "Having thus seen the Capitol, I went into the Noble Church of Ara Coeli which is joining to the Capitol upon the same hill, and built in the same place where anciently stood the Temple of Jupiter Capitolinus, or Jupiter Fererrius. Here it was the Sibyl showed unto Augustus Caesar, at the birth of our Savior, that a greater Lord than he was born; whereupon Augustus forbad, that any man should call him Lord from that time forward. In this Church is the tomb of St. Helen Mother of Constantine the Great." Lassels refers here to a medieval legend recorded in such works as Jacobus de Voragine's thirteenth-century *Legenda Aurea* and commonly known in the seventeenth and eighteenth centuries.[222] It is notable, in Lassels's iteration, for offering pagan confirmation (as it were) of the Incarnation and transforming an aspect of supposedly secular political history—Augustus's "absolute monarchy disguised by the forms of a commonwealth," which Gibbon attributes to the emperor having "a cool head, an unfeeling heart, and a cowardly disposition"—into testimony to a miracle.[223] It also tellingly plays on the phenomenon of ruins. The Church of the Ara Coeli holds the ground "where anciently stood" the Temple of Jupiter. As the memory of pagan antiquity has been subsumed by Christian history, so the Roman Church has replaced the ancient temple.

It is on this site that Gibbon sets his conversion: "In my Journal the place and moment of conception are recorded; the fifteenth of October, 1764, in the close of evening, as I sat musing in the Church of the Zoccolanti or Franciscan fryars, while they were singing Vespers in the Temple of Jupiter on the ruins of the Capitol."[224] The setting is recognizably the same that Lassels visited a century before. Gibbon places himself inside a Christian church. But within a sentence the space suddenly transforms for the musing visitor into "the Temple of Jupiter on the ruins of the Capitol." It is as if Gibbon closed his eyes in prayer and opened them onto the Christian world as Tacitus might have seen it: the Capitol in ruins, the Temple of Jupiter still strangely standing.

That version of the story was written sometime in late 1789 or early 1790 for the third draft of the *Memoirs*. A few months later Gibbon threw those pages back into the fire and recast the story:[225] "It was on the fifteenth of October, in the gloom of evening, as I sat musing on the Capitol, while the barefooted fryars were chanting their litanies in the temple of Jupiter, that I conceived the first thought of my history."[226] Gibbon no longer begins in a Christian church. He places himself somewhere on the Capitol (assuming we are to understand the "on" to indicate his location rather than the subject of his thought), probably within earshot of the litanies, though even that detail is not definitive. What is clear is that the friars (now barefooted) sing their litanies (not vespers) in the Temple of Jupiter. The scene is thoroughly dechristianized, and the change from ancient to modern Rome is all but eliminated. The Capitol is no longer in ruins. There is no church other than that of Jupiter in evidence. The only novelty are the barefooted friars, who are made to seem odd interlopers in an essentially classical tableau.

Having written one version of the epiphany that started in Christian Rome and turned back toward antiquity, and another that started in and hardly departed from ancient Rome, Gibbon wrote his third and final draft of the pivotal scene: "It was at Rome, on the fifteenth of October, 1764, as I sat musing amidst the ruins of the Capitol, while the barefooted fryars were singing Vespers in the temple of Jupiter, that the idea of writing the decline and fall of the City first started to my mind."[227] Gibbon is again among the ruins; the friars have returned to their vespers. And Gibbon is transformed into the historian who can approach the questions posed by the ruins (how did this all fall apart?) and by the barefooted friars (how did these men come to hold the high ground?) neither starting from the Christian and working back nor starting from the pagan and asserting that nothing has changed. Gibbon settled on a pagan view open to the possibility that something new and remarkable has happened in the world.

Gibbon's path toward this epiphany had crossed numerous, discordant contexts. To the memoirist it seemed evident that a long line of emulable ancestors had been available to the young man, but the young man knew nothing of them. The family history of the Gibbons, like the history of their country, had been disrupted by commerce and confessional controversy. Gibbon's grandfather, a self-made Jacobite, had refounded the family for this new world but had failed to act the part of the lawgiver. The education of his son (Gibbon's father) was outsourced to a "saint" and the scholars of Cambridge, neither of whom succeeded in transmitting the founder's virtues. The heir of the new prince was a louche, a lover, and ultimately a dabbler in this and that—in religion as in everything else. As a result, during a time of impressive confessional stability in England, Gibbon had been raised amid religious wreckage—the old Jacobite pieties, premonitions of the evangelical surge (thanks to Law), and freethinking redolent of the deist controversies and suggestive of the atheism he would soon encounter on the Continent. Gibbon rejected this mélange for Roman Catholicism, then conformed in Switzerland to the religion of his country. But this was largely a matter of outward practice. Gibbon's heart was now in his scholarship. As his pilgrimage across the Continent crossed Paris and Lausanne on the way to Rome, Gibbon came to realize his vocation as a scholar: to offer a secular account of religious transformation—not in his own life (though he would attempt that in the *Memoirs*) but in the history of Europe.

CHAPTER 3

Essai

Having described some of the contexts surrounding Gibbon as he became "the historian of the Roman Empire," we turn in the next three chapters to his texts. Gibbon's account of Christianity in the great work will naturally command most of our attention. But Gibbon's famously (or infamously) novel narration of Christian history as the effect of "secondary" or secular causes was in fact a return to a theme Gibbon had sounded as a young man in his first book, the *Essai sur l'étude de la littérature*. Considering the genesis of this early work, the philosophy of religion it contains, and the revisions it underwent as Gibbon's own religious commitments settled will allow us to warm up a bit in the foothills before setting out on a longer and more arduous trek through the great work. The *Essai* will also help to mark the trail we will take by introducing us to Gibbon's notion of "philosophical history."

THE RISE AND FALL OF THE *ESSAI*

The *Essai sur l'étude de la littérature* was the culmination of Gibbon's Swiss education. Begun in Lausanne in March 1758 and nearly completed at the Gibbon family home in Buriton less than a year later, the composition of the work straddled the Channel. But its origin, execution, and reception were thoroughly French.

D'Alembert's introduction to the *Encyclopedia*, published in June 1751, had divided the sciences according to intellectual faculties: philosophy was paired with reason, poetry with imagination, and history with memory. Although d'Alembert urged philosophers and artists to acknowledge their debts to scholars (*érudits*) engaged in history, the *érudits* were still relegated to a separate and, it seemed, lower branch of the "tree of knowledge."[1] D'Alembert at any rate quoted with approval Voltaire's quip that scholars "knew everything in the ancients except their grace and finesse."[2] This attack on erudition roused the spirited young classicist to take up his pen.[3] Having just passed several years reading the Latin canon, investigating arcane antiquities, and tussling with distinguished scholars over emendations, Gibbon rushed, as he later told the story, to "[vindicate] a favorite study from the unjust contempt of the French philosophers" and "prove, by my example as well as by my arguments, that all the nobler faculties, as well as memory, might be employed and displayed in the study of ancient literature."[4] What Gibbon ultimately urged on the *philosophes* was respect for erudition not as instrumental to their goal of ordering and promoting human knowledge but as partially constitutive of that goal.

The *philosophes*, as we have seen, took Gibbon's exhortation well. Written in Gibbon's naturalized French, the *Essai* was noticed warmly by journals on the Continent. In his native country, however, Gibbon's work "was received with cold indifference, little read, and speedily forgotten"—until the sensation of the *Decline and Fall*.[5] Readers then scoured bookstores throughout the British world for remaindered (or pirated) copies of his first book.[6] Gibbon decided not to authorize a second edition. The newly minted "historian of the Roman Empire" of 1776, like the memoirist of the 1780s and 1790s, considered the *Essai*—with a few caveats—a "juvenile performance."[7]

The most important of the memoirist's caveats concerned the *Essai*'s treatment of religion. In three of the four manuscripts of the *Memoirs* that touch on this period, Gibbon commends the essay's analysis of ancient polytheism. In his most common formulation, the *Essai* contained "the seeds of some ideas, especially on the Polytheism of the ancients, which might deserve the illustrations of a riper judgment."[8] The section Gibbon cites contains, in fact, the most explicit philosophy of religion to come down to us in his work.

The history of the *Essai*'s composition and revision also allows us to track Gibbon's religious commitments after his return to Protestantism in 1754. Gibbon records in his *Memoirs* that he had completed a draft of the *Essai* in February 1759. "Yet I still shrunk from the press with the terrors of virgin-modesty," he writes, and "the Manuscript was safely deposited in my desk."[9] In the spring of 1761, the desk opened. After a "last revisal," Gibbon's "literary maidenhead" was lost. For the *Essai*, alone of Gibbon's major works, literary remains allow us to trace Gibbon's revisions. (After completing the *Decline and Fall*, Gibbon allowed no manuscript drafts to survive; of the *Memoirs* we have only drafts without an authoritative edition.) Attending to Gibbon's revisions of the *Essai* produces an *apparatus criticus* of considerable consequence, for the differences between the *Essais* of 1759 and 1761 reveal the moment when and the manner in which Gibbon came to think that a work of history might account for the rise of Christianity.[10] The basis for this discovery was the *Essai*'s expansive vision of history rooted in the practice of textual criticism while reaching toward philosophy.

PHILOSOPHICAL HISTORY

From the opening lines of the *Essai*, Gibbon links the problem of disciplinary hierarchy to themes that will figure prominently in his later work.[11] "The History of Empires is the history of human misery," Gibbon writes. "The history of the Sciences is that of human greatness and happiness. The Philosopher must have a thousand different reasons to consider the study of the sciences as precious, but this one thought will endear it to any friend of humankind."[12] Science, progressive and cumulative rather than cyclical, seems to be governed by laws distinct from those that govern empire. If the philosopher could reduce or elevate the history of empires to a science, rendering it rational and predictable, he might make a significant contribution to human happiness. But Gibbon starts from the opposite perspective and suggests that science be understood according to the history of empires. Even the man of letters is subject to the "empire of fashion," Gibbon says. The succession of disciplinary regimes within the sciences resembles the rises and falls one observes in the political world. "At present," Gibbon writes, "Natural Philosophy and Mathematics are seated on the throne, from which they view their sisters prostrated before them, enchained to their chariot, or at best employed to decorate their triumphal procession. Perhaps their fall may not be far off."[13] Sciences dominate one another and grow corrupt, just as empires do. The history of empires, then, is the ruling discipline insofar as it accounts for politics and sciences alike.

Gibbon distinguishes history from the then-reigning disciplines of natural philosophy and mathematics, on the one hand, and skepticism, on the other. The power of natural science stems from the clarity and rigor of its "demonstrations." The spirit of geometry, as Gibbon elsewhere glosses the current regime, often seduces the "brilliant genius," "infatuation with his own systems" being "the sage's ultimate passion."[14] But mathematical precision is ill-suited to explain human action. "Speculators in their cabinets" err by making men into "systematic beings" like themselves: "Artfulness was detected in their passions, policy in their weaknesses, dissimulation in their inconstancy. In short, by insistently trying to honor the human mind, they have frequently done very little for the heart."[15] If history should not aspire to the precision of the mathematical system nor should it succumb to skepticism. The "friend of truth" rejects the skeptic's denial of all truth and all systems.[16] Similarly, he rejects "mere" or "crude" compilers of facts.[17] Gibbon's ideal stands somewhere between the lucid order of the system and the disarray left by the skeptic's doubts or the compiler's facts.

"Criticism" (*la critique*) is Gibbon's name for the practice of that ideal. The critic inhabits the realm of probability lying between mathematical certainty and skeptical denial of truth.[18] Gibbon defines "criticism" broadly as "the art of judging writing and writers; what they said, how well they said it, and how true." It is an art adapted not only to writing but to "everything that men have ever been, everything that genius has created, that reason has pondered and labor gathered."[19] As "criticism" seems to embrace all disciplines, so Gibbon's portrait of the critic seems to represent the highest type of man:

> [The true critic] weighs, combines, doubts, decides. Being exact and impartial he yields only to reason, or to authority, which is the reason of facts. Sometimes the most respectable name will give way before the testimony of writers to whom circumstances alone lend a momentary weight. Prompt and rich in resources, but bereft of false subtlety, he has daring enough to sacrifice the most brilliant, seemly hypothesis, and he never attributes to his masters the language of his own conjectures. A friend of truth, he seeks out the type of proof that suits his subject and contents himself with that. He never applies the sharp blade of his analysis to beauties that are so delicate they would wither at the least touch. But neither is he satisfied with sterile admiration. He delves into the most hidden principles of the human heart in order to

> account for its pleasures and disgusts. Modest and sensible, he never presents his conjectures as truths, his inductions as facts, his probabilities as demonstrations.[20]

Gibbon's critic is a greater lover of truth than either the mathematician or the skeptic because he is aware that different sorts of proof suit different subjects. He knows the difference between probability, certainty, and ignorance. Gibbon's high praise of the critic's character and his expansion of "criticism" beyond the evaluation of texts to include "everything that men have ever been," even "the most hidden principles of the human heart," suggest that the most fundamental rules of human life, the rules that govern empires and sciences alike, are probabilities.[21]

The critic's practice carries philosophical consequences. "For a philosophical spirit," Gibbon says, "history is what gambling was to the marquis of Dangeau. He saw a system, relations, a sequence, where others discerned only the caprice of fortune."[22] Dangeau considered card games to consist in fixed rules and tendencies that enabled an observer to weigh probabilities but not to predict the outcome of any game with certainty. Gibbon conceives of history in its broadest application to be a game like those analyzed by Dangeau. The challenge for the historian is to discern its rules and patterns.

In both editions of the *Essai*, a narrative of Rome illustrates this conception of history. Early Rome's poverty and independence of mind explained why the Romans resisted tyrants and conquered other peoples. As the Romans conquered, "the republic sank under the weight of its greatness and corruption" until, by the time of Sulla, it could not survive without a master.[23] Augustus's regime arose from the same general causes that explained Sulla and Caesar. To account for these events with precision required a historian to mention particular causes like "Antony's debauchery, Lepidus's weakness, and Cicero's credulity."[24] But the shape of the story was foreordained. Poor, pure peoples conquer rich, corrupt ones, themselves becoming rich and corrupt, until they are conquered by the pure and poor. Republics mature into empires that degenerate until they are conquered by new republics. The most general causes move human events in a cycle of virtue and corruption, rise and fall.[25]

Discerning general causes of this sort is the work of what Gibbon here calls "philosophical history." This concept combines an explanation of human events and an articulation of an ideal human type. The theory of events balances necessity and chance, or general and particular causes. "In the hands of a Montesquieu the theory of these general causes would comprise a philosophical history of man," Gibbon writes. "He would show us how they govern the greatness and the fall of Empires, successively taking the guise of fortune, prudence, courage, and weakness; acting without the help of particular causes and sometimes even defeating them." The mind capable of discerning general and particular causes resembles that of the critic, described above. It is content with probability and capable of withstanding the illusions of certainty that seduce both the dogmatist and the skeptic: "Being above infatuation with his own systems—the sage's ultimate passion—he would have recognized that though these causes may be extensive, their effect is still limited; and that they appear principally in those general events whose slow but sure influence changes the face of the earth, even if we cannot perceive when the change occurs, especially as concerns manners, religions, and everything that wears the yoke of opinion."[26] Here is the ideal of the "philosophic historian" and his project: to account for the general causes that govern "everything that wears the yoke of opinion."[27]

Gibbon's analysis of the disciplines aims to win a hearing for erudition, but that modest bid for recognition excuses a project that is considerably more ambitious. Gibbon's ultimate claim in the *Essai* is that "philosophical history" deserves to rule natural philosophy and mathematics insofar as it accounts better for the irreducible role of passion and chance—that is, forces other than reason—in everything that humans undertake, including the sciences. Philosophical history can explain the rise and fall of scientific disciplines, but science cannot explain the history of empires. History, as Gibbon presents it here, detects patterns and probabilities, and it confidently asserts that this is all one can ever hope to do.[28]

That is the core argument of the *Essai*. But Gibbon wrote two quite different versions of that argument. They diverged over the question of how universal the rule of philosophical history could aspire to be.

THE *ESSAI* OF 1759

Gibbon concludes the *Essai* of 1759 by considering how philosophical history relates to religion. He argues that the humanities are a better ally for theology than the natural sciences. Natural science defends religion by using the orderliness of the universe to suggest its creation by a supreme being. Few doubt that particular doctrine, Gibbon says. Critics of the divine authority of the Christian scriptures are far more "numerous and bold."[29] And it is against these enemies that the humanities are most useful. Critics can demonstrate that the scriptures are in fact as old as they claim to be and do not contain any overt errors in their depictions of their age.[30]

Humanists can also help to moderate certain disputes between Christians and their adversaries. For instance, when enemies of Christianity point out that morally excellent men lived before Christ and that Christians exaggerate the "vice and corruption that covered the earth when the legislator of the Christians came," the humanist can split the difference. Gibbon demonstrates the sort of moderation that results: "After paying homage to the virtue of a small number, we must tremble with horror at the general corruption." Gibbon continues, "A history like Suetonius's makes me feel how greatly men needed a new law. . . . It is only among the Roman Emperors that I see what men are when they are free of the yoke of religion, deaf to the voice of shame, raised above human punishments."[31] Gibbon acknowledges pagan virtue while portraying a world ripe for a "new law."

Gibbon proceeds to suggest that in the early Roman Empire paganism did not allow for its own renewal. Augustus failed to restore republican virtue owing to general causes outside of his control. Augustus's refounding of Rome would have been complete, Gibbon suggests, had Augustus been entered among the gods—on this point, gratitude and politics agreed.[32] Very little seemed to be wanting for the apotheosis to be achieved. The Senate voted divine honors; divine lineages and miracles were attested; and a Senator "swore an oath that the new divinity had appeared to him like that of Romulus in all the splendor of Celestian majesty."[33] But "the enlightened Philosophy of this age easily dissipated all these Illusions, the God Augustus was never taken for more than a machination of Politics; the people neglected him[,] the most superstitious of his successors scoffed at him."[34] An ancient version of the enlightened philosophy touted by Christianity's modern adversaries precluded the restoration of Roman virtue.

In this first draft of the *Essai*, the intellectual disciplines that comprehend decline arise toward the end of it, but they serve only to "soften" its harsh effects. Human industry, Gibbon says, generates luxury and science simultaneously: "The rudiments of art satisfy mankind's first needs. Once they are perfected, they procure new needs, form Vitellius's shield of Minerva to Cicero's philosophical discourses."[35] What would seem our highest need, not only to understand the process of corruption but to oppose it on the basis of our understanding, seems to be a need that the sciences cannot satisfy. "Even as luxury corrupts manners," Gibbon says, "the sciences soften them, like the prayers in Homer that always race across the earth following an act of injustice."[36] We might expect, then, that the sciences would play their role in the Roman Empire's descent into softness and subsequent replacement by the hard, in keeping with the paradigmatic "general cause" discerned by philosophic history.

But Gibbon confounds this expectation. After describing Augustus's failure to complete his refounding of Rome, the *Essai* of 1759 concludes with this paragraph:

> Eighteen years [after Augustus's death] an obscure man perished by the most sordid of ordeals. He issued from a nation despised by the whole earth. His disciples proclaimed him God, but god of a new order, destroyer of all the earth's gods. All the while his doctrine spread. Persecuted everywhere, it everywhere was reborn from its ashes. Its enemies obstinately fought against it, by their own avowals they refuted themselves. The cross was erected on the debris of the Capitol. The Magus and the Druid, the Stoic and the Epicurean, united in believing a doctrine that astonishes reason and that redeems.[37]

Gibbon makes us feel the shock of the Christian triumph by staging a dramatic conversion scene. It seems no general cause can account for it. Indeed, all the general causes that Gibbon had identified moved in the opposite direction.

What are we to make of this surprising conclusion? It seems at first glance to be the expression of Gibbon enlisting the humanities under "the banner of Theology."[38] The mission of the humanities would be to defend Christianity, without lapsing into the error of attempting to explain Christianity as just one effect among many. Christianity had to be allowed to erupt into the scene and succeed against all odds in order to appear as revelation. Its glory was all the greater for converting a world so inhospitable to it.[39]

Gibbon's *Essai* of 1759 secures the alliance of philosophic history and Christianity by allowing Christianity to escape explanation. The rise of Christianity seems miraculous; it is ungoverned by historical causality, and it is restorative rather than destructive. Indeed, there is a deep basis for the compatibility of philosophic history and revelation in Gibbon's understanding of the general causes that govern decline. In Augustus's time those who were capable of understanding the need for regeneration were, by virtue of what allowed them to understand, incapable of effecting that restoration. What astonished reason redeemed. Only by allowing for something outside of reason—something outside of the natural philosopher's systems, but also (here) outside of the general causes known to the philosophical historian—could a history of empires be something other than a story of descent into misery.

INTERLUDE

As we have seen, Gibbon finished the first complete draft of *Essai* early in 1759, but he hesitated to publish: "After marking the date (February 3rd 1759) by a short preface, the Manuscript was deposited in my bureau."[40] Gibbon served three years (June 1759–December 1762) in the Hampshire militia, reading Homer and several treatises on ancient tactics in his tent. He was otherwise largely (and reluctantly) disengaged from intellectual pursuits.[41]

Gibbon does, however, date a significant development in his own religious disposition to this time. Attending church each Sunday, "in conformity with the pious or decent custom of the family," Gibbon followed the readings in the "original text, or the most ancient version of the Bible."[42] The ironic conjunctions suggest Gibbon's skepticism, which he here (and only here) openly affirms: "The doubts, alas! or objections that invincibly rushed on my mind were almost always multiplied by the learned expositors whom I consulted on my return home."[43]

In the *Memoirs* Gibbon mentions in this context a correspondence with the Anglican bishop Richard Hurd (in fact from 1772) on the authenticity of the Book of Daniel.[44] That text, with its depiction of successive world empires, evoked Gibbon's mature themes. It also allowed Gibbon to articulate principles for interpreting sacred history that would prove fundamental to his later work. "May I not assume as a principle equally consonant to experience, to reason, and even to true religion; 'That we ought not to admit any thing as the immediate work of God, which can possibly be the work of man; and that whatever is said to deviate from the ordinary course of nature, should be ascribed to accident, to fraud, or to fiction; till we are fully satisfied, that it lies beyond the reach of those causes?'" Gibbon asked Hurd. "If we cast away this buckler, the blind fury of superstition, from every age of the world, and from every corner of the globe, will invade us naked and unarmed."[45] Gibbon goes on to suggest that the Book of Daniel is part fiction and part fraud: "If the prophecies were framed three or four centuries after the Prophet's death, it was much easier for the counterfeit Daniel *to foretell* great and recent events, than to compose an accurate history or probably romance of a dark and remote period."[46] Hurd replied courteously and, to a man of faith, persuasively. "I doubt, sir," he wrote, "you take for granted that the claim of inspiration is never to be allowed, so long as there is a possibility of supposing that it was not given."[47] Hurd's reply seems not to have persuaded Gibbon, however. In a fragmentary draft of a response, Gibbon concedes that a prophet can be rapidly promoted at court but seems otherwise to intend a full self-defense.[48]

Indeed, by the time of this correspondence, Gibbon had, with the aid of Grotius's *De veritate religionis Christianae,* made "a regular trial of the evidence of Christianity" and found it wanting. "By every possible light that reason and history can afford, I have repeatedly viewed the important subject," Gibbon wrote in a draft of the *Memoirs.* "The most accurate philosophers and the most orthodox Divines will perhaps agree that the belief of miracles and mysteries cannot be supported on the brittle basis, the distant report, of human testimony, and that the faith as well as the virtue of a Christian must be formed and fortified by the inspiration of Grace."[49] The human testimony to the central miracles of Christianity was brittle and distant; the inspiration of grace was not forthcoming. Not faith but "the love of truth and the spirit of freedom" set the horizons of Gibbon's trial of Christianity.[50] The *Memoirs* frames this episode with a view to Gibbon's earlier conversions: "Since my escape from Popery I had humbly acquiesced in the common creed of the Protestant Churches."[51] We are permitted, then, to date Gibbon's final break with Christian faith to the "latter end of 1759."[52]

THE *ESSAI* OF 1761

The *Essai* remained in the bureau during this time. It was not removed until the spring of 1761 when Gibbon's father recommended his son bolster his chances for appointment as secretary to the English delegation at the Peace of Augsburg with a "Classical performance in the French language."[53] Gibbon obeyed. He records in his journal that he "revised [the *Essai*] with great care, made many alterations, struck out a considerable part, and wrote the chapters from 57–78."[54] Then, on June 23: "We marched to Alresford where I received a Copy of my book."[55]

The differences between that book and the draft that Gibbon had placed in his bureau two years before are significant, and they have mainly to do with Gibbon's understanding of religion.[56] In the 1759 essay there are religious phenomena that escape the grasp of philosophical history. Although that discipline deserves to rule over natural philosophy and mathematics, its empire is not yet universal. In the 1761 version of the *Essai*, however, religion itself is conquered and assimilated. Philosophical history expands its empire to the limits of the known world.

Having removed the *Essai* from his bureau, Gibbon struck the captivating section we have just considered at length. Gone was the relation between literature and theology culminating in the paradox of the cross erected on the debris of the Capitol. In their place, Gibbon considers whether paganism can be understood as a "system"—that is, an ordered whole in which everything is accounted for and no room is left for fortune or chance.[57] These revisions make the theme of religion more prominent while removing Christianity from consideration.

This last effect is only apparent, however. Gibbon intends his exploration of the "cheerful but absurd system" of paganism to determine whether the pagan gods were originally "benefactors of the earth" (i.e., admired men) or "elements of the universe." Because this religious system was considered "absurd," Gibbon could follow Hobbes and others in excluding the orthodox opinion that the gods entered into human concern by revealing themselves. On this foundation an author could construct a subversive rhetoric of indirect analogy by nudging the reader to consider whether an account of "false" gods might also apply to gods considered "true."

In the *Essai* of 1761, Gibbon more than nudges. Immediately after stating the question—are pagan gods men deified or nature personified?—he comments on the difficulty of discovering objective evidence: "We know little about the system of Paganism except what comes from the poets and the church fathers, both of whom were addicted to fictions."[58] Fifteen years later Gibbon will praise pagan tolerance; here in the *Essai* he finds little to distinguish pagans from Christians.[59] Every enemy of a religious sect adopts "the vilest calumnies against it"; every votary considers doubt a crime and turns a number of unsavory techniques, among them "forging prophecies and miracles," to bolster his own side.[60] At least with a view to paganism, which consecrates temples "to those whose tombs we see," and Catholicism, which appeals to the senses for confirmation of doctrine yet denies the senses' authority with the doctrine of transubstantiation, Gibbon says, "Reasoning is of little use. . . . What can be too absurd for men?"[61] This can be taken as the thesis of this section of the text: there is no reasoning about religion—thus no possibility of a "system"—because religion is a realm where absurdity, prejudice, and persecutional passions reign.

Gibbon then gives the antithesis: where we cannot reason, "we must interrogate the facts." He proceeds to use facts derived mainly from Herodotus to develop a narrative history of paganism, a sequence of events in which the operative general causes are not made explicit. The pagan gods originated in Egypt rather than Greece, and they originally represented nature personified, *not* man deified. "Reason gleamed through [the Egyptians'] dark metaphysics enough to convey to them that man can never become a God, nor a God be transformed into a man," Gibbon writes. "Mysterious in their dogma and worship, these interpreters of the Heavens and of wisdom disguised in pompous language the truths of nature, whose majestic simplicity a rude people would have despised."[62] The Greeks, for their part, distinguished heroes from the Hellenized Egyptian deities they worshipped, while "bold philosophers" like Euhemerus of Messina, who derived gods from men alone, earned "a universal contempt and the title of Atheist."[63] It was not until the Roman Empire that the Messinian's heresy took hold. "In a slavish world in which the title of Gods was awarded to monsters unworthy of the appellation of men, to confuse Jupiter and Domitian was so much courtly flattery. . . . Euhemerus now reigned everywhere."[64] The Church fathers could attack the pagans for worshipping humans because that is what the pagans of the Empire understood themselves to be doing. Gibbon, on the other hand, has constructed a narrative that answers his question definitively—the pagan gods are originally nature personified—while explaining the conditions under which the alternative answer seemed most persuasive and thus produced plentiful evidence in the sources that have come down to us. He has used a few general assumptions—for instance, "rude people" cannot comprehend the wisdom of the few, a slavish world gives rise to flattery, and theology reflects political development—to structure the facts at his disposal, but he has allowed the emphasis to fall on the facts rather than the structure that orders them. To the extent we can reason about religion, it is only in a historical, not a philosophical, mode.

On the basis of this history, however, Gibbon returns to the beginning to build a system "not of facts, but of ideas"—a philosophy of religion.[65] Gibbon begins from human psychology; he asks what man is, such that he can be the subject of a religious history like the one Gibbon has sketched. To answer this question, one must "plumb the human heart and unravel this thread of errors which, starting from the true, simple, and universal feeling that there is a power greater than man, gradually led him to produce Gods he would blush to resemble."[66]

Gibbon proceeds to construct a state of nature theory all his own.[67] He presents man as naturally weak (as in Hobbes) yet capable of profound transformation (as in Rousseau).[68] Man is not naturally vainglorious and so not particularly prone to war (Rousseau, again) and yet he feels a "well-warranted contempt" for himself by comparing his own inability to meet his natural needs to the self-sufficiency and abundance of "the majestic oak."[69] The notion of divinity, "the existence of a higher power," is born from humanity's self-loathing. Divinity is rendered beneficent by man's "gratitude and admiration" for natural objects that he needs but that seem to have no need of him and by his hope that his appeals for aid will be answered. The root of religion, then, lies in man's situation vis-à-vis nature: man is fearful because he is weak and needy, but he experiences nature as at least partly beneficent. He can pray to, thank, and admire the world around him for meeting some needs and offering hope, at least, that they might continue to be met.

For Gibbon, religion and philosophy are of a piece. Man's notions of the world around him and his conception of the gods proceed in tandem. Initially, man has no "general ideas" and everything he encounters is a god: "Every forest and meadow teemed with them."[70] As the human mind groups particulars into universals, so there comes into being "a new Deity that was superior to any of his individual Gods." The more experience, the more universality. Gradually the Greeks reduce their gods and their conception of nature's elements to three: water (Neptune), earth (Pluto), and sky (Jupiter). The Egyptians had progressed further, arriving at two gods and elements: the "intelligent principle" (Osiris) and matter (Isis). Without questioning "the eternity of matter," Gibbon notes, a people could hardly go further.

After accounting philosophically-theologically for nature, man descends into the moral world to account for the "Gods of human nature."[71] As with gods of nonhuman nature, so these "Gods of man" are "assigned their provinces." Each initially constitutes a "generalized, personified" passion or faculty blended with the "Gods of nature" for the sake of acquiring some hold on the senses. Each god inspires human passions appropriate to its province; each favors those men and nations who resemble the god most in manners and temperament; and each takes the side of these men and nations when they struggle with others. Unsatisfied with the sensory access to these gods that natural objects provided, men demand "a shape that would decorate their temples and fix their ideas," and they settle on the most beautiful form known to them—their own.[72] With the human form came man's natural necessities: eating, sleeping, the sensation of pain. "Having become very powerful men, the Gods were often led to visit the earth, live in temples, enjoy human distractions, take part in the hunt or the dance, and sometimes even be charmed by a mortal beauty, which gave birth to a race of Heroes."[73] In this manner the gods descend over time from the heavens to the earth.

In the abrupt style characteristic of the *Essai* (the *Memoirs* would blame Montesquieu's influence), Gibbon leaves at this his demonstration of how general causes might constitute "a philosophical history of man."[74] Indeed, he has made a virtuosic display of method: the failure of philosophy alone to account for paganism necessitated a turn to the *érudit*'s "facts," which in turn opened into a concatenation "not of facts, but of ideas" so orderly and seemingly exhaustive as to merit Gibbon's calling it a "system." Gibbon has demonstrated the power of philosophical history on the relatively safe proving ground of ancient religious history.

Nevertheless, Gibbon's rhetoric of indirect analogy leaves his reader to consider whether his system applies only to paganism. On the one hand, Gibbon's accounts of both natural and moral gods indicate that monotheism is more theologically and philosophically satisfying than paganism. The natural gods progress from multiplicity (when nature teemed with gods) toward unity; the moral gods' multiplicity does not progress in the same way, but their descent toward mortality heightens the appeal of the hypothesis Gibbon seems to oppose to paganism: the Creator endows man with reason, will, and thus freedom to regulate his own actions.[75]

On the other hand, by rooting his account of paganism in "the human heart" Gibbon addresses not only paganism but religion simply. Insofar as religion has natural causes—no other causes appear here—it reflects man's attempt to make sense of the world around him.[76] Religion issues entirely from man, not from a god, and it does not differ fundamentally from philosophy. General ideas and conceptions of the gods move in the same direction at the same pace. Gibbon's critique of Euhemerus opens a safe space for a sustained (if indirect) attack on not only deification but incarnation.[77] In restating the views of the Egyptian "interpreters of the Heavens and of wisdom" who know "the truths of nature," for instance, anti-Euhemerianism requires him to report only "that man can never become a God." Gibbon adds, "nor a God be transformed into a mere man."[78] When he concludes the narration of the gods' corruption into mortal men by noting that they would "sometimes even be charmed by a mortal beauty, which gave birth to a race of Heroes," does he mean his reader to envision Zeus and Leda or the Incarnation? If the latter it is only by insinuation, but we have seen sufficient willingness to elide pagan and Christian as to make this a plausible reading. To the extent Gibbon's analysis of religion in this new section of the *Essai* extends beyond paganism to religion simply, it gives us reason to prefer monotheism to polytheism, to elide philosophy and theology, and to question whether man can ever become God or God man.

Where does that leave Gibbon? In describing the origin of religion among the savages, Gibbon pauses to make the following remark: "Indeed, without the lights that teach us how far reason alone is superior to all the necessary parts of an intelligent system, each of these parts is higher than man. But deprived of these lights, the savage conferred life and power on each of the parts. He bowed down before his own work."[79] To be enlightened entails knowing that reason is superior to "all the necessary parts of an intelligent system," and as a result man is higher than each of these parts. The savage understands himself to worship gods; the enlightened observer knows that the savage worships "his own work." Human rationality, not God, is the peak of nature. Man in his reason is the creator of nature—and, Gibbon has now argued, history—as an intelligent system.

Gibbon's scholarly ambitions expanded considerably between 1759 and 1761. In 1759 Gibbon envisioned philosophical history overthrowing natural philosophy and mathematics but not theology. In 1761, philosophical history supplanted theology as well by attending to the natural causes of religious belief. It is clear from the *Memoirs* and other literary testaments that this change in Gibbon's conception of history coincided with his loss of Christian faith. What is perhaps less clear, however, is what disposition toward Christianity's role in history Gibbon's settled skepticism ultimately entailed. In the *Essai* of 1759 Gibbon had claimed that "the enlightened Philosophy" of the Roman Empire had spread skepticism and precluded Augustus's attempts to avert decline.[80] Gibbon would repeat that claim in the *Decline and Fall*.[81] He would also, as we shall now see, attempt to distinguish his own practice of philosophical history from that of the enlightened pagans he championed in the *Essai*.

CHAPTER 4

The Rise of Christianity

"In the second century of the Christian Aera, the empire of Rome comprehended the fairest part of the earth, and the most civilized portion of mankind."[1] The first sentence of Gibbon's *Decline and Fall of the Roman Empire* hid the central puzzle of the work under a serene and conventional façade. The period from which Gibbon's narrative began was the "second century of the Christian Aera" only for Gibbon's readers. For Gibbon's Romans, it was the second century since the rise of the Empire, the ninth since the founding of the city. But theirs was not yet Christian time.[2]

How did the era of Gibbon's Romans come to be that of his readers? Gibbon would tell that story in the great work that followed this first sentence, but when the first of its six volumes appeared in 1776 this question seemed surprisingly peripheral. Gibbon's primary concern, as his title announced, was "to deduce the most important circumstances of [the Roman Empire's] decline and fall."[3] For pious and impious readers alike, the rise of Christianity figured prominently among the "circumstances" of the fall. In the first fourteen chapters of Gibbon's work, however, Christianity served merely to mark time and sometimes space; it occasionally came up for discussion in connection with a source.[4] But Gibbon stretched his narrative well into the fourth century of the Christian era before allowing the Christians to play their part among the circumstances. Even Constantine at the Milvian Bridge had only his "valour and ability" to thank for his success.[5] The first volume of Gibbon's work suggested that one could account for the decline of Rome without accounting for the rise of Christianity.[6]

If Christianity was notably absent from the bulk of Gibbon's first volume, the same was not true of other religions. In the second chapter, Gibbon analyzed Roman polytheism and praised its expansive toleration. A large section of the eighth chapter described Zoroastrianism and its role in Artaxerxes's reforms of the Persian Empire, while the ninth discussed the "religious system of the Germans (if the wild opinions of savages can deserve that name)."[7] And these larger studies were but the continents in an array of lesser islands: Druid priests sacrificing humans; Elegabalus converting humanity to the worship of a black, conical stone; Odin ("the Mahomet of the North") instituting a religion for the Goths.[8] All testified to the prominence of religious phenomena in Gibbon's narrative. Gibbon's account of Christianity in the concluding chapters of the first volume would prove controversial, but just as remarkable was his peculiar account of Rome's decline in the preceding chapters, so alive to religious phenomena of every variety except the Christian.

By the time Gibbon began his great work in 1773, his own religious experiences had ranged widely. As we have seen, he was a sixteen-year-old Catholic convert who returned eighteen months later to "implicit belief in the tenets and mysteries which are adopted by the general consent of Catholics and Protestants."[9] He proceeded to draft a book that depicted the rise of Christianity as inexplicable by "general causes" before making a trial of his own Christian faith, finding it wanting, and revising the book so that polytheism (at least) appeared the work of human passion while human rationality seemed the pinnacle of nature.[10] Gibbon was from that point forward a skeptic. But he was a skeptic reluctant to dismiss religious belief as merely a product of human fear manipulated by priests (though he thought it was that, in part). Instead, religion appeared to him a rich and varied phenomenon capable of revealing and engaging the whole man—passions and interests, mind and soul. During Gibbon's Tour of the Continent, this understanding of religion disclosed the beauty of Saint-Sulpice, the prudence of Abraham Davel, and the deficiency of Paul Henri Mallet's account of conversion, so blind to the transformative power of pilgrimage. Gibbon's was a mind open to the events of October 15, 1764, and willing, thirty years later, to narrate those events as a conversion experience.

We turn now to the first volume of the great work, where we will recognize the author we have come to know in the preceding chapters: a skeptic concerned to study and understand the worldly power of Christianity, not simply to sneer at it.[11] We will ask first what theory of religion can be discerned from Gibbon's general statements on that theme, before considering in greater detail his accounts of Roman polytheism, the Parthians' Zoroastrianism, and German paganism. Finally we shall trace the rise of what Gibbon called—with a perplexing blend of irony and earnestness—"the Christian republic."

GIBBON'S THEORY OF RELIGION

Gibbon did not present himself as a theorist of religion in the *Decline and Fall*.[12] The sheer diversity of religious phenomena in the work seems to militate against a unified account of religion, as does the genre of the work: a "history" (which Gibbon often praises in the text) as opposed to a "speculative system" (which Gibbon always derides).[13] Gibbon, however, uses a single word, "religion," to represent variants of polytheism and monotheism alike. And the *Decline and Fall* of 1776, like the *Essai* of 1761, reflects a notion of history far more welcoming to "theory" than we, reading after Ranke and others, might expect. As a historian, Gibbon evidently took as his models figures like Hume, Montesquieu, and, above all, Tacitus, whom Gibbon describes as "the first of historians who applied the science of philosophy to the study of facts," a "writer who had pierced into [nature's] darkest recesses," and a "philosophic historian, whose writings will instruct the last generations of mankind."[14] Even if the study of facts indicated nothing more than the diversity of religious phenomena, the science of philosophy might reveal some unity beneath this diversity. A reader would not be doing obvious abuse to the *Decline and Fall*, then, to search it for a theory of religion.

How would one conduct the search? One might be tempted to begin by extracting from their context all of the general comments Gibbon makes about religion in order to recast them as a universally applicable theory. For instance, in a footnote in the fifteenth chapter Gibbon cites Hume as a guide to the self-understanding of early Christians: "As the human heart is still the same, several of the observations which Mr. Hume has made on Enthusiasm (Essays, vol. i. p. 76, quarto edit.), may be applied even to real inspiration."[15] By "heart" Gibbon indicates the passions that constitute the nature of humans across historical time: avarice, pride, and a propensity toward devotion.[16]

With a view to these and other passions, illuminated as much by the philosophy of his own day as by his historical research, Gibbon could account for the "secondary causes" of true religion and (presumably) the primary causes of false religion.[17] In short, at least for his skeptical readers, he could account for religion.

At the root of religious belief, as Gibbon presents it in the *Decline and Fall*, is fear. This is "the original parent of superstition."[18] On Gibbon's understanding, humans excused their terror of the world around them by imagining hostile gods, and they alleviated this terror by inventing rites to assuage the gods' hostility.[19] Political leaders regularly exploited the capacity of religious rites to channel human fear toward productive action.[20] Divination, for instance, offered the gods' endorsement for political projects and punishment for failure to carry them out; "avenging gods" could be made to reinforce moral proscriptions that favored public order.[21]

This much Gibbon might have learned from Hobbes or Lucretius. But what is distinctive about the *Decline and Fall* is how Gibbon's psychology of religion expands beyond this low but solid foundation. Recall that already in the *Essai* published in 1761 Gibbon had traced man's belief in gods to not only his fear of nature but the gratitude and admiration he felt for the world around him.[22] Similarly in 1776 Gibbon adds to fear such passions as wonder, veneration, hope, and curiosity.[23] He is alive to the ways in which religion can serve as not only an instrument of political manipulation but a reflection of our moral sense. "Every mode of religion, to make a deep and lasting impression on the human mind," Gibbon says, "must exercise our obedience, by enjoining practices of devotion, for which we can assign no reason; and must acquire our esteem, by inculcating moral duties analogous to the dictates of our own heart."[24] Here is a register into which Hobbes rarely ascends.

That this is a skeptic's psychology of religion, there can be no doubt. We have seen that Gibbon's decisive break with his own Christian faith occurred in 1759. Even in the passages quoted above, Gibbon considers moral duties to issue from the human heart, not the Christian conscience and certainly not the divine law. Nevertheless, Gibbon's theory of religion is that of a generous rather than a sneering skeptic, one willing to view religious belief from above as well as from below. "As the human heart is still the same," Gibbon's theory of religion could be applied to "every mode of religion."[25]

Nevertheless it is significant that Gibbon did not present himself in the first instance as a theorist of religion. As we have seen, Gibbon did not understand philosophical history to entail history serving merely as the instrument for philosophy. Casting aside historical detail saps the power of narrative not only to embody theory but to refine it.[26] Better, then, to treat Gibbon's work as it asks to be treated—not as philosophy first, but as history, albeit history of a certain sort.

ROMAN POLYTHEISM

Gibbon initially views religion in the *Decline and Fall*, as in the *Essai*, through the lens of ancient polytheism. This was the "elegant mythology of Homer"—a poetic religion, beautiful in its variety rather than its regularity.[27] Rivers were powerful and so were gods. Rivers' influence was local (the Nile never having flooded the Palatine) and so was that of the gods they represented. The visible powers of the universe were gods too; although common to Egypt and Rome they were evidently plural. Similarly with the nations of the earth: there were many, and many gods seemed best to reflect their plurality. Polytheism in its diversity and beauty reflected the mind's wonder at the multifarious world surrounding it.

There were, nevertheless, forces for unity within polytheism. "A republic of gods of such opposite tempers and interests required, in every system," Gibbon says, "the moderating hand of a supreme magistrate, who, by the progress of knowledge and flattery, was gradually invested with the sublime perfections of an Eternal Parent, and an Omnipotent Monarch."[28] The principles of theology and politics were of a piece.[29] Unity seemed more elusive in heaven than on earth, the gap between two gods and one being far larger than the gap between two and three. But even on earth a single ruler had sometimes to hide his power and appear as the prince of a "republic."[30]

Presiding over the religion of Homer, Gibbon says, were the disciples of Plato.[31] Gibbon understood the philosophers of Greece to have divided into sects in their meditations on the nature of the gods but to have reached consensus on several other points. They agreed, for instance, that the best way of life could be deduced from the nature of man. They agreed, too, that most humans were ill-suited for rational contemplation of man's nature, much less that of the gods. The affairs of the people could therefore not be guided in the first instance by reason or nature; they were bound to convention, "the commands of law and custom."[32] For these philosophers popular religion was an object of contempt. Their only concern was to secure "the independent dignity of reason."[33] They wanted only to be left alone to contemplate the nature of gods and man.

Nevertheless, Gibbon says, the philosophers of Greece recognized that securing their independence required that they engage in politics at one remove: through education of the Roman elite. Philosophers "had given laws to the senate" by instructing "the ingenuous youth, who, from every part, resorted to Athens."[34] These ingenuous youth grew into Roman magistrates and priests, the custodians of law and custom, who learned to conceal "the sentiments of an Atheist under sacerdotal robes."[35] For them religion appeared a tool of policy that might or might not be useful, rather than a system of theology or belief that might be true or false. They found religion quite useful indeed. Religious festivals "humanized" the people's manners, the arts of divination buttressed policy decisions, and the fear of divine punishment for moral transgressions like perjury reinforced the "firmest bond of society."[36] Since *all* religions served these salutary purposes, there was no advantage (and considerable risk) in overturning "the form of superstition, which had received the sanction of time and experience, [and] was the best adapted to the climate and to its inhabitants."[37] An atheist magistrate could not do without sacerdotal robes, but he was indifferent to which robes he put on. Even the religion of Homer—even for a Platonist—would do.

Gibbon presents the religious policy of these Roman elites with a tone of admiration verging on wonder. Here was a religion for mankind, expressive of man's awe in the face of nature, capable of reconciling the few and the many, and politically useful—both in Rome and throughout the Empire. Although derived from Homer, Roman polytheism was not distinctly Greek or Roman. Because Homer's gods reflected nature as it was experienced by minds unconcerned with the strict coherence of a "speculative system," barbarians could easily translate their gods into Homeric.[38] Roman polytheism was pliable. Adding or diminishing the number of gods, or recognizing that a single divinity might answer to many names, was not exceedingly difficult. As a result Rome could rule its provinces by turning religious toleration toward political assimilation. The people of the provinces could keep their gods, while provincial elites were gradually brought into the class of rulers who understood religion as an instrument of policy. The system as a whole was fundamentally hostile to the "spirit of persecution," and it contributed in no small measure, in Gibbon's eyes, to Rome's greatness.[39] The "greatness of Rome," after all, lay not in the extent of its conquest—"the sovereign of the Russian deserts commands a larger portion of the globe"—but in how it governed what it had conquered.[40] For Gibbon, polytheism figures prominently in the benignity of Rome's rule over its provinces.

More subtle are Gibbon's reservations. He first hints at the weakness of Roman polytheism in the third footnote of the chapter we have been exploring. There he recommends Herodotus and Hume on polytheism, opposes to them Bossuet on monotheism, and notes exceptions to his claim regarding the tolerant spirit of ancient religion: the Egyptians, the Christians, and the Jews.[41] The last two cases will require "a distinct chapter of this work," but for the first Gibbon cites Juvenal's fifteenth satire, which describes a holy war between two neighboring Egyptian towns. "Each people is filled with fury against the other," Juvenal says, "because each hates its neighbors' gods, deeming that none can be held as deities save its own."[42] One town attacks the other during a religious festival and ends up eating its enemies. Juvenal laments the fragility of human compassion. A quiet allusion to this story—a citation without quotation in the middle of a long footnote—introduces Gibbon's critique of the Roman elites he seems, at first glance, simply to praise. The trouble is not only that the Egyptians persecute one another but that the Romans are powerless to stop them.

As Gibbon's study of Roman polytheism draws to a close, he extends this critique along three lines. First, Gibbon notes that though the Romans did not prevent provincials from exercising their ancestral religions, "avarice and taste very frequently despoiled the vanquished nations of the elegant statues of their gods, and the rich ornaments of their temples."[43] Gibbon stresses that this looting is not an attempt at religious persecution. It is nevertheless persecution of a sort. The Roman magistrates view objects of religious significance to their believing subjects as objects of aesthetic appreciation or commerce; their power enables them to enact their own view and to exclude that of their subjects. Looted temples testify to an imperfect application of religious toleration, just the sort of failing one might expect from magistrates who had been trained in philosophical schools to consider all gods false idols.

Second, Gibbon brings up the Romans' persecution of the Druids, ostensibly to demonstrate its consistency with the general policy of toleration. "Under the specious pretext of abolishing human sacrifices," Gibbon writes, "the emperors Tiberius and Claudius suppressed the dangerous power of the Druids: but the priests themselves, their gods and their altars, subsisted in peaceful obscurity till the final destruction of Paganism."[44] By noting the suppression and survival of the Druids, Gibbon presents his reader with both an outlying case of religious intolerance and, more importantly, a failed persecution. The sources Gibbon cites heighten the significance of this failure. Suetonius praises Claudius for "utterly abolishing the cruel and inhuman religion of the Druids among the Gauls," while Pliny says both that Tiberius "did away with the Druids and this tribe of seers and medicine men" and that "the debt owed the Romans is incalculable, for sweeping away the monstrous rites, in which to kill a man was the highest religious duty and for him to be eaten a passport to health."[45] We are presented, then, with not only a failed policy but Roman elites (Suetonius and Pliny) who failed to anticipate the failure. The ominous and ironic conclusion of Gibbon's sentence—"till the final destruction of Paganism"—links this broad failure of early imperial policy to the Empire's subsequent conversion to Christianity. Like the Druids, the Jews and the Christians were victims of ultimately unsuccessful Roman persecution. And Gibbon has already given us license to link these cases with that of Egypt.[46]

The worship of the Egyptian gods Isis and Serapis illustrates Gibbon's third line of critique—a failed persecution not in distant Gaul but in the city of Rome. Recall that the Roman magistrates' policy of religious toleration was rooted in the belief that "in every country, the form of superstition, which had received the sanction of time and experience, was the best adapted to the climate, and to its inhabitants."[47] What was one to do when forms of superstition escaped their native countries? Rome's empire had gathered the world's goods and people into a great cosmopolis. Religions sanctioned by the experience and climate of distant lands came with them. The same theory that favored toleration abroad promoted persecution in Rome and the Empire's other great cities. Magistrates considered themselves justified in attempting to prevent "the inundation of foreign rites."[48] But justification did not guarantee success. Despite persecution, Gibbon says, devotees of Isis and Serapis multiplied in Rome and eventually secured their gods a place in the Roman pantheon. The magistrates of the imperial Senate could not exclude even "the most contemptible and abject" of religions. As with the Druids, so with Serapis and Isis: "The zeal of fanaticism prevailed over the cold and feeble efforts of policy."[49]

Gibbon's study of Roman polytheism ends on a superficially appealing note. "Rome gradually became the common temple of her subjects; and the freedom of the city was bestowed on all the gods of mankind."[50] But Gibbon has given ample reason to suspect so straightforward a conclusion. He has shown, in fact, that the skepticism and elitism of the Roman magistrates limits their understanding of religion and the effectiveness of their religious policy.[51] For them, religion is not the sort of thing one kills for; there are things like that, but religion is not among them. When it comes to comprehending the sort of person for whom religion *is* that sort of thing, the Roman magistrates consistently fall short. They treat as objects of aesthetic appreciation (and appropriation) what their subjects consider worthy of veneration; they are consistently blind to the depth and durability of fanaticism. Their religious policy runs aground in particular when it is opposed by priests—thus the premature declarations of victory over the Druids and disciples of Serapis and Isis. Above all, the Roman elite fails to appreciate fully the religious consequences of their empire. They act as though subjected peoples can be left to their own gods even while their elites are coopted. Gibbon shows that the line between elite and people is blurrier than this policy allows, and the gods are not so easily confined to their localities.[52] They and their devotees had flooded into Rome, detaching religion from the "climate" and tradition for which, on the Roman elites' understanding, it was uniquely adapted. The Empire had opened the door for religions not tied to local and limited gods to come into being, even while extending its elites' own insensitivity to the varieties of religious experience. Gibbon indicates that the philosophical historians who informed and recorded this moment, however astute as guides to its politics, were poorly suited to describe its religion.

GIBBON'S *GERMANIA* AND *PERSIA*

Where Gibbon relates Roman political history, he mostly follows these guides in tone and purpose. Indeed, the bulk of the first volume of Gibbon's *Decline and Fall* is narrative history focused on Rome from the fall of Marcus Aurelius in 180 CE to the "elevation of Constantine" over a reunified Empire in 324 CE. A three-chapter study of the imperial regime (including the sections on Roman religion we have just discussed) precedes this narrative; a two-chapter analysis of Christianity follows it. Chapters on Persia and Germany interrupt the sequence and divide the volume in two. Their style differs markedly from what precedes insofar as it contains elements of philosophy and what we would call ethnography: time is no longer primarily sequential but congeals into national "character, forces, and designs."[53] We glimpse the author's hand most clearly in this departure from the structure of narrative; its topic, which recalls the *Essai*'s "manners, religions, and everything that wears the yoke of opinion," suggests that the hand is that of a philosophical historian.[54]

Gibbon justifies his digression in two ways. First, he imitates Tacitus. Just as the first philosophical historian indulges "in those beautiful episodes, in which he relates some domestic transaction of the Germans or the Parthians," so his successor can relieve his reader's attention from the "uniform scene of vice and misery" that has occupied chapters four through seven covering the fall of Aurelius in 180 to the rise of Philip in 244. Although this period was unknown to Tacitus, who died under Hadrian in the 120s, its outlines would have been familiar to him, Gibbon suggests. It could thus be narrated and interrupted in a Tacitean mode.[55] Second, Gibbon justifies his digression with a view to the narrative itself. Having reached the point where "the barbarians of the north and of the east . . . boldly attacked the provinces of a declining monarchy," Gibbon provides "a previous idea of the character, forces, and designs of those nations" to facilitate "clearer knowledge" of the events to come.

While a tour of Persia and Germany might simultaneously relieve and inform Gibbon's reader, these justifications nevertheless stand in some tension with one another. What has come down to us of Tacitean history does not, in fact, interrupt narrative with the sorts of extensive ethnographies that Gibbon will deploy.[56] Tacitus interrupts his Roman narratives only with other narratives; his ethnographic work comes down to us primarily in the *Germania*, a separate (and, it seems, preliminary) study.[57] Also, not all Tacitean interludes provide relief from misery at Rome. Tacitus's Germany, to be sure, is a land of admirable if barbaric liberty; Tacitus can therefore use German vigor, so redolent of Rome's own republican past, to hold an unflattering mirror up to the Empire. Tacitus's Parthia, however, is a land of luxury, despotism, and corruption; any relief it offers his reader has to do with *variatio* rather than the "beautiful episodes" contained in its domestic transactions.[58] Tacitus had good reason to write a *Germania*. We have no record of his having written a *Parthia*.

Gibbon's eighth chapter on "the state of Persia" fills this gap in the Tacitean project.[59] The ultimate significance of Gibbon's addition, however, is ambivalent. Gibbon might be understood merely to extend Tacitus's reach, as if filling out one of the lacunae in the *Annals'* broken manuscripts. Alternatively, we might understand Gibbon to have discovered within longstanding empires more potential for relief from vice and misery—that is, for renewal—than Tacitus seems to have allowed. Gibbon's Persia is an empire more entrenched and advanced than Rome. "Whilst the forest that covered Europe afforded a retreat to a few wandering savages"—when even Italy resembled Tacitus's Germany (or "almost"[60])—"the inhabitants of Asia were already collected into populous cities, and reduced under extensive empires, the seat of the arts, of luxury, and despotism."[61] Gibbon pierces this illusion of stability. "The Assyrians reigned over the East," he says, "till the scepter of Ninus and Semiramis dropt from the hands of their enervated successors."[62] Even in an established empire enervated hands cannot hold scepters. The East reveals the rhythm of empires across large swaths of time: Empires decline and then fall to more vigorous powers.[63] But since every fall is a rise and every rise a fall, there is a story of virtue and acquisition to accompany and alleviate each tale of descent and loss. Gibbon's *Persia* describes a lowborn captain who earned "great reputation in the armies of Artaban, the last king of the Parthians" only to be driven into "exile and rebellion by royal ingratitude, the customary reward for superior merit."[64] The outlines of this story at this point in Gibbon's narrative are familiar. We have heard early and often of emperors' fears of great captains.[65] Artaxerxes's rise through the military to a stable throne reminds us of Septimus Severus; his low birth recalls Maximin. Tacitus, however, was as alive to these phenomena as Gibbon. His emperors feared their generals; they and he knew that the military empowered emperors to be made "elsewhere than at Rome."[66] And if Syme is right to think that Tacitus intended to comprehend and facilitate the rise of emperors like Trajan, he could hardly be said to be blind to prospects for imperial renewal. Gibbon's novelty would then lie only in the discovery that imperial renewal could be studied elsewhere than at Rome.

Artaxerxes differs from both his Tacitean models and his predecessors in Gibbon's narrative in one crucial respect, however. His ambition is not only to reign securely or to reform the military order (as Roman emperors had attempted to do, with mixed success) but to restore "in their full splendor, the *religion* and empire of Cyrus."[67] Like Gibbon's Roman magistrates, Artaxerxes uses religion as a tool of policy. But the religion he uses and the manner in which he uses it differ fundamentally from their Roman analogues. Tacitus had known the religions of the East and was aware of how they differed from religions closer to home, but what we have of his history does not explore the latent political significance of these differences.[68] Comprehending how politics and religion interact in the empires of the East allows Gibbon's *Persia* to surpass, at least in this respect, the work of his master.

Gibbon's analysis of Persian religion begins where his analysis of Roman religion left off. The Roman elites held that long-established religions were well adapted to a region's climate and inhabitants—a theory that did not account for the cultural mixing inherent in empires and evident especially in great cosmopolitan cities like Alexandria and Rome.[69] In this crucial respect, the religious scene in Persia was imperial centuries before Rome. "During the long servitude of Persia under the Macedonian and the Parthian yoke," says Gibbon, "the nations of Europe and Asia had mutually adopted and corrupted each other's superstitions."[70] The religion of Persia reflects what might become of Roman religion once the weakness of the Roman elites' localizing theory has been revealed.

The differences between the two religious systems are stark indeed. Zoroaster, "the ancient prophet and philosopher of the Persians," stands for Homer.[71] "The obsolete and mysterious language" of the Zendavasta replaces the "elegant mythology" of the *Iliad* and *Odyssey*. Instead of infinite national variants on the polytheist theme, all of them tolerated and promoted by quietly skeptical magistrates, there are "seventy sects, who variously explained the fundamental doctrines of their religion, and were all indifferently derided by a crowd of infidels, who rejected the divine mission and miracles of the prophet."[72] Most fundamentally, Persia's priests differ from Rome's. Prior to Artaxerxes's revolution, the Persian priests constitute a "very numerous" class unto themselves, set apart from the Arsacid magistrates and supported by returns on their lands and tithes.[73] Rome's priests are part-timers who possess political authority and do not have to seek it by ecclesiastical means.[74] Persia's priests are professionals, trained in the arts of spiritual warfare and eager to play a part on the political scene.[75] A host of religious phenomena that will figure prominently in subsequent volumes of Gibbon's great work—priestly religion rooted in a philosophical sacred text, fears of "hell tortures," "general councils" to resolve religious doctrine and mute sectarianism—emerge suddenly in the heart of this first volume, owing to their presence in his Persia.[76]

Also emerging for the first time is religious persecution. The Zoroastrians destroy Parthian temples and statues of deified monarchs. "The sword of Aristotle (such was the name given by the Orientals to the polytheism and philosophy of the Greeks) was easily broken; the flames of persecution soon reached the more stubborn Jews and Christians; nor did they spare the heretics of their own nation and religion."[77] Gibbon had earlier praised Roman toleration for producing "religious concord" and foreclosing the very possibility of persecution.[78] There, persecution was said to arise from three motives: a "blind, though honest bigotry," ambition, and avarice.[79] The Roman magistrates' philosophical training tempered their bigotry, and the preexisting union between temporal and ecclesiastical powers closed off an independent priesthood (as distinct from the rather more independent military) as a route to fame or fortune. The Persian priests had also found ways to satisfy avarice with religious rather than political power. Gibbon quotes from the Sadder a justification of tithing: "If the destour be satisfied, your soul will escape hell tortures."[80] Gibbon's Persian priests are also "philosophical," after a fashion, but their reasoning bears a more dogmatic than skeptical aspect. Gibbon notes that they were "of a speculative genius" and "preserved and investigated the secrets of Oriental philosophy"; in discussing the Persian, but not the Roman, philosopher-priests, Gibbon notes Hume's observation that "the most refined and philosophic sects are constantly the most intolerant."[81] Prior to Artaxerxes's revolution, however, these priests "sighed in contempt and obscurity"; their ambition for political power was not fulfilled. And so the persecution that accompanies their rise to power is one Gibbon's readers rather expect.

They would expect it to be related, however, in a tone of condemnation. Gibbon had praised Roman toleration, and he will later lament the religious persecutions that afflicted Christendom.[82] All the more remarkable, then, is his evaluation of the persecution Artaxerxes oversees. "This spirit of persecution reflects dishonor on the religion of Zoroaster," Gibbon writes, "but as it was not productive of any civil commotion, it served to strengthen the new monarchy, by uniting all the various inhabitants of Persia in the bands of religious zeal."[83] Gibbon takes full measure of the novel power Artaxerxes wields and acknowledges that, in this case, persecution strengthens the new monarchy. Indeed, the Persian priests succeed in suppressing the same sects that had eluded the Roman magistrates.[84] Not only rival Persian sects but Greeks, Jews, and Christians are all overcome. Gibbon's Persians conduct a spiritual conquest analogous to nothing in Tacitus's experience, save perhaps for the territorial conquests of the Roman Republic.

The temporal power of the Persian priests stems in part from distinctly religious phenomena. Indeed, it is in this section of the work that many of

Gibbon's insights into religious psychology appear. "Every mode of religion," he says in a passage we have already had occasion to notice, "to make a deep and lasting impression on the human mind, must exercise our obedience, by enjoining practices of devotion, for which we can assign no reason; and must acquire our esteem, by inculcating moral duties analogous to the dictates of our own hearts."[85] In the latter category, moral duties, Gibbon mentions, in addition to broad endorsements of justice, mercy, and liberality, the condemnation of fasting and celibacy; the saint's obligations to engage in agriculture, destroy noxious animals, and irrigate the desert; and festivals that commemorated "primitive equality."[86] In the former category, practices of devotion, Gibbon places the "mysterious girdle" worn by mature Persians and the injection of the gods into every aspect of daily life: "All the actions of his life, even the most indifferent, or the most necessary, were sanctified by their peculiar prayers, ejaculations, or genuflexions; the omission of which, under any circumstances, was a grievous sin, not inferior in guilt to the violation of the moral duties."[87] Fear of grievous sin, and with it the prospect of "hell tortures," empowers Persia's priests, whom Gibbon presents as exciting, alleviating, and exploiting this fear. Their power reaches not only into "all the actions of [the Persian's] life" but across the empire. The priests are also "extremely numerous"—Gibbon counts eighty thousand at the general council that begins Artaxerxes's reign.

Even more decisive than their numbers, Gibbon says, is the priests' "discipline."[88] For Tacitus, *disciplina* had been an attribute of soldiers, not priests.[89] Prior to this chapter on Persia, Gibbon had followed his master's lead. "Military exercises were the important and unremitted object of [the Romans'] discipline," Gibbon writes as his work begins.[90] From this point forward "discipline" serves as a measure of Roman military strength and a leading point of contention between the civil and military powers. The Praetorian guards' dread of "the strictness of the ancient discipline" motivates their overthrow of Pertinax; Septimus Severus achieves a death by old age by allowing himself to be "reduced to relax the nerves of discipline"; and fear of "slow revenge, colored by the name of discipline" turns the Praetorians against the "emperors of the senate," Maximus and Balbinus.[91] Just prior to decamping for Persia Gibbon offers this valedictory: "The discipline of the legions, which alone, after the extinction of every other virtue, had propped the greatness of the state, was corrupted by the ambition, or relaxed by the weakness, of the emperors." "The fairest provinces," he continues, "were left exposed to the rapaciousness or ambition of the barbarians, who soon discovered the decline of the Roman empire."[92] Tacitus, who worried that Nero's reign had squandered the legions' *veterem disciplinam,* would hardly be surprised.[93]

Gibbon adds to Tacitus recognition of a new source of power—the discipline not of legions but of priests. This new power carries important political consequences. In Rome, religious devotion had been subordinate to policy; in old regime Persia, policy was largely independent of religious devotion. Artaxerxes's attempt to restore the religion and empire of Cyrus, however, shows how a new sort of religion is compatible with a new vision of empire. "Those of more active dispositions mixed with the world in courts and cities," Gibbon writes, "and it is observed, that the administration of Artaxerxes was in a great measure directed by the counsels of the sacerdotal order, whose dignity, either from policy or devotion, that prince restored to its ancient splendor."[94] At the conclusion of the revolution the Roman order has been inverted: instead of magistrates using religion as a tool of policy, the Magi use politics as a tool of religion. In accounting for this transformation Gibbon reveals himself as a philosophical historian concerned to overtake and surpass his Roman guides.[95]

When Gibbon turns from the Persians to the Germans, his ostensible project shifts from filling a gap in the Tacitean project to following modestly in the master's footsteps. In antiquity, "the Germans were surveyed by the discerning eye, and delineated by the masterly pencil, of Tacitus"; in modern times, "innumerable antiquarians" and "philosophic historians" have explicated and elaborated Tacitus's portrait. Little is left for a writer like Gibbon to add. He therefore contents himself with "observing, and indeed with repeating, some of the most important circumstances . . . which rendered the wild barbarians of Germany such formidable enemies to the Roman power."[96] Thus Gibbon presents himself meekly bringing up the rear of Tacitus's train.

Tacitus's *Germania* had won such an enthusiastic following among modern readers because it presented a flattering and paradoxical origin story. "The most civilized nations of modern Europe," Gibbon says, "issued from the woods of Germany, and in the rude institutions of Germany, we may still distinguish the original principles of our present laws and manners."[97] This line of approach to the Germans involves tracing unchanging virtues that span barbarism and civilization; in its simplest forms, it writes the Roman Empire largely out of the narrative linking modern to ancient Europe. As an example of this sort of "well-labored system of German antiquities," Gibbon offers up the work of one "Olaus Rudbeck, professor in the university of Upsal," who ascribes to Sweden (part of Germany when Tacitus wrote) "whatever is celebrated either in history or fable."[98]

Gibbon considers Rudbeck and other nationalist antiquarians poor historians but not necessarily poor readers of Tacitus.[99] Tacitus's *Germania* presented a beguiling image of German liberty and, with it, a thinly veiled critique of Roman civilization.[100] By contrast to Rome's extravagant luxury, Tacitus shows the Germans moderate in their food, entertainment, and burials.[101] Among the Germans, military command follows virtue rather than political connection, and political authority is not corrupted by freedmen and slaves.[102] Debtors are not exploited by the rich; farm land, used only for grain, is not depleted by "the planting of orchards, the setting apart of water-meadows, the irrigation of vegetable gardens."[103] Most praiseworthy—"you will find nothing in their character to praise more highly," Tacitus stresses—marriage bonds and family obligations are taken seriously. "No one laughs at vice [in Germany]; no one calls seduction, suffered or wrought, the spirit of the age."[104] Above all, the Germans are free. Their freedom marks for Tacitus the main point of contrast between them and the Parthians: "The German fighting for liberty has been a keener enemy than the absolutism of Arsaces."[105] If modern Europeans are free as well, their liberty must have issued from the woods of Germany rather than the absolutist East or the Roman Empire that Tacitus made to resemble Parthia in contrasting it so vividly to the free people to its north.

Gibbon can also write in this vein. In describing Severus's war with the Caledonians, for instance, he pauses to contemplate the contrast between Romans and barbarians. "The parallel would be little to the advantage of the more civilized people," Gibbon writes, if one were to compare "the mercenary chiefs, who, from motives of fear or interest, served under the imperial standard, with the free-born warriors who started to arms at the voice of the king of Morven . . . , the untutored Caledonians, glowing with the warm virtues of nature, and the degenerate Romans, polluted with the mean vices of wealth and slavery."[106] Immediately prior to announcing the digression of the eighth and ninth chapters, *in imitatio Taciti*, Gibbon resounds the theme in a panoptic view of a millennium of Roman history (also imitating Tacitus, though Gibbon doesn't say as much).[107] For the first four centuries of their history the Romans acquired "in the laborious school of poverty" the "virtues of war and government"; for the next three, they used these virtues to conquer much of the known world and acquire considerable wealth; they then passed three centuries under the empire "in apparent prosperity and internal decline."[108] When Gibbon says of the Germans that "poverty secured their freedom, since our desires and our possessions are the strongest fetters of despotism," he invokes a Tacitean theory of rise and fall—one that he had seemingly made his own. Poverty instills the hard, manly virtues. The hard conquer and expropriate the soft, growing rich and soft all the while, until they are themselves conquered by a poor, hard people "glowing with the warm virtues of nature."[109] Gibbon seems on this point to agree with Tacitus.

But he is nevertheless willing to depart from his master on a number of smaller matters.[110] Gibbon considers Tacitus's claim that the Germans were "natives of the soil," for instance, "a rash inference, condemned by religion, and unwarranted by reason."[111] Tacitus is "somewhat too florid" on the chastity of German women.[112] Gibbon defends a number of modern emendations to Tacitus's manuscripts, one of which he praises as a correction of Tacitus himself.[113] Gibbon goes so far as to claim that two (of five surviving) books of Tacitus's *History* are "more remarkable for [their] eloquence than perspicuity."[114] This last suggests a broader departure.

Indeed, Gibbon strikes out farthest when he leaves his foil respectfully unnamed. Tacitus's Germans were strong and free. Gibbon's live "in a state of ignorance and poverty, which it has pleased some declaimers to dignify with the appellation of virtuous simplicity."[115] Tacitus spoke frequently of the Germans' *virtus*; he praised the simplicity of the German bartering economy, divination, and diet.[116] Tacitus's Germans, like Herodotus's Persians, turned even drunken banquets toward a serious purpose by debating issues once drunk and then again once sober (a kind of bicameral legislature); the drunkenness was crucial, since "at no other time are minds more open to obvious [and simple], or better warmed to larger, thoughts."[117] Gibbon's Germans hardly think at all. Tacitus's Germans used runes; Gibbon's are illiterate. And on Gibbon's understanding their illiteracy is a more consequential condition than Tacitus and modern admirers of the Germans allowed. Without letters, Gibbon says, "the human memory soon dissipates or corrupts the ideas intrusted to her charge; and the nobler faculties of the mind, no longer supplied with models or with materials, gradually forget their powers; the judgment becomes feeble and lethargic, the imagination languid or irregular."[118] Lacking knowledge, reflection, and the mind's nobler faculties, Gibbon's Germans are savages hardly distinct from animals; Gibbon draws this parallel more than once.[119] Tacitus praised the simplicity of the German barter economy. Gibbon considers the Germans' ignorance of money to reflect broader incapacities. Money, in a word, "is the most universal incitement, iron the most powerful instrument, of human industry; and it is very difficult to conceive by what means a people, neither actuated by the one, nor seconded by the other, could emerge from the grossest barbarism."[120] Gibbon's Germans are a people without "industry," a term Gibbon uses to signify man's manipulation of nature for human purposes.[121] Owing to ignorance of money and letters, Gibbon's Germans lack the mental capacity to extend themselves imaginatively into the future.[122] Tacitus's Germans were simple and virtuous. Gibbon's are stupid and lazy.

Gibbon's critique extends to Tacitus's view of German religion. "Some applause has been hastily bestowed on the sublime notion, entertained by that people, of the Deity, whom they neither confined within the walls of the temple, nor represented by any figure," Gibbon writes.[123] Gibbon's reference to the unnamed Tacitus is hard to miss. "The Germans," Tacitus wrote, "deem it incompatible with the majesty of the heavenly host to confine the gods within walls, or to mould them into any likeness of the human face: they consecrate groves and coppices, and they give the divine names to that mysterious something which is visible only to the eyes of faith."[124] For Gibbon, by contrast, it is misleading to describe the Germans as consciously performing an intellectual act like deeming or naming. Their religious system—"if the wild opinions of savages can deserve that name"—arises from "their wants, their fears, and their ignorance."[125] Missing from Gibbon's initial religious psychology are gratitude, curiosity, and other noble sentiments.

The centrality of fear serves the purposes of German priests, a class mentioned by Tacitus but always in conjunction with Germany's civil leaders, rather in the manner of Gibbon's own portrayal of Roman polytheism.[126] For Gibbon, however, Germany's priests show more initiative. "The priests, rude and illiterate as they were, had been taught by experience the use of every artifice that could preserve and fortify impressions so well suited to their own interest."[127] It is these priests who exploit the "religious horror" inspired by the "secret gloom" of the sacred groves, made all the more fearsome by the lack of any distinct object to fear.[128]

At the root, then, of German religion Gibbon finds a powerful and pervasive terror of the unknown.[129] This fear stems from an ignorance deeper than what Tacitus and his modern followers had allowed, owing largely to their inadequate reflection on the psychological consequences of German illiteracy and innumeracy. Tacitus's Germans, brave and free, revered gods who reflected their freedom; Gibbon's are exposed "naked and unarmed to the blind terrors of superstition," exploited by priests who—contra Tacitus, yet again—supplant rather than supplement the German magistrate.[130] In Germany, as in Persia, the priests rule.

Gibbon's excursion into Persia and Germany, far from tracing the path of his master, marks his departure from Tacitus and the tradition of elite Roman historiography he crowned. Tacitus had viewed the threat of Germany and, to a lesser extent, Parthia in political-military terms. His Germans were not only brave and free but extremely numerous. Only divisions among them—their too-spirited hostility to the title "Germans" as distinct from tribal names—kept Rome safe.[131] United, as they sometimes were in Tacitus's historical works, the Germans' *virtus* posed an existential threat to the corrupt and degenerating Empire to their south, summoning its own last, dying remnants of republican *virtus*.[132] Although "the German fighting for his liberty was a keener enemy than the absolutism of Arsaces," the Parthian threat remained.[133] As Tacitus's Germans invoked the defeat of Varus in the Teutoburg Forest, his Parthians cited the defeat of Crassus at Carrhae.[134]

Gibbon views these political-military threats rather differently. The numbers of the Persians and Germans are both of them exaggerated; both militaries are undisciplined.[135] Gibbon says of the Persians that "they trusted more to their numbers than to their courage; more to their courage than to their discipline. The infantry was a half-armed spiritless crowd of peasants."[136] The Germans, by contrast, were strong in infantry but "knew not how to rally or to retire." "When we recollect the complete armor of the Roman soldiers, their discipline, exercises, evolutions, fortified camps, and military engines," Gibbon writes, "it appears a just matter of surprise, how the naked and unassisted valor of the barbarians could dare to encounter, in the field, the strength of the legions, and the various troops of the auxiliaries, which seconded their operations."[137] In both cases, Gibbon narrates successful Roman campaigns. Strategic blunders on the part of Roman commanders do little to prevent the strength of the legions from holding sway.[138] For the future, Gibbon offers ominous prophecies, which are shortly fulfilled, but his description of the Persians and Germans themselves gives little reason to think either people will soon threaten the Empire.[139]

For Gibbon, it is not on the political but on the spiritual plane that the vigor and power of these peoples are to be found. The political map shows territory conquered and held by the arms of Rome, owing to their discipline, union, and the vast manpower and material resources at their disposal. A spiritual map, by contrast, shows a polytheistic political-theological system covering the Roman Empire and spilling out over its boundaries to the ends of the known world—except for the relatively small holdouts Gibbon gestures at in his footnotes (Druids, Jews, and Egyptians) and, as we now understand after Gibbon's chapters on Persia and Germany, two giant spiritual masses to Rome's north and east. These spiritual masses are the priestly religions, in which some men devote their lives to ministering to human fear, curiosity, and wonder without wielding formal political authority. The office of priest in Persia and Germany has political consequences, to be sure, but it is theological before it is political, in the same proportion as the Roman priests are political before they are theological. On the political plane, the Roman legions' discipline and unity allow them to conquer and hold territory; on the spiritual plane, Rome has no such force on the field. The priests of Persia and Germany stand to the Roman priests as Roman soldiers stand to undisciplined barbarian hordes.

The crucial break Gibbon makes from Tacitus turns on this power of priestly religion. Persia and Germany are for Gibbon what Germany alone was for Tacitus; the relief Gibbon offers his reader "from a uniform scene of vice and misery" describes the new *virtus* with respect to which Rome appears weak.[140] The virtue and fatal flaw of Roman polytheism, we come to understand in these chapters, is its elision of magistrate and priest. In Persia and Germany these roles are kept distinct. Among both peoples, professional priests perfect the art of caring for and controlling the human soul by means that, while not immediately political, nevertheless have profound political consequences. Professional priests generate a form of power that Rome, for all of its military and political dominance, is ill-equipped to confront. With his studies of Roman, Persian, and German religion, Gibbon equips his reader to understand the power of the early Christians better than did the pagan establishment—intellectuals, magistrates, and priests—that failed to control their expansion.

THE CHRISTIAN REPUBLIC

In the concluding chapters of the *Decline and Fall*'s first volume, Gibbon turned the theory of religion he had developed with a view to Rome, Persia, and

Germany to account for the progress of Christianity. The view of Christianity contained in these chapters is often said to hide a contemptuous sneer or to undercut pious pronouncements with characteristic "irony." But it is more accurate to say that Gibbon's contempt is half-hidden, at best, and his irony so overt as to shade into sarcasm. Few were fooled. Although he would later feign surprise at the controversy these chapters caused, Gibbon had in fact anticipated that his readers, both skeptics and believers, would catch his drift.[141]

How could he not have? His fifteenth chapter opposed the orthodox claim that Christianity's rapid progress revealed God's hand in history by showing that "secondary" or human causes could account for it. Other claims to miraculous intervention were debunked or undermined along the way, culminating in an investigation of the darkness at noon—the "preternatural darkness of the Passion"—so skeptical as to be unmistakable for anything but a denial.[142] There followed the sixteenth and final chapter, a narration of the early Church's persecution that diminished the guilt of the persecutors, both through critical evaluation of pagan and Christian source materials and by comparison to the more severe persecutions that Christians themselves had initiated. "The number of Protestants, who were executed in a single province and a single reign," Gibbon wrote of the Netherlands under Charles the Fifth, "far exceeded that of the primitive martyrs in the space of three centuries, and of the Roman empire."[143] Gibbon seemed here, as in so much of the *Decline and Fall*, to resurrect the spirit he had discovered under the sacerdotal robes of Roman magistrates and philosophers. As they viewed Roman polytheism so Gibbon viewed Christianity.

Nevertheless, in these concluding chapters there appears a new, countervailing rhetoric critical of not only early Christians but skeptical Romans. Earlier Gibbon had said that Roman polytheism was considered true by the people, false by philosophers, and useful by magistrates.[144] In these concluding chapters these distinctions are not so clearly drawn:

> The contagion of [Cicero and Lucian's] skeptical writings had been diffused far beyond the number of their readers. The fashion of incredulity was communicated from the philosopher to the man of pleasure or business, from the noble to the plebeian, and from the master to the menial slave who waited at his table, and who eagerly listened to the freedom of his conversation. On public occasions the philosophic part of mankind affected to treat with respect and decency the

> religious institutions of their country; but their secret contempt penetrated through the thin and awkward disguise; and even the people, when they discovered that their deities were rejected and derided by those whose rank or understanding they were accustomed to reverence, were filled with doubts and apprehensions concerning the truth of those doctrines, to which they had yielded the most implicit belief.[145]

Once philosophers had led the people to doubt their religion, Gibbon suggests, their pieties were no longer useful to the magistrate. The seemingly steady balance that sustained a valuable civic institution and freedom of philosophical inquiry had broken down, owing not to proselytizing Christians but to indiscreet skeptics.

Gibbon does not exactly retract his admiration for the ancient philosophers' skepticism, but amid his narration of Christianity's rise the practical and political consequences of that skepticism seem much less benign than before, for their hostility or indifference toward religion extended past polytheism to the new faith. Gibbon notes eight sages—Seneca, both Plinies, Tacitus, Plutarch, Galen, Epictetus, and Marcus Aurelius—who either "overlooked or rejected the perfection of the Christian system."[146] If Gibbon's own apparent contempt for Christianity inclines us to read this list as evidence that we should join the sages, his criticisms of the sages in these late chapters give us some pause. Might *their* reluctance to take Christianity seriously suggest a gap in their wisdom? Might a latter-day author, one who shared these sages' view of the early Christians as "obstinate and perverse enthusiasts" but could not dismiss them on that account, repair that failing?[147]

The pervasive contempt and irony of Gibbon's account of Christianity have the ironic effect of hiding from most of his readers his penetrating analysis—we might almost say appreciation—of Christianity's power. For what Gibbon describes in these concluding chapters is, in fact, a conquest as stunning in its own way as the Roman Republic's subjection of the inhabited world in a period of fifty-three years.[148] By what means and under what system of government did Christianity obtain "so remarkable a victory over the established religions of the earth," raise "the triumphant banner of the cross on the ruins of the Capitol," and, resisting the forces that caused Rome's decline and fall, extend its influence beyond the Empire's boundaries "to the most distant shores of Asia and Africa . . . from Canada to Chili, in a world unknown to the ancients"?[149] Polybius and Cicero could not be faulted for having neglected this question; Tacitus and the other Antonine sages might be. But regardless of who deserves blame or praise, in asking how Christianity conquered the world, Gibbon poses a question that the ancient philosophers and historians he most admired had failed not only to answer but to ask.

Gibbon explains the progress of Christianity by appealing to five "secondary causes" (the primary cause, God's Providence, is sounded once and then silenced): the Christians' intolerant zeal, promise of a future life, miraculous powers, austere morals, and finally "the union and discipline of the Christian republic, which gradually formed an independent and increasing state in the heart of the Roman empire."[150] Gibbon uses the word "republic" with varying shades of irony; the governments of ancient Greece and Rome are "republics," but the Roman Empire after the Republic has been "restored" under Augustus's government of names can assume this title as well.[151] That Gibbon means us to read the "Christian republic" in the first sense—as resembling the regime that preceded Augustus—is suggested by the restatement that follows his elaboration of these secondary causes:

> It was by the aid of these causes, exclusive zeal, the immediate expectation of another world, the claim of miracles, the practice of rigid virtue, and the constitution of the primitive church, that Christianity spread itself with so much success in the Roman empire. To the first of these the Christians were indebted for their invincible valor, which disdained to capitulate with the enemy whom they were resolved to vanquish. The three succeeding causes supplied their valor with the most formidable arms. The last of these causes united their courage, directed their arms, and gave their efforts that irresistible weight, which even a small band of well-trained and intrepid volunteers has so often possessed over an undisciplined multitude, ignorant of the subject, and careless of the event of the war.[152]

Gibbon's theory, in short, is that early Christians stood to the Romans in something like the relation that early Romans had to the decadent empires to their east. The early Romans conquered people and extended their empire over the "globe of the earth"; the early Christians were "spiritual conquerors" who won souls for the Church.[153] Gibbon intended to adapt the theories explaining the rise of the old, temporal republic—theories that, as we have seen, he deployed as early as the *Essai* of 1759[154]—to account for the rise of a new, spiritual republic. He does so via an extensive analogy between the two, which we shall examine under the heads Gibbon's restatement suggests: valor, arms, and discipline.

Gibbon begins from the phenomenon of valor, or the willingness, most evident in military settings, to sacrifice on behalf of the group to which one belongs. Gibbon's political history of this virtue runs from the ancient republics into the Roman Empire. First, under the Greek and Roman republics, arms had been reserved to "citizens who had a country to love, a property to defend, and some share in enacting those laws, which it was their interest, as well as their duty, to maintain"; the "patriotism" that resulted from the citizen-soldiers' self-interest, ennobled and enlarged as the common interest, rendered the legions "almost invincible."[155] Under the Empire, "honor and religion"—motives "which derived their strength from the imagination"—replaced patriotism; a soldier fought to win glory, if not for himself then for the unit he considered his own, and to avoid divine punishment for violating his oath or abandoning the unit's standard.[156] Under both regimes, republic and empire, material incentives like pay and corporal punishment buttressed these nobler motives.[157] Gibbon's analysis of the political orders that preceded Christianity, then, suggests that men could be rendered courageous—willing to sacrifice themselves on behalf of an order—by appealing to their patriotism, honor, religion, love of money, and fear of punishment.

In considering why Christians were so willing to sacrifice for *their* order, Gibbon begins from the "obstinacy" of the Jews. Why did the Jews alone of all the peoples Rome conquered "refuse to join in the common intercourse of mankind" by syncretizing "with the institutions of Moses the elegant mythology of the Greeks"?[158] Gibbon first offers an explanation adapted from Montesquieu: "The current of zeal and devotion, as it was contracted into a narrow channel, ran with the strength, and sometimes with the fury, of a torrent."[159] Having been deprived of worldly rewards and signs of divine favor, the Jews had only their laws and traditions to love, and so they loved them fiercely, to the point where death seemed preferable to "idolatrous profanation."[160]

In this singular case, Gibbon suggests, being conquered justified neither the abandonment of gods who had failed to protect nor the assimilation or subordination of one's gods to those of the conqueror but a more spiritual, less material, notion of divinity than had previously existed. "In contradiction to every known principle of the human mind," Gibbon writes, "that singular people seems to have yielded a stronger and more ready assent to the traditions of their remote ancestors, than to the evidence of their own senses."[161] The God of the Jews was not bound to the worldly success of his people and could elicit devotion no matter how low their worldly fortunes had sunk.

Even at their weakest the Jews were unassimilable; at their strongest they were unconcerned to assimilate those they conquered. "In the admission of new citizens," Gibbon writes, "that unsocial people was actuated by the selfish vanity of the Greeks, rather than by the generous policy of Rome."[162] As "patriotism" was the motive of republics in Greece and Rome, so "zeal" is common to both Jews and Christians. As Rome "sacrificed vanity to ambition, and deemed it more prudent, as well as honorable, to adopt virtue and merit for her own whosesoever they were found, among slaves or strangers, enemies or barbarians," so Christianity refines the Jewish ceremonial law into "a pure and spiritual worship, equally adapted to all climates as well as to every condition of mankind."[163] Gibbon's Christians relate to the Jews as the Roman Republic related to Athens and Sparta.[164]

Gibbon understands the Christians' conquering zeal, like the valor of Romans in the early Republic, to be fueled by fear as much as greed. The Christians are surrounded on all sides and are forced to fight: "The superstitious observances of public or private rites were carelessly practised . . . as often as they occurred, [and] they afforded the Christians an opportunity of declaring and confirming their zealous opposition." Gibbon continues, "By these frequent protestations, [the Christians'] attachment to the faith was continually fortified; and in proportion to the increase of zeal, they combated with the more ardor and success in the holy war, which they had undertaken against the empire of the demons."[165] What we are left with, then, is a view of Christianity that is simultaneously contemptuous and admiring. Gibbon does indeed (as many have noted) engage his readers' anti-Semitism to taint early Christianity. Nothing he says diminishes our strong impression that he denies the central doctrines of the faith. And yet the analogy he draws between the Roman and the Christian republics complicates the conclusions we would otherwise be too quick to draw. Both the citizens Gibbon seems to esteem and the Christians he seems to condemn are obstinate and ultimately "invincible."[166]

Gibbon now turns to consider the "most formidable arms" that allowed obstinate Christians to conquer paganism: the doctrine of a future life, miracles, and austere morals. The arms that had allowed the Roman Republic to expand were literally the swords and shields of the legions as well as the allurements of Roman commerce and citizenship.[167] Those methods of worldly conquest had been well understood by ancient and modern historians alike.

To comprehend their analogues in spiritual conquest, Gibbon stresses repeatedly, the modern observer and the ancient skeptic must extend their frames of reference. In presenting the doctrine of a future life, Gibbon says that "the ancient Christians were animated by a contempt for their present existence, and by a just confidence of immortality, of which the doubtful and imperfect faith of modern ages cannot give us any adequate notion."[168] Similarly with miracles: "In modern times, a latent and even involuntary skepticism adheres to the most pious dispositions. Their admission of supernatural truths is much less an active consent than a cold and passive acquiescence," Gibbon writes. "But, in the first ages of Christianity, the situation of mankind was extremely different. The most curious, or the most credulous, among the Pagans, were often persuaded to enter into a society which asserted an actual claim of miraculous powers."[169] Moderns and skeptics also have trouble acknowledging the extremity of Christian austerity. The "zealous fathers . . . carried the duties of self-mortification, of purity, and of patience, to a height which it is scarcely possible to attain, and much less to preserve, in our present state of weakness and corruption."[170] There is irony here, to be sure, and it carries with it a tone of incredulity. Gibbon in these passages permits his reader, and he will do so again, to consider whether we should discount entirely the testimony of a credulous age to events that would be incredible in the present day.

Nevertheless, a correction to ancient and modern skepticism is also at work. Gibbon suggests that we cannot understand the human causes of Christianity's rise if we refuse to extend our understanding beyond the explanations that our own age, or our own skepticism, makes immediately available to us.[171] To understand the rise of Christianity we cannot make the Romans Englishmen. We must allow them a greater share of earnestness, credulity, and self-discipline than would otherwise be credible—to us.

Gibbon understands Christianity's essential appeal to pagans to rest in its promise of eternal happiness or punishment. The prospect of a life after the present one was either denied or anticipated only hazily by pagan poets and skeptical philosophers; it was not present in the revelation Moses received. As a result, when Christians described, earnestly and in vivid detail, a "blissful kingdom . . . adorned with all the gayest colors of the imagination" and "the lowest abyss of darkness," where persecuting magistrates would "liquefy" in "fiercer fires than they ever kindled against the Christians," pagans could easily be swept up: "The careless Polytheist, assailed by new and unexpected terrors, against which neither his priests nor his philosophers could afford him any certain protection, was very frequently terrified and subdued by the menace of eternal tortures. His fears might assist the progress of his faith and reason; and if he could once persuade himself to suspect that the Christian religion might possibly be true, it became an easy task to convince him that it was the safest and most prudent party that he could possibly embrace."[172] For Gibbon, the power of Christianity's attack on its spiritual rivals came from its uncontested hold on this higher ground.

The miracles Christians performed made this message all the more credible. Gibbon relates these miracles of the early Church with deep skepticism. (Middleton's *Free Inquiry*, an unwitting apology for Catholicism no longer, figures prominently.) "The resurrection of the dead was very far from being esteemed an uncommon event," Gibbon notes, before proceeding to draw out the implication under the thinnest of ironic veils. "It seems difficult to account for the skepticism of those philosophers, who still rejected and derided the doctrine of the resurrection."[173] The central mysteries of Christianity, we are to understand, are the residue of an age when highly credulous Christians (and pagans) "perpetually trod on mystic ground."[174] Within such a world, miracles still "conduced . . . very frequently to the conviction of infidels."[175] They offered this-worldly confirmation of the nascent Church's authority over the soul's fate in the world to come.

When Gibbon goes on to consider how Christians translated their anticipation of imminent life in another world to a way of life in this world, we find a by-now-familiar ambivalence. On the one hand, Christians are drawn from the criminal, the poor, the ignorant, the indolent, and the dour. On the other hand, many of these very qualities make them resemble early Romans. "The virtue of the primitive Christians, like that of the first Romans, was very frequently guarded by poverty and ignorance"; we might add (though Gibbon only implies) that Christians resembled the early Romans in their austerity and the welcoming hand they extended to criminals.[176] Likewise, Gibbon describes the Christians' attachment to their church in terms that recall his analysis of republican "patriotism," with its mixture of interest and duty:

> Any particular society that has departed from the great body of the nation, or the religion to which it belonged, immediately becomes the object of universal as well as invidious observation. In proportion to the smallness of its numbers, the character of the society may be affected by the virtues and vices of the persons who compose it; and every member is engaged to watch with the most vigilant attention over his own behavior, and over that of his brethren, since, as he must expect to incur a part of the common disgrace, he may hope to enjoy a share of the common reputation.[177]

The patriotism of the early Romans, recall, "derived from a strong sense of our own interest in the preservation and prosperity of the free government of which we are members."[178]

The crucial difference between the early Romans and the early Christians turns on whether this world or the next is man's proper home. The early Romans and the civilization they established placed man's happiness in this world. For them, a good man was one who harmonized the pleasant and the useful, the "feelings of nature and the interest of society."[179] From this view the disposition of Christians seemed "insensible and inactive," which is to say the inverse of the ideal. Gibbon agrees with this view in its fundamentals—man's home is in this world, and the best man is agreeable and useful—but he challenges the simplest analysis of Christianity it opens up. First, it is incorrect to say the Christians are "insensible and inactive" and leave it at that, because "it was not in *this* world that the primitive Christians were desirous of making themselves either agreeable or useful."[180] There is all the difference in the world between the "insensible and inactive" man who does not believe in another world and the man who does believe; the first deserves our contempt for negating the goals proper to man, the latter transposes them into another register. Second and related, the latter sort of man cuts a rather different figure in this world than the first. Gibbon's Christians do not simply check out of the "active life" on offer in the Empire—though insofar as they do, Gibbon shines a harsh light on them.[181] But what most interests Gibbon is the new "active life" that the Christians establish in this world, one that occurs within a new sort of institution—indeed, a new sort of republic.

Gibbon's account of the rise of Christianity culminates in the fifth of the human or secondary causes: "The union and discipline of the Christian republic, which gradually formed an independent and increasing state in the heart of the Roman empire."[182] Later, Gibbon credits this fifth cause for uniting the Christians' "courage, [directing] their arms, and [giving] their efforts that irresistible weight, which even a small band of well-trained and intrepid volunteers has so often possessed over an undisciplined multitude, ignorant of the subject, and careless of the event of the war."[183] The Christians were disciplined "troops" like those of the early Republic; the Romans, in this spiritual conflict at least, the "undisciplined multitude."[184]

As we have seen, discipline and union are normally qualities Gibbon (following Tacitus) invokes to explain Rome's military and political success against other peoples. Gibbon says that "as long as the empire retained any vigor, their military instructions were respected as the most perfect model of Roman discipline," while "domestic peace and union" enabled the Romans to exploit the disunion of provincial subjects and northern tribes, among whom "every quarrel . . . was fomented by the intrigues of Rome; and every plan of union and public good was defeated by the stronger bias of private jealousy and interest."[185] Discipline and union are in fact closely linked to one another. "The advantages of military science and discipline cannot be exerted, unless a proper number of soldiers are united into one body, and actuated by one soul," Gibbon observes. "With a handful of men, such a union would be ineffectual; with an unwieldy host, it would be impracticable; and the powers of the machine would be alike destroyed by the extreme minuteness or the excessive weight of its springs."[186] Union precedes discipline and enables it; discipline also sustains union. Gibbon understands a disciplined and united body of soldiers to punch well above its weight against enemies not only foreign but domestic. "A hundred thousand well-disciplined soldiers will command, with despotic sway, ten millions of subjects," Gibbon writes, "and a body of ten or fifteen thousand guards will strike terror into the most numerous populace that ever crowded the streets of an immense capital."[187]

The ultimate source of union under the Roman Republic was patriotism—that "public virtue" arising from "our own interest in the preservation and prosperity of the free government of which we are members."[188] This was also the source of the Christians' union. "The safety of [the Christian commonwealth], its honor, its aggrandizement," Gibbon writes, "were productive, even in the most pious minds, of a spirit of patriotism, such as the first of the Romans had felt for the republic, and sometimes of a similar indifference, in the use of whatever means might probably conduce to so desirable an end."[189] Like the patriotism of the Roman Republic, that of the Christian republic, on Gibbon's understanding, was a public virtue arising from private interests.[190] The early Romans "had a property to defend"; the early Christians benefitted from "a generous intercourse of charity" that "very *materially* conduced to the progress of Christianity."[191] The early Romans' love of country had been buttressed by their fear of exile, enslavement, or harsh punishment; the Christians,' by fear of excommunication, the consequences of which "were of a temporal as well as a spiritual nature."[192] In Gibbon's moral alchemy, the individual's attachment to property and fear of pain and death transformed into virtue, the willingness to risk property and even life for the body that protected those goods.

Overseeing this alchemy were Church leaders whom Gibbon frequently compares to the great statesmen of the ancient republics. These "active prelates," Gibbon says frequently, are motivated by "ambition."[193] The third-century bishop Cyprian of Carthage is Gibbon's model in the concluding chapters of the first volume, as Athanasius, Ambrose, and John Chrysostom will be in subsequent volumes, of a form of statesmanship at once ancient and quite new.[194] Cyprian reconciles "the arts of the most ambitious statesman with the Christian virtues which seem adapted to the character of a saint and martyr."[195] His resistance to Roman rule recalls his countryman Hannibal.[196] Of Cyprian's declamations Gibbon writes that "sometimes we might imagine that we were listening to the voice of Moses. . . . We should sometimes suppose that we hear a Roman consul asserting the majesty of the republic, and declaring his inflexible resolution to enforce the rigor of the laws."[197] The Jewish and Christian virtues are here presented not as the subversion of the old Roman ones but as an amplification of them. In his ambition and the "patriotism" he inspires, Cyprian's statesmanship can be made to seem a restoration of an older type. What is new in Cyprian is the immediacy of his access to his subjects' souls. "Cyprian had renounced those temporal honors, which it is probable he would never have obtained," Gibbon writes. "But the acquisition of such absolute command over the consciences and understanding of a congregation, however obscure or despised by the world, is more truly grateful to the pride of the human heart, than the possession of the most despotic power, imposed by arms and conquest on a reluctant people."[198] Here Gibbon speaks from the perspective of an ambitious man rather than a saint, a type from the old regime rather than the new. On this basis of ambition alone, one would prefer the sort of rule Christianity opens up to the projects of conquest that motivated the statesmen of the Republic.[199]

Not only did Christianity open up the possibility of new sorts of conquest and rule, it made possible, even under the aegis of a stable Empire, a new form of the most characteristic project of the ambitious soul: that of founding. Gibbon describes the institutional history of the Church, too, with analogies drawn from the old republics. "Every society formed within itself a separate and independent republic," Gibbon writes, and these republics entered into increasingly greater union with one another just as *poleis* had before them.[200] "The churches of Greece and Asia . . . may justly be supposed to have borrowed the model of a representative council from the celebrated examples of their own country, the Amphictyons, the Achaean league, or the assemblies of the Ionian cities."[201] As these associations deepened, "the catholic church soon assumed the form, and acquired the strength, of a great foederative republic."[202]

A subtle, bivalent irony suffuses these passages. On the one hand, Gibbon consistently exposes for the reader's ridicule the Church's pretension to otherworldly motives. When he writes, for instance, of "the love of power, which (under the most artful disguises) could insinuate itself into the breasts of bishops and martyrs," Gibbon hardly allows his reader to suppose that loftier loves ever moved in the bishops' breasts.[203] On the other hand, his assessment of the Christians' achievement and its novel features—understood merely as a project of worldly ambition—is more earnest. If the bishops are at bottom lovers of power, Gibbon suggests, one can simultaneously expose their pretenses and evaluate them on honest terms. On those terms Gibbon finds reason to admire their achievement in this world.

This is especially so when Gibbon compares the arms the bishops acquired to those the Empire opposed to them. Recall that on the field of spiritual war, the Christians resemble the Romans of old, and the Romans, "an undisciplined multitude, ignorant of the subject, and careless of the event of the war."[204] The "ministers of polytheism" had always been part-timers; "their zeal and devotion were seldom animated by a sense of interest, or by the habits of an ecclesiastical character."[205] Their flock, for its part, prayed to thousands of gods and felt no "sincere or lively passion for any of them."[206] What passion the Roman people did feel had been weakened by the progressive revelation of their ministers' "secret contempt" for religious belief. When Christianity comes onto the field armed for spiritual war, Roman polytheism has largely abandoned it to them, as Gibbon describes in a remarkable passage:

> So urgent on the vulgar is the necessity of believing, that the fall of any system of mythology will most probably be succeeded by the introduction of some other mode of superstition. Some deities of a more recent and fashionable cast might soon have occupied the deserted temples of Jupiter and Apollo, if, in the decisive moment, the wisdom of Providence had not interposed a genuine revelation, fitted to inspire the most rational esteem and conviction, whilst, at the same time, it was adorned with all that could attract the curiosity, the wonder, and the veneration of the people. In their actual disposition, as many were almost disengaged from their artificial prejudices, but equally susceptible and desirous of a devout attachment; an object much less deserving would have been sufficient to fill the vacant place in their hearts, and to gratify the uncertain eagerness of their passions. Those who are inclined to pursue this reflection, instead of viewing with astonishment the rapid progress of Christianity, will perhaps be surprised that its success was not still more rapid and still more universal.

Again Gibbon relates the drama of Christian history in falsely pious tones ("the wisdom of Providence . . . interposed a genuine revelation"), deflates the Christian achievement ("surprised that its success was not still more rapid"), and heightens the mystery at what had transpired. Wonder at Christianity's conquest of the field now shifts into wonder at polytheism's abandonment of it.

The story of how the Temple of Jupiter was abandoned points forward to the volumes yet to come and back to the chapters that precede.[207] The first volume of the *Decline and Fall* began with praise of polytheism for its tolerance and universality. It concludes with a candid condemnation of polytheism for its weakness. On the spiritual plane, the once-admired magistrate-philosopher-priests are exposed as amateurs. The priests, whom we might expect to be condemned as otherworldly fanatics, are (when they are not that) shown to be far savvier statesmen than even the old Romans who had conquered "the globe of the earth."[208] Gibbon praises polytheism while hinting parenthetically and finally demonstrating why it is doomed.

The concluding chapter of the *Decline and Fall*'s first volume sustains this ambivalence. Gibbon offers a virtuosic display of the critical historian's capacity to separate "a few authentic as well as interesting facts from an undigested mass of fiction and error" in order to challenge received opinion regarding the extent to which pagans persecuted early Christians.[209] The total number of Christian martyrs, after a careful interrogation of the sources, is "reduced to somewhat less than two thousand persons."[210] Gibbon hints that a more prompt and less restrained persecution might have curtailed the new religion. Nevertheless, the first volume ends where it began: with ostensible admiration for the tolerance and beneficence of the pagan elites.[211] "Christians, in the course of their intestine dissentions, have inflicted far greater severities on each other, than they had experienced from the zeal of the infidels." To the "somewhat less than two thousand" Christian martyrs Gibbon contrasts the "more than one hundred thousand of the subjects of Charles the Fifth" and concludes that "the number of Protestants who were executed in a single province and a single reign, far exceeded that of the primitive martyrs in the space of three centuries, and of the Roman empire."[212] Here are grounds to admire the ancients but still more to admire the modern historian who, by contrast to his ancient predecessors, has confronted and comprehended religious extremism. As Tacitus related to ancient magistrates, so Gibbon, extending and surpassing Tacitus, relates to modern statesmen. In the midst of the narrative sweeping from Aurelius to Constantine, Gibbon takes his readers for study abroad in Persia and Germany. The point of this "reprieve," we have seen, is to understand how priestly religions work and how persecution might serve politically salutary purposes. Here Gibbon trains his readers in the new arts and new powers that will threaten the Empire—not, primarily, those stemming from the worldly virtues that Tacitus and others knew and lamented Rome's having lost. There is something beyond the frontiers that Rome, for all of its power, never lost for never having had. And this is the spiritual power possessed by experts in religion. Priests are to religion what the legions were to republics.

Having used every artifice to keep Christianity locked offstage, having shown the Empire's decline to be quite explicable without any appeal to the Christians' transvaluation of its values (the secular Empire having achieved *that* transvaluation long before Christianity exerted much influence[213]), Gibbon introduces the historical development his readers, believers and skeptics alike, have been waiting for. Gibbon accounts for the spread of Christianity in human or secular terms; in doing so, he removes one of the central pillars of Christian history. This challenges believers. However, in showing us the sort of explanation Christianity's spread demands, he challenges skeptics as well. For all its irony, Gibbon's account of Christianity's rise, though secular, is not deflationary. Gibbon adapts the ancient historians' theories of the rise of republics to a new sort of regime: the "Christian republic." His Tacitean narrative opens by the end of the first volume into one that is more Polybian. Gibbon's decline and fall transforms into an ascent and triumph.

CHAPTER 5

General Observations

Gibbon dramatized the triumph of Christianity with jarring diptychs. In the third volume of the *Decline and Fall* he relates the "Fable of the Seven Sleepers," in which seven young Christians escape the emperor Decius's persecution by hiding in a cave, where they sleep for 187 years. They wake to a Christian empire that they can scarcely believe to be true. These young men would sense the profundity of historical change, Gibbon says, in a way that men who lived through it *and* historians accustomed to linking distant revolutions by a "perpetual series of causes and effects" could not. "If the interval between two memorable eras could be instantly annihilated," Gibbon wrote, "if it were possible, after a momentary slumber of two hundred years, to display the *new* world to the eyes of a spectator, who still retained a lively sense of the *old*, his surprise and his reflections would furnish the pleasing subject of a philosophical romance."[1] Gibbon's own conversion experience in Rome resembled the shock of these seven young men. The sight of bare-footed friars in the Temple of Jupiter, like the sight of Theodosius's Empire where Decius's should be, set the new world against the old.[2]

In the fable of the seven sleepers, however, only the worlds of paganism and Christianity collided. Gibbon's conversion story included a *tertium quid*, neither Christian nor pagan: the person of Gibbon himself.[3] By the time of his "pilgrimage" to Rome in 1764, Gibbon had converted to Catholicism, returned to "implicit belief" in Christian doctrine, and then abandoned his faith altogether. He had written an *Essai* exploring the roots of religious belief in human fear, wonder, and curiosity, and he had applied this theory of religion to the Christian art and liturgy he encountered on Tour. Even when he imagined himself alongside Romulus on the Palatine Mount, however, he was not a pagan; even when he warmed to a bishop's patriotic sermon or swooned before Correggio's *Madonna del S. Girolamo,* he was not a Christian. As he traveled toward Rome Gibbon could imagine himself in both worlds and could not belong to either of them.

Gibbon was in that sense a modern, but a modern of a certain sort. He wanted to understand how modernity related to the epochs that preceded it, and he was reluctant to conceive of that relation simply as a negation or a return. The point of his history was not merely to juxtapose enlightened Europe to the dark ages of barbarism and religion, nor to disinter and reanimate Tacitus. The point was rather to tally the "perpetual series of causes and effects" and the more fundamental "general causes" that linked the epochs of Europe's history without losing sight of what distinguished those epochs. This was a historical project, but it was equally a philosophical and even a pragmatic project. "This awful revolution," Gibbon asserted, "may be usefully applied to the instruction of the present age."[4]

What did Gibbon intend his age to learn from the work? For many of his readers, the essential lesson of the *Decline and Fall* had to do with religion. These readers thought that Gibbon sneered and scoffed at the early Christians, even blamed them for Rome's decline, in order to eradicate the religious faith of his contemporaries. Other readers discovered an essentially political message. On this reading, Gibbon charts the decline and fall of the most powerful ancient empire in order to prevent, or at least delay, the decline of modern empires. These readings continue to have purchase in our own age, although, as we shall see, Gibbon cautioned against both of them.

The present study has attempted to open a line of approach to Gibbon's understanding of religion by exploring some elements of his context as he matured and embarked on his great work. Our inquiry has been primarily historical. But as Gibbon's history shaded into philosophy and even pragmatic "instruction," so we might conclude by considering what Gibbon might teach us about the present age. When we observe not only friars where the priests of Jupiter once presided but the historian observing that odd overlay, what do we learn? How, in Gibbon's view, are we to understand not only the diptych of paganism and Christianity but the triptych of paganism, Christianity, and modernity?

THE HISTORY OF THE "GENERAL OBSERVATIONS"

Gibbon addresses this question most directly in his "General Observations on the Fall of the Roman Empire in the West," a short text appended to the third volume of the *Decline and Fall.* Here Gibbon explains what caused Rome's fall and what lessons a modern reader might learn from it. The simplicity of the account has made some readers suspicious.[5] Many have found the "General Observations" superficial, as if it was an early draft or at best a précis of the great work. Indeed, some fifteen years after the "General Observations" was first published, Gibbon's *Memoirs* revealed it to have been his first foray into the history of Rome's decline.[6] While relating the reception of the second and third volumes of 1781, Gibbon notes that "a passage in the third was construed as a personal reflection on the reigning [French] Monarch."[7] The offending passage held that modern Europe's division into multiple states marked a distinct advance over the Roman Empire, since "the happiness of an hundred millions" no longer depended on the merit of one man: "A Julian, or a Semiramis, may reign in the North, while Arcadius and Honorius slumber on the thrones of the house of Bourbon."[8] The allusion was as flattering to Frederick and (probably) Catherine as it was unflattering to the French and Spanish kings.[9] But, Gibbon's *Memoirs* continues, "the concluding observations of my third volume were written before [Louis XVI's] accession to the throne" in May 1774. Although they were indeed meant to allude to contemporary politics ("I shall neither disclaim the allusion nor examine the likeness," Gibbon says), their target was Louis XVI's grandfather.[10] On Gibbon's testimony, then, the "General Observations" was earlier in composition than the bulk of the great work, and many readers have testified to its inferior literary quality. It is tempting simply to scrape it off the main text.

Gibbon's claim that he composed the "General Observations" first should not be a serious impediment to our taking it seriously, however. Gibbon seems to have revised it just prior to its publication in 1781; it is certain that he edited it well after 1774.[11] More important, prior to writing the fifth draft of his *Memoirs* (probably early in 1791), Gibbon gave no indication in private or public that he intended the "General Observations" to be read differently than the text to which it was appended.[12] The fact that Gibbon chose in 1781 to include the "General Observations" without qualification suggests he understood it to reflect his views at that time. Indeed, the fact that Gibbon wrote some version of the "General Observations" first *and* inserted it after the third volume might serve to heighten its significance. We might read it as the alpha and omega—the *archê*, the end that Gibbon started from—for the work as a whole.[13]

It is important that we approach the "General Observations" in this way because both its literary quality and its broader significance have been underrated. This short text not only corrects several common misreadings of Gibbon's intent. It articulates a penetrating critique of Gibbon's own project.

THE CYCLE OF EMPIRES

"The rise of a city, which swelled into an empire," Gibbon writes, "may deserve, as a singular prodigy, the reflection of a philosophic mind." But, he continues, the decline of an empire does not. Not every city rises; every empire falls. It is the motion of particular cities, not empires, that most calls for explanation.

Gibbon gives two examples of how one might explain the rise of a city. One attributes the rise to fortune, as Plutarch does; the other, to human causes like manners, constitutions, and military systems, as Polybius does.[14] The latter approach constitutes philosophical history, the discovery and display of the fundamental secular causes of human events.[15] Gibbon naturally prefers Polybius's explanation to Plutarch's.[16]

Although Gibbon resembles Polybius in this respect, he presents his own topic as far less promising than his predecessor's. After nearly a million words describing three centuries of Roman decline, Gibbon's reader is startled to hear this: "The decline of Rome was the natural and inevitable effect of immoderate greatness. Prosperity ripened the principle of decay; the causes of destruction multiplied with the extent of conquest; and as soon as time or accident had removed the artificial supports, the stupendous fabric yielded to the pressure of its own weight. The story of its ruin is simple and obvious; and instead of inquiring *why* the Roman empire was destroyed, we should rather be surprised that it had subsisted so long."[17] Gibbon had embraced this simple story as early as the *Essai* of 1761: The strong and poor, having acquired empire by conquering the weak and rich, themselves grow rich and weak until they are overthrown by the poor and strong. It is a song to be sung as a round, in which politics resembles the cycles of nature and dust always returns to dust.[18] It is also a song sung long before Gibbon by authors well known to him, including Polybius himself.[19]

This simple, obvious, and powerful story suggests there is no essential difference between ancient and modern and no fundamental novelty in Gibbon's own work. The problem of empire is for him what it was for the ancients. Gibbon begins the "General Observations," then, by suggesting he has done nothing more than transpose an old melody, the song of empire, into a new key.

Readers from Gibbon's time to our own have found this a profitable way to approach the work. Many of Gibbon's initial British readers held their own empire up to his Roman mirror. Richard Sheridan, for instance, crowned the publication of the great work's concluding volumes by describing one of Warren Hastings's crimes as unparalleled "in the correct periods of Tacitus or the luminous page of Gibbon"—a nice compliment to the author, a strong condemnation of the accused, and a foreboding reflection on Britain's fate.[20] Opponents of the British Empire could draw much the same lessons as the imperialists did, with the opposite intent. Benjamin Franklin followed up an encounter with Gibbon in Paris with an invitation to dinner. When Gibbon demurred, Franklin quipped, "I shall be happy to furnish materials to so excellent a writer for the Decline and Fall of the British Empire."[21] Several works with the title Franklin recommended have since appeared, though not by Gibbon's hand, and each has indeed drawn on the materials provided by Gibbon-steeped revolutionaries.[22] These readers, imperialists and anti-imperialists alike, understood Gibbon to have traced empire's—every empire's—inescapable downward slope.[23]

Gibbon himself was not altogether hostile to this reading. Although he famously conceived the *Decline and Fall* while "musing amidst the ruins" of the Roman Capitol, Gibbon composed much of the work while residing in London. His life in the imperial capital was hardly one of scholarly seclusion. In his *Memoirs*, Gibbon would recall that when he was writing the *Decline and Fall* "there were few persons of any eminence in the literary or political World to whom I was a stranger."[24] Indeed, Gibbon regularly attended late-night sessions of Parliament as he began work on the first volume in 1773; as he approached its conclusion in the fall of 1774 he was himself elected a Member.[25] Gibbon would later describe his eight sessions in Parliament as "a school of civil prudence, the first and most essential virtue of an historian."[26] Throughout this time he cultivated a passionate interest in the American Revolution—on the floor of Parliament, in social encounters with leading protagonists like Thomas Hutchinson and Lord North, and in his own reading—all while deeply engaged in writing Rome's fall.[27]

The potential parallels between his political and literary interests could not have been lost on him. But it is difficult to say just how Gibbon understood them.[28] He would sometimes elide Rome and London playfully, as when he quotes Horace's farewell to the *fumum et opes strepitumque Romae* to signal his own departure from "the Metropolis," or when he refers to members of Parliament as "senators" and his father as a "new Cincinnatus."[29] At other times he juxtaposed the two empires in a suggestive but not particularly clarifying manner, as when he reports to Holroyd: "On Thursday [there will be] an attempt to repeal the Quebec Bill, and then to the right about, and for myself having supported the British I must destroy the Roman Empire."[30] Even the peak of Gibbon's political action—his composition of the *Mémoire Justificatif*, the British government's official French-language appeal to "intelligent and disinterested men of every nation" after France had joined the Revolutionary War—is recognizably Gibbonian in style only.[31] Although France's past transgressions are detailed, the *Mémoire* reads more as a lawyer's brief than a historian's narrative. Where we might expect a Roman parallel we find "an act of perfidy unprecedented in the history of nations."[32]

Few writers have been better situated than Gibbon to explore the parallels and divergences between ancient and modern empires. In his letters, memoirs, and occasional writings, however, Gibbon indicated only that the British "senator" influenced the Roman historian. To what degree or in what respects he did so, Gibbon does not say.[33]

BREAKING THE CYCLE

Gibbon's clearest explanation of how ancient and modern empires relate to one another occurs in the "General Observations." The lessons he offers to imperialists and revolutionaries interested in empire's unchanging cycles are surprising. "The same reflections will illustrate the fall of that mighty empire, and explain the causes of our actual security," Gibbon writes. He then proceeds to offer a series of reasons—some practical, others philosophical—why his readers should not search for modern parallels to Rome's decline and fall.

Let us begin with the practical reasons. Suppose, as the most superficial and least controversial account suggests, that the Roman Empire fell because it could not reconstitute its forces following a series of decisive battles with the barbarians.[34] Are European states likely to relive this military history? Gibbon suggests not.[35] Since there are fewer dark spots on modern than ancient maps, he says, Europeans cannot easily be caught off guard by barbarian hordes.[36] And even if barbarians were to rush the gates, Gibbon continues, modern military technology has rendered the gates impenetrable and mere physical vigor immaterial. The ancient cycle had turned on wealth sapping military virtue and with it the ability to win battles. Applying the modern sciences to war, however, allows industrious peoples to protect themselves with arts that "survive and supply the decay of military virtue."[37] Modern barbarians, for their part, cannot supplement their vigor with advanced weapons without becoming civilized and losing their vigor. "Before they can conquer," Gibbon says, barbarians "must cease to be barbarous."[38]

The *Decline and Fall* gives grounds to question these arguments. Gibbon's barbarians adopted Rome's critical "technologies" (especially the discipline of the legion but also siege engines and ships), remained "barbarous" nevertheless, and overthrew Romans whose mastery of military arts, not only their "military spirit," had declined. Gibbon seems purposefully to overstate the link between technological advancement and civilization.[39] Similarly, he understates the potential for both rebarbarization and the rise of sudden, unanticipated threats. Gibbon acknowledges, for instance, that "the Arabs or Saracens, who spread their conquests from India to Spain, had languished in poverty and contempt, till Mahomet breathed into those savage bodies the soul of enthusiasm."[40] At best, Gibbon's analysis of modern military strategy suggests why civilized moderns might fear barbarians less than their predecessors did. But these arguments alone seem not to shatter the ancient cycle.

Gibbon's remaining argument for the invulnerability of modern Europe, however, is more compelling. Europe's division into nations, Gibbon says, constitutes a distinct advance on the Roman Empire. National rivalry maintains military spirit and prevents Europe's being "peopled by a race of pygmies."[41] Security competition also favors technological progress and economic growth. "In peace, the progress of knowledge and industry is accelerated by the emulation of so many active rivals," Gibbon writes, while "in war, the European forces are exercised by temperate and undecisive contests."[42] The always-elusive prospect of conquering one's neighbors or defending against conquest serves, under modern conditions, to turn martial energies toward ends that are "dual-use"—constitutive of the Europeans' "general state of happiness" and military strength.[43] Europe's division into nations also presents difficult military challenges to prospective invaders, while multiplying "the chances of royal and ministerial talents" insofar as Europe contains many kings (not one emperor) and even several republics.[44] Europe has diversified and divided to the point where Gibbon can envision, as the last resort in an unlikely barbarian invasion, a continental Dunkirk.[45] "Should the victorious Barbarians carry slavery and desolation as far as the Atlantic Ocean," Gibbon writes, "ten thousand vessels would transport beyond their pursuit the remains of civilized society; and Europe would revive and flourish in the American world, which is already filled with her colonies, and institutions."[46] All nations are kept in a kind of perpetual rise, enjoying luxury and absolute (if not relative) strength insofar as threats to national security are never mortal but never fade. Gibbon suggests that the watchword of modern politics, economics, and military science is the opposite of Cato's: *Carthago non delenda est*!

Abstracting from the practical concerns of a citizen partial to his or her nation and assuming the perspective of a "philosopher," Gibbon presents Europe as "one great republic, whose various inhabitants have attained almost the same level of politeness and cultivation."[47] This European republic is quite different from the "republic" that Augustus founded. Augustus's regime—an "absolute monarchy disguised by the form of a commonwealth"—unified the provinces both through the "gentle, but powerful influence of laws and manners" and politically, with the result that "public courage which is nourished by the love of independence, the sense of national honor, the presence of danger, and the habit of command" faded away.[48] Modern Europe shared manners across political divisions, and these divisions maintained "public courage." Thus Gibbon could reiterate in the "General Observations" an argument that he had anticipated throughout the three volumes that preceded it: "The division of Europe into a number of independent states, connected, however, with each other by the general resemblance of religion, language, and manners, is productive of the most beneficial consequences to the liberty of mankind."[49] This argument is the centerpiece of the "General Observations" and, arguably, of the *Decline and Fall* as a whole.

CHRISTIANITY AND MODERNITY

Gibbon understood the triumph of Christianity to be as indispensable to the genesis of modern politics as the polite paganism of the Antonines. Christianity opened a new plane of conquest separate from the political, such that the spirits of barbarians could be Romanized even as they destroyed what remained of Rome's political institutions. The union of manners, religion, and politics had formed both the strength and the weakness of ancient politics.[50] Christianity, by dividing manners and religions from politics, allowed a remnant of civilization to float away from the flotsam of political decay. The "Christian republic" that conquered the pagan Empire opened the suprapolitical realm that unified modern Europe above its division into a number of independent states.

Christianity's separation of manners and religion from politics had been the focus of early modern critique. Some moderns blamed Christianity for facilitating political division. Others blamed Christian valorization of passivity and humility for undermining the political virtues of the pagans.[51] On both accounts, Christianity bore considerable responsibility for Rome's decline.

Gibbon disagrees. Dividing the empire, he says, may have exacerbated but did not cause the "oppressive and arbitrary" system of imperial government nor the courts' "vain emulation of luxury, not of merit."[52] Christianity, for its part, discouraged the active virtues and buried "the last remains of military spirit . . . in the cloister," but those virtues and that spirit were long past when the new religion began to influence men's mores: "The sacred indolence of the monks was devoutly embraced by a servile and effeminate age; but if superstition had not afforded a decent retreat, the same vices would have tempted the unworthy Romans to desert, from baser motives, the standard of the republic. Religious precepts are easily obeyed, which indulge and sanctify the natural inclinations of their votaries."[53] The fundamental transformation that explained Rome's fall was the Empire's eclipse of the Republic, not Christianity's conquest of paganism. The logic of the imperial regime accounted for the growth of luxury and accompanying decline of military spirit as well as the centralization of power in the emperor and accompanying decline of the senatorial and provincial aristocracies.

These dynamics had been anticipated by Herodotus and Polybius. An authoritative account of their relevance to Rome had already appeared in Tacitus. What these authors did not anticipate was what accompanied and followed Rome's fall.

Gibbon not only opposed accounts of Rome's decline that blamed political division and Christianity; he turned these accounts on their heads. These very developments allowed Rome to survive itself. Constantine's construction of a new Rome "more essentially contributed to the preservation of the

East, than to the ruin of the West."[54] Christianity, Gibbon says, "broke the violence of the fall, and mollified the ferocious temper of the conquerors."[55] Political division made Rome less dependent on fortune or necessity; the Empire could fall in the West and still leave volumes to be written about its 1,058-year span of "premature and perpetual decline" in the East.[56] Christianity opened a suprapolitical realm capable of uniting independent states. Gibbon understood the Roman Empire to have invented ways of transforming itself that allowed it, or a form of it, to escape the ancient cycle.

What role did Gibbon intend his philosophical history to play in sustaining this new world? Polybius thought that Romans (and Greeks) would rule more effectively for knowing the cause of Rome's success, but he had no hope of an "eternal republic" even in the wake of his articulation of the mixed regime. Although the divisions in Rome's constitution were a powerful force for stability, the cycle of nature was still all-powerful. Gibbon departed from Polybius on this point. Gibbon understood the division of nations to mirror and augment the institutional divisions Polybius described. Decline was no longer inevitable. According to Gibbon, luxury would not weaken Europe as it had Rome so long as political division and transpolitical union were maintained.

One could imagine threats to each of these principles. Gibbon did not live to witness Napoleon's rise, but he would have shared the perennial alarm of British strategists at a united continent, and not only with a view to Britain's security.[57] Similarly, Gibbon would have criticized the romantic nationalism of the nineteenth and twentieth centuries in the same spirit that he condemned the religious wars of the sixteenth and seventeenth centuries. Gibbon meant to assert Roman universality and national particularity simultaneously. The path between homogenization and fragmentation was not some arithmetic mean between the two but the relegation of each to its appropriate sphere: homogeneity in manners and fragmentation in politics.

That Gibbon was able to hold both principles simultaneously and to acknowledge the importance of paganism and Christianity in enabling their combination was a sign of his moderation. His moderation was closely linked to his modernity. By 1759 Gibbon had lost his personal faith; his service in the Hampshire militia had dissipated any desire *pro patria mori*. He was neither a pagan patriot nor a pious believer. He was instead a skeptic and a scholar concerned to contemplate and understand commitments that were not his, except insofar as they had formed the modern world around him. This was the spirit that Gibbon contributed to the scene that confronted him on October 15, 1764. Without the moderate, modern spirit Gibbon had acquired, the diptych could hardly have generated the great work that followed.

Gibbon's intent in that work is commonly thought to have been anti-Christian. All of its sneering and scoffing toward the miraculous and the credulous certainly fits that bill. But Gibbon was—and presented himself as being—closer to the wars of religion than to anything resembling the twentieth century's secular ideologies. He tilted against the nearer threat without any hope or fear of eradicating Christianity from the minds of men. "So urgent on the vulgar is the necessity of believing," he wrote, "that the fall of any system of mythology will most probably be succeeded by the introduction of some other mode of superstition."[58] Gibbon diagnosed clearly the failures of those who tried to resist this rule. Both Julian and the French *philosophes* contracted Christian vices in their opposition to Christianity. Gibbon also held the seeping skepticism of a Roman elite he largely admired responsible for the religious transformation he partly (but only partly) regretted. For all of his sneering, Gibbon had no desire for his own skepticism to trace the diffusive path of the Antonine historians'.

That Gibbon nevertheless has come down to us as "the infidel historian" suggests the fragility of the persona he attempted to create. A modernity that contemplates patriotism and faith generously and skeptically, without embracing or compromising either, is an achievement. It is possible to admire that achievement in Gibbon's work, even if observing the triptych of paganism, Christianity, and modernity makes us more skeptical than Gibbon that the modern world has escaped the ancient dynamics of decline.

Conclusion

This book has attempted to use Gibbon's context as he conceived of the *Decline and Fall* to open a new, or at least neglected, window on that great work. Although, as we have seen, Gibbon lost his Christian faith as a young man of twenty-two, his encounters during his own life with Christians and the monuments of Christian civilization were rich and varied. They left him with sentiments toward Christianity rather more subtle and sympathetic than the "sneer" that is usually attributed to him.

We have seen how Gibbon's early experience of Christianity informed his analysis of religion in the *Essais* of 1759 and 1761, the first volume of the *Decline and Fall* in 1776, and finally the "General Observations on the Fall of the Roman Empire in the West." In these texts Gibbon developed a psychology of religion sufficiently expansive to include not only fear but nobler passions like wonder and curiosity. He accounted for the decline of the Roman Empire without reference to Christianity using only a "simple and obvious" story, known to the ancients, of rise, corruption, decline, and fall. Gibbon adapted that same story to a novel phenomenon: the rise of a "Christian republic." He cast priests as centurions, bishops as statesmen, and Roman polytheism, hollowed out by the skepticism of Rome's elites, as a decadent old empire like the ones that fell to the legions of the Roman Republic. Christianity's successful conquest of Roman polytheism ultimately dissolved the Empire's union of politics and religion and made possible a civilization that Gibbon not only endorsed but considered invulnerable to decline. So long as states retained their political division and their "general resemblance of religion, language, and manners," Gibbon held, the decline of a particular nation need not entail the decline of civilization.

Gibbon's readers have proven more eager than Gibbon himself to translate historical reflection into political prescription. Despite serving as a British "senator," Gibbon did not quite say what he meant modern statesmen to learn from Roman history. Gibbon's leading desire was to understand rather than to advise, much less rule. The manner in which Gibbon pursued understanding, however, carries something of a prescription. If modern states, in their political divisions and the "general resemblance" of manners across these divisions, stem from the Romans' patriotism and the Christians' faith, comprehending their genesis requires minds capable of balancing opposing forces, never allowing one to subsume the other. Gibbon's reputation for infidelity suggests that he hewed more closely to pagan philosophical historians than to Christian chroniclers, as indeed he did. But this reputation also obscures our appreciation of the richness of Gibbon's approach to Christianity. We understand both the historian and the greatness of his work better when we start from Gibbon's understanding of himself.

NOTES

INTRODUCTION

1. Loftus, "Reply," 146. The origins of this particular phrase can be traced back at least to Berkeley's description of Spinoza in 1732 as "the great leader of our modern infidels" (Berkeley, *Works*, 3:473–74). See Robertson, *Short History*, 2:168.

2. Loftus, "Reply," 159.

3. Gibbon depicts the response to these later volumes as muted in his *Memoirs*, though he notes without further comment that upon the work's conclusion in 1788 "the religious clamor revived" (*A*, E:322–24, 337–38). In a letter of 1781 Gibbon attributes the relative silence to the clergy's successful attacks on his reputation in the controversy over his first volume: "The clergy (such is the advantage of total loss of character) commend my decency and moderation" (*L*, 2:266; see also 3:100). Scholars have had much more to say about the reactions to the volumes of 1781 and 1788 than Gibbon. See especially Craddock, *Edward Gibbon*, 168–72, 263–65; Aston, "'Disorderly Squadron'"; and Turnbull, "Marionette Infidèle." Womersley, "Introduction to *Religious Scepticism*," notes that "the attacks on Gibbon, judged in terms of number of publications, peaked in 1789" (xx).

4. The epithet "infidel historian" comes from Whittaker, "Review," 390. Quoted in Craddock, *Edward Gibbon*, 353. For the origin of the persona to whom the epithet replied, see Turnbull's "Marionette Infidèle."

5. Watson, "Apology," 97.

6. Gibbon's friend Lord Sheffield attributed Gibbon's indelicacy regarding religion to the "extreme levity of conversation" he had encountered in Europe. See Womersley, *Watchmen*, 347, 371; and Womersley, "Gibbon's Religious Characters," 69–70. Gibbon assesses the influence of his continental education in a 1767 letter to Hume: "The five years, (from sixteen to twenty one) which I passed in Switzerland formed my style as well as my ideas; I write in French, because I think in French; and strange as it may seem, I can say with some shame, but with no affectation, that it would be a matter of difficulty to me, to compose in my native language" (*L*, 1:222). In the *Memoirs* Gibbon claimed that owing to the "success of [his] Swiss education" he "had ceased to be an Englishman" (*A*, B:152). See also Craddock, *English Essays*, 3–4; and Craddock, *Young Edward Gibbon*, 54, 76, 133–34. For Gibbon linked to Bolingbroke, see, for instance, Watson, "Apology," 53; Loftus, "Reply," 129; Milner, "Gibbon's Account," 216; and the title, if not the substance (as Turnbull, "Marionette Infidèle," 281, notes), of Ogilvie's *Inquiry*. As Womersley and many others have noted, Gibbon was also linked to Bolingbroke through David Mallet, a family friend and literary figure who served as Bolingbroke's literary executor (Womersley, *Watchmen*, 39n109, 78). We discuss Gibbon's links to Hume in chapter 1.

7. Watson, "Apology," 53.

8. Davis, "Examination," 187. In the same vein, James Chelsum claims that "even the licentiousness of modern infidelity, has been only able to revive old arguments, disguised under some new form" ("Remarks," 2n2).

9. Chelsum, "Remarks," 42.

10. Hobbes, *Leviathan*, 67 (12.12).

11. Spinoza, *Tractatus*, 89–91.

12. Chelsum, "Remarks," 40; Watson, "Apology," 97.

13. Loftus, "Reply," 133. Writing in 1830, with the whole of the *Decline in Fall* in view, William Jones wrote that "the apostate Julian is the hero of the tale" ("The Difficulties," 2:388, quoted in Aston, "'Disorderly Squadron,'" 272). This interpretation has since been revised and extended by Ziegler ("Edward Gibbon and Julian the Apostate"), Bowersock ("Gibbon and Julian"), and Baridon (*Edward Gibbon et le mythe de Rome*, 693–98). Womersley, by contrast, notes

the ambivalence of Gibbon's portrait, which he attributes both to historiographical challenges and to Gibbon's mixed judgment of Julian himself (*Transformation*, 156–68; *Watchmen*, 126–46). Pocock considers Gibbon's Julian not a skeptical philosopher-king but an intolerant enthusiast (*Barbarism and Religion*, 6:166, 171; see also Bremmer, *Rise of Christianity*, 8).

14. Young and Pocock present compelling arguments that Gibbon is best understood to have died a skeptic rather than an atheist (Young, "'Scepticism in Excess,'" 179, 187; Pocock, *Barbarism and Religion*, 1:250, 306, 2:107, 6:128). For Ghosh, Gibbon holds that "timeless values were found in nature and human nature—the latter exemplified, above all, by the culture of Latin antiquity—rather than in Christian doctrine" ("Gibbon's First Thoughts," 154, 158; "Gibbon's Timeless Verity," 127–28). Turnbull, "'Supposed Infidelity,'" 38–39, and, more cautiously, Carnochan, *Gibbon's Solitude*, 160–75, do all one can to place Gibbon's soul among those of "enthusiasts who sing Hallelujahs above the clouds" (*A*, E:349).

15. In the volumes of the *Decline and Fall* published in 1788 Gibbon judges Voltaire "a bigot, an intolerant bigot" for his hostility to Christianity (*DF*, 3:916n13, 6.67). Pocock quips that "an impressive *Schimpflexicon* could be compiled" from this and numerous other jabs at Voltaire in Gibbon's work (*Barbarism and Religion*, 2:156). That it is therefore incorrect to view Gibbon as a disciple of the great *philosophe* is widely agreed; still, the extent and nature of the latter's influence on Gibbon is a matter of dispute. See especially Turnbull, "Marionette Infidèle"; Womersley, "Gibbon's Religious Characters"; Pocock, "Clergy and Commerce," 556–57; and Pocock, *Barbarism and Religion*, 2:72–159.

16. Machiavelli, *Discourses*, 6; Machiavelli, *Prince*, 45.

17. For these criticisms of the *Spirit of the Laws* and Montesquieu's denial of them, see Montesquieu, *Complete Works*, 4:218–25. Montesquieu praises Julian in *Spirit of the Laws*, 466 (book 24, chapter 10). For Christianity softening mores, see Montesquieu, *Spirit of the Laws*, 461–62 (book 24, chapters 3–4). For the passions that give rise to religion, see Montesquieu, *Spirit of the Laws*, 467–68 (book 24, chapter 13), 479–84 (book 25, chapters 2–4).

18. Rousseau, *Social Contract*, 149 (4.8.28).

19. Turnbull, "Marionette Infidèle," offers a succinct history of Gibbon's transformation, among scholars, from an "anti-Christian *philosophe*" to a more generous student of Christianity: "Since the mid-1950s works by a number of scholars have slowly begun to disclose the true complexity of Gibbon's thinking about religion and history" (279). Especially salient for Turnbull are Giarrizzo's *Edward Gibbon* and Baridon's *Edward Gibbon et le mythe de Rome.*

20. Porson, *Letters*, xxix.

21. *A*, B:165, C:248, E:340. The libraries of the Academy of Lausanne and several friends and relatives supplemented Gibbon's vast collection.

22. Craddock, *Edward Gibbon*, 50.

23. *L*, 1:127.

24. Bowersock, "Reflections," 41. Keynes, *Library of Edward Gibbon*, and Mankin, "Gibbon's Mind and Libraries," collect a wealth of information on the contents of Gibbon's collection and how he seems to have used it while writing. See also *Vindication*, 279, 281.

25. *A*, E:340.

26. The difficulty of determining the appropriate context in which to view the *Decline and Fall* has been an important theme in the reception of Pocock's six-volume monument to Gibbon's first three volumes. Rosenblatt contends that Pocock's elaborate contextualization diminishes the work in question and obscures its author's intent ("On Context and Meaning," 149, 152–54). In response, Pocock has presented his work as "a history of historiography" as much as a study of the contexts immediately relevant to Gibbon's text ("Response and Commentary," 157–58; *Barbarism and Religion*, 6:8–9; see also *Barbarism and Religion*, 1:13). My own attempt to understand Gibbon's approach to religion is necessarily an exercise in contextualization—one that owes great debts to Pocock's research, as becomes clear. Since I am not attempting a history of historiography (or theology), however, I hew rather more closely to Gibbon's texts and his own indications of relevance than does Pocock. The guiding thought behind my own approach has been elegantly expressed by another great scholar of Gibbon: "I take it as an elementary courtesy that we should at least begin with the modest belief that a great writer means what he says; for those who recoil from close

scrutiny of Gibbon's prose in effect maintain that they know what he meant better than he himself" (Womersley, *Transformation*, 49).

27. For scholarly introductions to Gibbon's use of irony, consider especially Rawson, "Gibbon, Swift, and Irony"; Wootton, "Gibbon, Irony, and Faith"; Pocock, *Barbarism and Religion*, 1:80; and Lerner, "Smile of a Philosophic Historian." Womersley, *Watchmen*, offers this valuable insight into the development of Gibbon's irony: early in his career, irony was "a means of sarcastic dismissal"; later, it is "a way of suspending his prose between a number of more simple positions, each of which is partially true (and therefore not to be renounced) but none of which is entirely the case" (310n147; compare Womersley, *Transformation*, 264–66).

28. For Gibbon's infamous "sneer," see Loftus, "Reply," 149, and Paley's better-known formulation: "An eloquent historian, besides his more direct, and therefore fairer, attacks upon the credibility of Evangelic story, has contrived to weave into his narration one continued sneer upon the cause of Christianity, and upon the writing and characters of its ancient patrons.... Who can refute a sneer? Who can compute the number, much less, one by one, scrutinize the justice, of those disparaging insinuations, which crow the pages of this elaborate history?" (*Principles*, 289).

29. *A*, E:302; see also C:270–71, D:405–6. The influence of Gibbon's epiphany is itself a fascinating episode in literary history. Not long after the publication of Gibbon's *Memoirs* nineteenth-century pilgrims to Rome were "posing for a Gibbon" on the steps of the Ara Coeli. Henry Adams, visiting in May 1860, insisted that "the thought of posing for a Gibbon never entered his mind" (*Education*, 803–4). The scene also had a profound influence on Macaulay and subsequently on Churchill; Brendon's *Decline and Fall of the British Empire* discusses both cases (95, 210). On Gibbon's influence on Churchill more generally, Quinalt's "Winston Churchill and Gibbon" is invaluable. See also Edwards's *Roman Presences*.

30. See, for instance, a comment in Gibbon's *Memoirs* to which we return below: "Every man who rises above the common level has received two educations: the first from his teachers; the second, more personal and important, from himself. He will not, like the fanatics of the last age, define the moment of grace; but he cannot forget the aera of his life in which his mind has expanded to its proper form and dimensions" (*A*, C:231; compare B:137).

31. *A*, B:104.

32. David Womersley notes that Gibbon seems to have intended five of the six drafts of his *Memoirs* for posthumous publication. Draft E, which Gibbon initially intended to publish during his lifetime, is the least critical of English institutions. See Womersley, *Watchmen*, 236–40, 276–81.

33. *DF*, 1:447 (1.15).

34. Gibbon's neglect of Christianity in the bulk of the first volume has seemed to some an expression of contempt; to others, an artful piece of rhetoric, whereby the secret cause of Rome's decline was hidden to heighten the surprise of its revelation. See, for instance, Womersley, *Transformation*, 102. The position I take here—that Gibbon delays discussion of Christianity because he understands it to be inessential to the decline of the Empire prior to Constantine—is best defended by Pocock (e.g., *Barbarism and Religion*, 3:497–98, 6:43).

35. *DF*, 1:59 (1.2).

36. *DF*, 1:447 (1.15).

37. *DF*, 1:106 (1.3).

38. Ibid.

CHAPTER 1

1. *A*, E:302; see also C:270–71, D:405–6.

2. Ghosh articulates "the emotional premise" of Gibbon's work: "It cannot be too strongly emphasized that the source of the emotional appeal of the *Decline and Fall* is the principle of regret for *temps perdu*, the period of 'correct' classical taste" ("Gibbon's Dark Ages," 5n24).

3. *A*, C:258, 270. As Spacks, *Imagining a Self*, has noted, Gibbon's autobiography "describes his life in terms of his vocation" (17). See also Womersley, *Watchmen*, 210–12; and Pocock, *Barbarism and Religion*, 1:262, 306, 3:7. Jordan goes so far as to consider the *Memoirs* "a history of 'the historian of the Roman empire' rather than an autobiography of Edward Gibbon" (*Gibbon and His Roman Empire*, 4).

4. On the "dark ages" preceding Gibbon's work on the *Decline and Fall*, see especially Ghosh, "Gibbon's Dark Ages"; Womersley,

Transformation, 42–43; and Pocock, *Barbarism and Religion*, 1:124–34, 288–89, 2:375–96. Craddock, *Edward Gibbon*, 21, notes that Gibbon's first reference to his "great Work" occurs in a letter to Holroyd of September 10, 1773 (*L*, 1:377). By that time Gibbon had already completed several preliminary studies, including the first draft of his "General Observations on the Fall of the Roman Empire in the West," which would appear after the *Decline and Fall*'s third volume in 1781.

5. The vision is first mentioned, without the precision of the *Memoirs*'s account, at *DF*, 3:1085 (6.71). Craddock, *Young Edward Gibbon*, 222–23, 352n112, discusses Trevor-Roper ("Edward Gibbon after Two Hundred Years") and Badian's ("Gibbon and War") doubts about the scene's historicity before reaching the sensible conclusion that "it was clearly important to [Gibbon] that posterity share his view that the confrontation of the ruins of the city and the rituals of present-day Catholicism inspirited the writing of the *Decline and Fall*. My own opinions is that the incident really happened" (223). Womersley expresses a similar sentiment with characteristic elegance: "It may be that Gibbon refined and clarifies this moment not out of a desire to mislead, but from loyalty to a truth deeper than that of circumstance" (*Transformation*, 42). See also Ghosh, "Gibbon's Dark Ages," 6; and Edwards's "Gibbon and the City of Rome," 62–63, which notes a number of details that Gibbon must have embellished or invented.

6. Jordan, *Gibbon and His Roman Empire*, refers to the events of October 15, 1764, as "the one lasting conversion of [Gibbon's] life" (14; see also 22–23), following Giarrizzo, who spoke of Gibbon's "*conversione alla storia*" (*Edward Gibbon*, 13). Cartledge refers to Gibbon's "'Damascus Road' experience" ("'Tacitism' of Edward Gibbon," 253).

7. Womersley notes Gibbon's recollection of the precise date (October 15, 1764) and links it to Gibbon's account of Othman's invasion of Nicomedia "on the twenty-seventh of July, in the year twelve hundred and ninety-nine of the Christian aera"; "the singular accuracy of the date," Gibbon continues, "seems to disclose some foresight of the rapid and destructive growth of the monster" (*DF*, 3:810, 6.64; *Transformation*, 227). Compare Craddock, *Young Edward Gibbon*, 341n79.

8. On the role of conversion in early Methodism, see Hempton, *Methodism*, 60–68.

9. Carnochan says that Gibbon's account of the *Decline and Fall*'s genesis "hints at self-impregnation" (*Gibbon's Solitude*, 19).

10. The similarity of the setting of Gibbon's conversion to a palimpsest is too striking not to have been noted before; see, for instance, Bann, "Envisioning Rome," 35. Melvyn New has discovered a precedent for Gibbon's overlaying monks on ancient ruins in Conyers Middleton's description of Cicero's family home, now inhabited by Dominican friars (Middleton, *Life and Letters*, 2; "Gibbon, Middleton, and the 'Barefooted Fryars'").

11. By Gibbon's "maturity" I mean roughly the thirty-six years between his arrival at Oxford in April 1752 to the publication of the *Decline and Fall*'s final volumes in 1788.

12. See especially Field, "Measuring Religious Affiliation in Great Britain," 359–60; and Field, "Counting Religion in England and Wales," 710–11. Bossy, *English Catholic Community*, 184–86, suggests a rough figure of eighty thousand English Catholics in 1770 in a total population of roughly six million (Wrigley, *Population History of England*, 527–35).

13. On the eighteenth-century *nachleben* of the *Book of Martyrs*, see Haydon, *Anti-Catholicism*, 28–29, 45.

14. As we shall see in chapter 2, many members of Gibbon's household sympathized with the Jacobite cause. Turnbull, "'Buffeted for Ancestral Sins,'" surveys the evidence for these sympathies and their influence on Gibbon's own development.

15. For a helpful review of prospective Jacobite invasions after 1745—and a critique of historians for not taking their prospects for success more seriously—see Zimmermann, *Jacobite Movement*.

16. These proscriptions help us to appreciate the stakes of the sixteen-year-old Gibbon's conversion to Catholicism, which we shall discuss at length in chapter 2.

17. For accounts of politeness and enthusiasm in the early eighteenth century, see especially Pocock, "Enthusiasm"; *Barbarism and Religion* 1:107, 2:20; Heyd, *"Be Sober and Reasonable."*

18. More, *Enthusiasmus Triumphatus*, 2, 36–39.

19. Locke, *Essay Concerning Human Understanding*, 46, 699.

20. For this phrase, see for instance: Hobbes, *Leviathan*, 249; and Shaftesbury, *Characteristicks*, 2:185. Aldridge cites a number of sermons repeating the "perfectly orthodox" position that miracles had ceased during or shortly after the historical periods discussed in Scripture ("Shaftesbury and the Deist Manifesto," 361).

21. Locke, *Reasonableness*, 18–20, 32–33, 84–85; Locke, *Essay*, 667.

22. Shaftesbury, *Characteristicks*, 2:186–87. See also Aldridge's judgment of Shaftesbury's "underlying purposes" in the *Letter concerning Enthusiasm* ("Shaftesbury and the Deist Manifesto," 361).

23. See Collins, *Discourse*, 26. For Collins's questioning of the Church's authority, see in particular *Priestcraft* and *Historical and Critical Essay*.

24. I follow Peter Gay and J. C. D. Clark's dating here (Gay, *Deism*, 9; Clark, *English Society*, 280–81). Leland's *View* traces the origins of deism to Herbert of Cherbury's *De Veritate* of 1624.

25. Leland, *View*, 1:v–viii.

26. Wayne Hudson has noted that many of the most famous English deists are best understood as enlightened Protestants rather than enemies of Christianity (*English Deists*, 79; *Enlightenment and Modernity*, 8–9, 141–42). On this point, see also the first volume of Pocock's *Barbarism and Religion* and Clark's conclusion that eighteenth-century "political and social spheres were conceived to overlap with the religious to such an extent that the roots of reform lay in theology" (*English Society*, 348).

27. See, for instance, Gay, *Deism*, 10; Clark, *English Society*, 280–81; and Hudson, *Enlightenment and Modernity*, 142.

28. Burke, *Reflections*, 184–85. Hudson claims that contrary to Burke's "celebrated dismissal, the writers known as the English deists were not forgotten in England" (*Enlightenment and Modernity*, 144–45).

29. Burke, *Reflections*, 185.

30. Ibid., 159.

31. Ibid., 99.

32. Charles Taylor emphasizes the significance of deism as a forerunner of and contributor to modern secularism (*Secular Age*, chapters 6–7).

33. Jordan, *Gibbon and His Roman Empire*, xii, 57; and Kelly, "Grand Tour," 49, compare the *Decline and Fall* itself to an "elegantly planned and stylishly executed Grand Tour," in Kelly's words. Jordan dubs Gibbon an "urbane, witty, and philosophic Cicerone" (57).

34. Lassels himself had died on tour in September 1668, leaving the manuscript of his *Voyage* to the care of his charge, Lord Lumley, and an "old friend and fellow traveler," Sheldon Wilson, who oversaw its posthumous publication (Chaney, *Grand Tour*, 134–40). Note that though Lassels's work will help us to understand the history of the Grand Tour in which Gibbon participated, Lassels seems to have had no direct influence on Gibbon himself, as Gibbon does not cite him in *Decline and Fall* and *Voyage* does not appear in Keynes's catalogue of Gibbon's library.

35. Lassels, *Voyage*, xiii. Hurd, *Dialogues*, 11–12, assigns this argument to Lord Shaftesbury. Hurd's Locke suggests that ancient philosophers traveled to increase "their reputation with the people"—that is, in their capacity as politicians and legislators, not as philosophers. He also points out that Socrates did not travel (citing Plato's *Phaedrus* 230d-e).

36. Chaucer, *Canterbury Tales*, 31 ("General Prologue," lines 463–67). Hill's translation into modern English renders the passage discussed here: "Thrice at Jerusalem this dame had been, / And many a foreign river she had seen, / And she had gone to Rome and to Boulogne, / To Saint James's in Galicia, and Cologne. / Much lore she had from wandering by the way" (Chaucer, *Canterbury Tales*, 12). Bissons, *Chaucer*, 99–119, offers an illuminating discussion of pilgrimage in late-medieval Europe.

37. Bacon, "Copy of a Letter," 6:43–44; compare Bacon's essay "On Travel." Wilson, "How it Began," 18, called my attention to the significance of travel in Chaucer and Bacon.

38. Lassels, *Voyage*, v; note that the Roman numerals are my own, as the pages of the "Preface" to Lassels's *Voyage* are unnumbered in the 1670 edition. This passage paraphrases one of Lassels's favorite passages in Augustine, which also appears as an epigraph in an early manuscript of the *Voyage* (see Chaney, *Grand Tour*, 121). See Augustine's letter to Eleusis (Epistle 43, from 397) and his commentary on Psalm 45. As Losovsky, *Earth Is Our Book*, 142–43, notes, Augustine's intent in these passages was not to encourage his readers to travel but rather to search for correspondences

between the revealed text and the "text" around them. "Pilgrimage" (*peregrinatio*) is of course a central theme in Augustine's thought; Clark's "Pilgrims and Foreigners" suggests that Augustine generally uses the term to evoke being away from one's home, as opposed to making a trip to a holy site. Kaufman's *Agamben* offers a valuable reflection on the political implications of conceiving humans as pilgrims.

39. Lassels, *Voyage*, vii–viii. In a discussion of the route from Rome to Naples, Lassels writes: "It is true, a man is ill lodged, and badly treated in that journey, but it doth a gentleman good to be acquainted with hardship" (*Voyage*, part 2, 258). Sweet, *Cities*, especially 23–64, argues that the Grand Tour was "deeply implicated in the construction of elite masculinity" (20); Chard's *Pleasure and Guilt*, especially 126–56, is also quite instructive on this topic.

40. Lassels, *Voyage*, viii–x.

41. Ibid., xi–xii.

42. The Oxford English Dictionary traces the term "bear-leader" to a 1749 letter from Horace Walpole to Horace Mann, where Walpole defines the term as a "travelling governor" and worries that he will be mistaken for one (*Letters*, 2:387).

43. Lassels, *Voyage*, xiii–xiv.

44. Ibid.

45. Ibid., xvii–xviii.

46. Ibid., iv.

47. Ibid., part 2, 4–5.

48. Ibid., part 2, 4–6.

49. Ibid., part 2, 94–95.

50. Lassels bolsters the faith of English Catholics in part by showing them sites where English and Church history intersect. In Florence and Rome Lassels shows the tombs of prominent English bishops (*Voyage*, part 1, 203; part 2, 78); in Rome we visit the English College (part 2, 8–9, 131) and read letters concerning the English schism (part 2, 64–66). At one point even Constantine is Anglicized: he is "our most noble countryman and the first emperor that publicly professed Christianity" (part 2, 112; for background, see Mulligan, "British Constantine").

51. For Lassels's biography, see especially Chaney, *Grand Tour*, and Chaney, "Lassels [Lascelles], Richard."

52. Wood's *Athenae Oxonienses*, 3:818, had Lassels as "an hospes for some time in this university, as those of his persuasion have told me, but whether before or after he left England they could not tell." See Chaney, *Grand Tour*, 131–32.

53. This trip was the occasion for Lassels's *Voyage of the Lady Catherine Whetenhall from Brussels into Italy in the Holy Year, 1650*. For background, see Chaney, *Grand Tour*, 70–91. Lassels's memories of this trip surface frequently in the *Voyage*, as, for instance, in his description of the *Scala Santa*: "It's painful enough to go up these stairs upon your knees; yet I saw it done hourly in the Jubily year, by continual flocks of devout people both men and women; of great condition as well as of great devotion" (*Voyage*, part 2, 113–14; see also 248 and 253, where Lassels praises Rome's *Sbiri* (police) for going undercover as pilgrims).

54. Lassels, *Voyage*, part 2, 95.

55. Chaney argues that the warm reception moderate Protestants received from Lassels and other continental Catholics in the 1640s contributed materially to the tumults of the 1680s: "Without the experience of exile it is doubtful whether the monarchy would have become first secretly and then openly and in the event disastrously Catholic" (*Grand Tour*, 12).

56. Burnet, *Some Letters* (Keynes, *Library*, 84); the passage quoted, in which Burnet discusses the intent of this work, appears in Foxcroft, *Supplement*, 251, and in Martin Grieg's entry for Burnet in the *Oxford Dictionary of National Biography*. Burnet's and Lassels's treatment of Geneva and Rome offer a nice point of contrast. From a detailed consideration of the two cities' corn laws, Burnet draws this broad lesson: "If one will compare the faith of *Rome* and *Geneva* together by this particular, he would be forced to prefer the latter: For if *good Works* are a strong presumption, if not a sure indication of a *good Faith*, then *Justice*, being a good work of the first form, *Geneva* will certainly carry it" (*Some Letters*, 6–7). Upon arriving at Rome, Burnet returns to the corn laws, blaming the desolation of the papal lands on the pope's "oppression and cruelty" (*Some Letters*, 193–98). Lassels's contrasting views in the *Voyage* are discussed above. Chaney, *Grand Tour*, 140–41, discusses Burnet's relationship to Lassels; he also notes that the second edition of Lassels's *Voyage* (printed in London) redacted passages like this one from the first edition (printed in Paris): "Geneva, like a good sink at the bottom of three

streets, is . . . fit to receive into it the corruption, of the Apostates of the Roman Church."

57. Misson, *New Voyage*, 1:674–75.

58. Addison, *Remarks*, 138–39; Keynes, *Library*, 45. In the preface to his work, Addison expresses with admirable brevity his place in the literary tradition we have been considering here. Addison is grateful to Burnet "for his masterly and uncommon Observations on the Religion and Governments of Italy," while "Monsieur Misson has wrote a more correct Account of Italy in general than any before him, as he particularly Excels in the Plan of the Country, which he has given us in true and lively Colours." Lassels, by contrast, appears rather diminished: he is useful only for "giving us the Names of such Writers as have treated of the several States through which he pass'd" (ii–iii, note that the numbers are my own, as the pages of Addison's preface are unnumbered in the edition cited).

59. Addison's "Letter," a poem published in 1704, nicely expresses this relationship between Rome and Britain. Addison writes of Rome: "Here pillars rough with sculpture pierce the skies: / And here the proud triumphal arches rise, / Where the old Romans deathless acts display'd, / Their base degenerate progeny upbraid." The poem concludes in a paean to the goddess liberty "that crowns Britannia's Isle, / And makes her barren rocks and her bleak mountains smile" ("Letter," 1:33, 37).

60. Addison, "Letter," 1:29: "For wheresoe'er I turn my ravish'd eyes, / Gay gilded scenes and shining prospects rise, / Poetic fields encompass me around, / And still I seem to tread on classic ground."

61. Smollett's *Travels* offer many examples of the contrasting tendency to elide beauty and theology. "What pity it is," Smollett writes, "that the labours of painting should have been so much employed on the shocking subjects of the martyrology. Besides numberless pictures of the flagellation, crucifixion, and descent from the cross, we have Judith with the head of Holofernes . . . and a hundred other pictures equally frightful, which can only serve to fill the mind with gloomy ideas, and encourage a spirit of religious fanaticism, which has always been attended with mischievous consequences to the community where it reigned" (266–67 [Letter 31]).

62. Addison, *Remarks*, 110–11.

63. Ibid., 110.

64. Ibid., 111. Smollett's *Travels* would continue this tradition of British Tourists imagining attacks, this time on Rome itself: "Rome has nothing to fear from the catholic powers, who respect it with a superstitious veneration as the metropolitan seat of their religion: but the popes will do well to avoid misunderstandings with the maritime protestant states, especially the English, who being masters of the Mediterranean, and in possession of Minorca, have it in their power at all times, to land a body of troops within four leagues of Rome, and to take the city, without opposition" (259 [Letter 30]).

65. Addison, *Remarks*, 112.

66. Ibid.

67. The scholarly literature on eighteenth-century theorists' attempt to control passions with other passions—such as Hirschman's classic *The Passions and the Interests*—tends to underestimate the role played by aesthetics. Sensitivity to beauty, especially the beauty of form rather than moral nobility, can be thought to ally with avarice in counterbalancing the more dangerous passion of ambition or love of glory. In Adam Smith's work the two passions—avarice and the love of beauty—come so close as to be inseparable.

68. Addison, *Remarks*, iii. Note that the Roman numerals are my own, as the pages of the "Preface" to Addison's *Remarks* are unnumbered in the edition I cite.

69. Ibid., 21, 111.

70. Ibid., 242.

71. Ibid.

72. Machiavelli, *Discourses on Livy*, 6 (book 1, preface).

73. Addison, "Letter."

74. The outcome of that war made them resemble a parade of victors. "The British name was respected," Gibbon would later record in his *Memoirs*. "Our opinions, our fashions, even our games, were adopted in France; a ray of national glory illuminated each individual, and every Englishman was supposed to be born a patriot and a philosopher" (*A*, B:200, C:261).

75. Smollett nevertheless found something to admire, albeit without much aesthetic distance: "The back parts especially are executed so happily, as to excite the admiration of the most indifferent spectator" (*Travels*, 234–36 [Letter 28]).

76. Sterne, *Sentimental Journey*, 24. Sterne's dialogue with Smollett continues throughout *Sentimental Journey*, as, for instance, on the question of swaddling infants (Sterne, *Sentimental Journey*, 49; Smollett, *Travels*, 254 [Letter 30]).

77. Smollett discusses his "pulmonic disorder" in *Travels*, 8 (Letter 1). The tone of Smollett's self-diagnoses is captured well in his third letter, from Boulogne: "In consequence of a cold, caught a few days after my arrival in France, I was seized with a violent cough, attended with a fever, and stitches in my breast, which tormented me all night long without ceasing. At the same time I had a great discharge by expectoration, and such a dejection of spirits as I never felt before" (*Travels*, 13 [Letter 3]).

78. Smollett is disarmingly frank in acknowledging his limitations as a critic of art: "I do not set up for a judge in these matters," he says at one point, "and very likely I may incur the ridicule of the virtuosi for the remarks I have made: but I am used to speak my mind freely on all subjects that fall under the cognizance of my senses; though I must as freely own, there is something more than common sense required to discover and distinguish the more delicate beauties of painting" (*Travels*, 240–41 [Letter 28]).

79. Sterne, *Sentimental Journey*, 10.

80. Locke's placement of his thoughts on travel at the conclusion of the *Thoughts* offers the opportunity to reflect on the fate of his enterprise in education, which he sums up at the end "[to] give some small light to those whose concern for their dear little ones makes them so irregularly bold that they dare venture to consult their own reason in the education of their children rather than wholly to rely on old custom" (161). Locke does not expect the customary travel to change, because it serves the interests of the parents: they unreasonably fear for the child, but for the man in his twenties they require marriage—the father for his daughter-in-law's dowry, the mother "for a new set of babies to play with" (161, sect. 215). Locke stresses that as far as the interests of the young man go, it would do no harm at all to wait a few more years to marry.

81. See *Spectator*, no. 364 (April 28, 1712); *World*, no. 205 (December 2, 1756). These and many other corroborating passages appear in Mead, *Grand Tour*, 380–95. Gibbon himself echoed Locke's sentiment in a 1755 letter to Catherine Porten: "I never liked young travelers, they go too raw to make any great remarks, and they lose a time which is (in my opinion) the most precious part of a man's life" (*L*, 1:10). Samuel Johnson put the ideal age after twenty-four (Boswell, *Life of Samuel Johnson*, 714).

82. Rousseau, *Emile*, 448, 452. Compare Locke, *Thoughts*, 158–59 (sect. 212).

83. Locke, *Thoughts*, 160 (sect. 214); Rousseau, *Emile*, 467–68.

84. Rousseau, *Emile*, 455.

85. Rousseau, "Emile and Sophie, or the Solitaires," 13:685–721.

86. Howell, *Instructions*, 16. Howell continues, "Such a one, I mean he that is well Instructed in his own Religion, may pass under the torrid Zone, and not be Sun-burnt. . . . So such a one may pass and repass through the very midst of the Roman See (or Geneva lake either) and shoot the most dangerous Gulf thereof, and yet return home an untainted [English] Protestant; nay he will be confirmed in zeal to his own Religion, and illuminated the more with the brightness of the truth thereof" (17).

87. On loose morals, consider the proviso to Samuel Johnson's condemnation of the Tour (at least before the age of twenty-four): "If a young man is wild, and must run after women and bad company, it is better this should be done abroad" (Boswell, *Life of Samuel Johnson*, 714).

88. Hurd, *Dialogues*, see especially 18–21, 132–35. Smith, *Wealth of Nations*, 773. Smith attributes the vogue for travel to "the discredit into which the universities are allowing themselves to fall" (774). Smith's travels from 1764 to 1766 with the Duke of Buccleuch (to whose case Smith's critique of travel seems not to have applied) are described in Phillipson, *Adam Smith*, 180–99, 204, and Ross, *Life of Adam Smith*, 209–33. Mead's *Grand Tour* quotes an anonymous 1756 entry in the *World*: "The majority of our young travelers return home, entirely divested of the religion of their country, without having acquired any new one in its place" (385).

89. This 1785 report from the British envoy in Turin is quoted in Black, *Italy*, 124–25.

90. As late as 1785 Gibbon could report to Lord Sheffield from Lausanne: "The only disagreeable circumstance is the increase of a race of animals with this country has been long infested, and

who are said to come from an Island in the Northern Ocean. I am told, but it seems incredible, that upwards of 40,000 English masters and servants are now absent on the continent, and I am sure we have our full proportion of both" (*L*, 3:33).

91. Boswell, *Life of Samuel Johnson*, 537.

92. *A*, B:198.

93. Acts of the Apostles 9:3–6. Although it is conventional to refer to "Saul" prior to the conversion and "Paul" following the conversion, Acts and Paul's letters use the two names interchangeably. See, for instance, Acts 13:9: "Then Saul, (who also is called Paul,) filled with the Holy Ghost, set his eyes on [Elymas the sorcerer]." I refer to "Paul" unless quoting biblical text.

94. Acts of the Apostles 9:7, 9:15.

95. Ibid., 22:1–21, 26:2–23.

96. Tristram Shandy's humorous account of his own conception and birth might be thought to mark the limit of this third-person view. (Charlotte Roberts notes that the first draft of Gibbon's *Memoirs*, "like the early volumes of *Tristram Shandy*, does not get as far as narrating the birth of its protagonist" ["*Memoirs*," 206].) Misch, *Geschichte*, stresses ancient biography's portrayal of "fixed" character: "The origins [of biography] lie in the philosophy of Plato and Aristotle, and its basis was the same conception of *bios*: it did not narrate simply to narrate, and its deepening into an individual's development lay outside of its horizons: it was essentially concerned with the enduring essence of fully developed men" (1:44). Momigliano places the origins of ancient biography and autobiography earlier than Misch, whose notion of autobiography he criticizes while largely agreeing that the *bios* set the standard for autobiography, at least prior to Augustine's *Confessions* (*Development*, 14–18). Swain's discussions of "character change" in Plutarch is also helpful on this point ("Character Change").

97. We might expect pre-Christian autobiography focused on internal events—such as those that compose a philosopher's *Life*—to be fertile ground for distinctly autobiographical forms of writing. Misch, for instance, traces the origin of autobiographical "conversion" narratives to Socrates's speeches in Plato's *Apology* and *Phaedo* (*Geschichte*, 1:79–80).

98. Augustine, *Confessions*, 8.12.

99. Ibid.

100. Jane Shaw's *Miracles* offers a helpful summary view of Augustine's doctrine on miracles and its reception in Gibbon's day.

101. Augustine, *Confessions*, 3.4.

102. Luther, "Preface," 337. Luther's encounter with Paul was followed by a reading of Augustine's *The Spirit and the Letter*.

103. Bishop, *Pascal*, 40–43, notes that Pascal's "conversion of the heart" in 1654 was preceded by a prior, intellectual conversion to Jansenism in 1646. Bishop describes the night of fire (168–80) and suggests that "[Pascal's] reading may have had a considerable influence in determining the form of the second conversion. Saint Augustine, one of Pascal's closest spiritual companions, had also a philosophic, intellectual conversion at nineteen, and a later emotional one. . . . Pascal knew also (though possibly only later) Saint Theresa; he may have read her descriptions of the intellectual vision, of her certitude, and of her helplessness to report that certitude and its reasons" (181).

104. Hebrews 12:29. Bishop helpfully links Pascal's comment in the "Memorial"—"I am the God of Abraham, the God of Isaac, the God of Jacob, not of the philosophers and the scholars"—to their "scholium" in the *Pensées* (*Pascal*, 172). Natoli, *Fire*, 110, is still correct to notice the "surprising silence" of the *Pensées* regarding Pascal's second conversion.

105. Petrarch, *Letters*, 1:177. Augustine attributed this method of reading to Anthony (*Confessions*, 8.12).

106. Teresa, *Life*, 56.

107. Baxter, *Reliquiae Baxterianae*, 3.

108. Ibid., 6.

109. Wesley, *Journal*, 1:465–78.

110. Hume regularly appears in Gibbon's work prior to the autobiography accompanied by his friend and compatriot, William Robertson. As a young man Gibbon had read Robertson's *History of Scotland* alongside Hume's *History of England*, two works that he would later judge to have disproven "the old reproach, that no British altars had been raised to the muse of history" (*A*, B:166–67). Upon the publication of the first volumes of the *Decline and Fall*, Gibbon thanked Robertson and Hume for inspiring the work. "When I ventured to assume the character of historian, the first, the most natural, but at the same time the most ambitious wish which I

entertained was to deserve the approbation of Dr Robertson and of Mr. Hume, two names which friendship united and which posterity will never separate" (*L*, 2:152). Twelve years later, while inviting Robertson to a celebration of the *Decline and Fall*'s concluding volumes, Gibbon said that the most flattering praise he had received was to have his name associated with Robertson and Hume in a "triumvirate" of British historians (*L*, 3:100). In this letter, and elsewhere, Gibbon does not hesitate to refer to both Hume and Robertson as his "masters" (*L*, 3:100). (In Gibbon's letter to Deyverdun of May 7, 1776, Robertson and Hume are "*mes Maitres*" [*L*, 2:106]. Gibbon's relation to his masters is a leading theme in the second volume of Pocock's *Barbarism and Religion*. "As Gibbon describes the problem which Hume and Robertson have solved," writes Pocock, "it is that of providing a grand narrative, written in polite prose and satisfying the newly emerging canons of philosophical explanation" [2:175]. See also Stuart-Buttle, "Gibbon and Enlightenment History," 110–18.) For the *Memoirs*, then, Gibbon maintains one master and swaps another. If the fact that Robertson's vast *ouvre* did not include a self-portrait explains his exclusion, we might still wonder at his replacement.

111. On de Thou's reception in the eighteenth century, see especially Kinser, *Works*, 1–5. Kinser, *Works*, 5, notes Samuel Johnson's praise of de Thou's *Life*, a model biography, for laying "open to posterity the private character of a man . . . whose candor and genius will to the end of time be by his writings preserved in admiration" (Boswell, *Life of Samuel Johnson*, 22–23; later Johnson considers translating de Thou's works, 994–95). Grafton links de Thou and Gibbon as predecessors to Ranke in "critical history—the sort of history whose author agonized about a mistake of a few months in chronology, as well as about the ascription of motives and the identification of causes" (*Footnote*, 138).

112. Gibbon links Hume and de Thou's approach to religious controversy in the *Vindication*: "Since the original of theological factions, some historians, Ammianus Marcellinus, Fra Paolo, Thuanus, Hume, and perhaps a few others, have deserved the singular praise of holding the balance with a steady and equal hand" (299).

113. *L*, 2:101. For Gibbon's description of Hume as "*un des plus grans hommes qu'ait jamais produit notre isle*," see Baridon, "Lettre inédite," 80.

114. At the age of thirty Gibbon thrilled to Hume's praise of his work: "Your approbation will always flatter me infinitely more, than the applause of an undistinguishing multitude" (*L*, 1:222). Hume's subsequent praise of the *Decline and Fall*'s first volume, Gibbon said, "overpaid the labor of ten years" (*A*, E:311). (In this fifth draft of the *Memoirs* Gibbon proceeds, rather immodestly, to reproduce Hume's letter in a footnote.) For illustrative criticisms of Hume, see *J1*, 42; and *DF*, 1:135n30 (1.5), 2:494n128 (3.38), 3:605–6 (6.58), 3:1058 (6.70). At *DF*, 3:983 (6.69), Gibbon gives Hume the rare honorific of "philosophic historian." Already "the Great David Hume" for Gibbon at twenty-one, Hume would become "*bon David*" after the two were better acquainted (*L*, 1:117, 2:106). Compare to this last Gibbon's letter to Holroyd during the latter's visit to Edinburgh: "You tell me of a long list of Dukes, Lairds, and Chieftains of Renown to whom you are recommended; were I with you, I should prefer one David to them all. When you are at Edinburgh, I hope you will not fail to visit the Stye of that fattest of Epicurus's Hogs, and inform yourself whether there remains no hope of its recovering the use of its right paw." Prothero, *Private Letters*, 190n1, notes Gibbon's allusion to Mason's satire *An Heroic Epistle to Sir William Chambers on his Book of Gardening*, in which Hume is "The fattest hog in Epicurus's sty."

115. Carte and Buckley's seven-volume 1733 edition of de Thou's *History*, which includes de Thou's *Life* in the seventh volume, appears in the Bentinck Street catalogue of Gibbon's library, a "classified manuscript list containing nothing later than 1777" (Keynes, *Library*, 37, 267). Gibbon must therefore have been familiar with de Thou's *Life* and *History* well before he began to work on the concluding volumes of the *Decline and Fall*. De Thou, however, appears neither in the early volumes of the *Decline and Fall* nor in Gibbon's *Essai* of 1761, despite the latter work's discussion of French erudition.

116. For citations of de Thou on points of fact, see *DF*, 2:632n19 (4.41), 3:511n105 (5.56), 3:733n77 (6.61), 3:1015n100 (6.69), 3:1058n91 (6.70), 3:1059n95 (6.70). While discussing the foundation of Cairoan in Tunis Gibbon corrects

historians who confound it with the Greek Cyrene, located a thousand miles to its east: "The great Thuanus has not escaped this fault, the less excusable as it is connected with a formal and elaborate description of Africa" (3:297n155 [5.51]). In the third volume of the *Decline and Fall* Gibbon refers to Thuanus's son, François-Auguste, as "the virtuous de Thou" (2:244n19 [3.32]).

117. Kinser, *Works*, 7, notes that the material published in 1603 would subsequently be divided into twenty-six books. Thuanus's "Preface" was "immediately translated into French at the king's request" and was published as a stand-alone work six times between 1603 and 1617 (*Works*, 8).

118. The spirit of de Thou's case for toleration is nicely captured by this passage from his dedicatory letter to Henry IV: "Experience has taught us that fire and sword, exile and proscription, rather irritate than heal the distemper, that has its seat in the mind. Religion alone is not subject to command, but is infused into well prepared minds from a preconceived opinion of the truth, with the concurrence of divine grace. Tortures have no influence over her: in fact, they rather tend to make men obstinate, than to subdue or persuade them" (de Thou, *Jacobi Augusti Thuani Historiarum sui temporis libri CXXXVIII* [hereafter *JATH*], 1:3).

119. Kinser, *Works*, 299–300, notes that the defense of toleration in Thuanus's "Preface" was "one of the major reasons for condemning the *History* to the Index." See de Thou, *Vie*, 904–5 (5.5.7), and Gallus [Machault], *Notationes*, 7.3:36–39.

120. Machault published under the pseudonym Joannis Baptista Gallus. Kinser, *Works*, 168n1, discusses the authorship and credits Fouqueray, *Histoire*, 3:316n4, with the decisive identification. De Thou's *Life* relates the premarital examination and confession of his fiancée, whose parents "had once adhered to Protestant beliefs," in order to satisfy "ill-natured men who, not content to calumniate de Thou's historical work, pry into his domestic life" (*Vie*, 606–9 [3.4.18–19]); also consider Teissier-Ensminger's discussion of the sanctity of minor orders at 559n14 and 609n88. Machault's attack was condemned as libel in 1614 (Kinser, *Works*, 173; de Smet, *Thuanus*, 274; de Thou, *JATH*, 7.3:71). Prominent among the polemicists apart from Machault was Kaspar Schoppe, one of Nisard's *gladiateurs de la république des lettres*, the second volume of which provides an excellent account of Schoppe's life and literary contests. The attack on de Thou in the *Ecclesiasticus* was preceded by a portion of the *Scaliger Hypobolimaeus* in 1607, both of which are printed, along with related letters, in de Thou, *JATH*, 7.3:1–31. See also Kinser, *Works*, 72, and de Smet, *Thuanus*, 265–66n11.

121. Teissier-Ensminger, "Introduction," 184, nicely captures the spirit of the counterattack with the phrase *juris-biographie*. See also "Introduction," 14–16, on Thuanus's training as a jurist and the role of the *Life* in the history of law.

122. The complex manuscript history of the *Life* is related in Kinser, *Works*, 170–84, and Teissier-Ensminger, "Introduction." Teissier-Ensminger makes a number of insightful comments on the title of the work. See especially her general discussion of the issue ("Introduction," 21–26), and the links she makes between "Commentaries" and the juridical ("Introduction," 125–32) and classical ("Introduction," 45, 126–27) background of the text. She also comments on the aspect of the title that I stress here: "The fact is that the word *comentarii*, describing the practice of erudition, and especially juridical humanism, is extremely widespread at this time" ("Introduction," 127–28).

123. The early history of the commentary as a literary form is glossed in Reynolds and Wilson, *Scribes and Scholars*, 31–33; Kraus and Stray, "Form and Content," explore the multivalence of the form. Foucault's comments on early modern commentary are predictably illuminating and provocative (*Order of Things*, 39–42, 78–81).

124. De Thou's narrator claims that he can praise Thuanus and defend his works more freely than Thuanus himself. On the link between praise and defense, Plutarch's "On Praising Oneself Inoffensively" is instructive, as Plutarch excuses self-praise in self-defense (540c–541d; see also Teissier-Ensminger, "Introduction," 39–40). The apologetic purpose of the *Life* is made explicit in 5.4.8 (869): "It was at this same moment that the historical work was started, for the defense of which the writing of this text has been principally begun." Teissier-Ensminger nicely expresses this aspect of the relationship between *Life* and *History*: the *Life* is "un texte-satellite, asservi à une enterprise de

réhabilitation du grand oeuvre" ("Introduction," 17; see also 35).

125. De Thou, *Vie*, 386–87 (2.1.70); compare 558–59 (3.1.29–31) and de Smet, *Thuanus*, 108–11.

126. De Thou, *Vie*, 592–93 (3.3.39). On de Thou's verse paraphrases of biblical texts, see especially Kinser, *Works*, 202–3, who claims that Thuanus's themes were "chosen and treated for their moral rather than theological or mystical significance." Teissier-Ensminger, "Introduction," 151–52, links the themes of Job to the persecutions described in the *Vita*; de Smet, *Thuanus*, 66, links de Thou's interest in Job to recent deaths in his family.

127. De Thou's elision of Christianity and classicism is neatly expressed in the writing routine he describes in the *Commentaries*: "Besides the prayers, which every faithful man is bound to offer God at his first rising in the morning, [Thuanus] used a peculiar one for the work which he had undertaken; and never applied himself to writing, till his mind had been purged from passion and prejudice by prayer; imploring the Deity, that he would be constantly assisting him, and enlighten his mind, that, from amongst the heats of factions and animosities, he might pick out the hidden truth, and bring it to light without envy or adulation" (*Vie*, 870–73 [5.4.12]). These daily devotions to the God of impartial history reflect de Thou's conviction that religious faith and writing *sine ira et studio* are hardly incompatible.

128. De Thou, *Vie*, 460–61 (2.7.4).

129. Ibid., 422–23 (2.5.11), 438–39 (2.5.48).

130. Ibid., 522–23 (2.10.16–17). The Hume of "My Own Life," by contrast, hardly registers his parents' passing. Hume says his father "died, when I was an infant"; his mother, "a woman of singular merit, who though young and handsome, devoted herself entirely to the rearing and educating of her children," cuts a more striking figure, but passes almost silently: In 1749 Hume rejoins only his brother at the family house, "for my mother was now dead" ("My Own Life," 611–12). The unflappable tone is more revealing of the work than Hume's sentiments, for his letters reveal he indeed mourned the "immense void" his mother had left (Hume, *New Letters*, 17; Mossner, *Life of David Hume*, 27).

131. De Thou, *Vie*, 868–69 (5.4.8). See the discussion of Thuanus's plans for the *History* in Kinser, *Works*, 80.

132. De Thou, *Vie*, 252–53 (1.5.20).

133. Ibid., 414–15 (2.4.1).

134. Although Thuanus continues to feel torn between his scholarly and political callings, it is impossible to say which of the two predominates at any moment. What we might think to be the centerpiece of an autobiographical work "principally written for the sake of" the *History* (*Vie*, 868–69 [5.4.8])—the genesis of the *History*—dissolves into the narration of the *Life*. We might also consider the extent to which not only political but personal narrative influenced Thuanus's composition of the *History*: Kinser, *Works*, 82, reports that for a time Thuanus planned the last event of the *History* to be the death of de Thou's wife in 1601. See de Smet, *Thuanus*, 136, and Kinser, *Works*, 110–11, for the continuation of the story and the relatively late transposition of this material into the *Life*. The distance between the two works seems narrower than one might expect, as indeed Teissier-Ensminger stresses in her interpretation of the *Life*.

135. This is the origin of the saying attributed to Henry IV by legend (albeit apocryphally): "Paris is worth a mass." For background, see Pitts, *Henry IV*, 169–75. Pitts notes that one of Henry's most important clerical supporters, the Archbishop Renaud de Beaune, compared the conversion of the French king to that of Constantine (*Henry IV*, 170). Gibbon's homage to Henry IV via de Thou might be compared to an episode involving Laurence Sterne and a statue of the French king preserved in Suard's *Mémoires* and engagingly retold by Sterne's biographer: "Stopping one day in front of the statue of Henry IV on the Pont-Neuf, Sterne was quickly surrounded by a crowd attracted by his behavior, whereupon he turned round crying. 'Why are you looking at me? All of you, follow me,' and dropped to his knees before the statue, persuading the crowd to do likewise. . . . By kneeling to him was Sterne—who knew his history well enough—proclaiming his adherence to the Protestant faith, dramatizing a cynical willingness to adopt any identity willed on him, provided the reward were real enough, or—as so often—delighting in the ambivalence of his actions?" (Ross, *Laurence Sterne*, 282).

136. Voltaire followed suit in the *Henriade*. A wise hermit prophesies Henry's conversion at the beginning of his epic and Truth herself confirms the prophesy as the poem ends. See

Voltaire, *Complete Works*, 2:379 (1, line 270), 616–17 (10, lines 481–94).

137. De Thou, *Vie*, 912–13 (6.1.3).

138. Anthony Grafton's beautiful comment on de Thou and Scaliger's friendship deserves quotation: "[Scaliger's] closest friends, the jurists de Thou and Dupuy, reacted to religious war and social dissolution by turning to honest scholarship and accurate history. In the compiling of data, rather than forging an ideology, they found an escape from chaos if not a remedy for it. And in scholarship they created a forum where they could carry on reasonable debate with men of different faiths" (*Joseph Scaliger*, 2:356; see also Grafton, *Footnote*, 133–34). De Thou also praised Spaniards despite the Inquisition's attacks on his works; see *Vie*, 754–55 (4.5.8–10).

139. On Hume's loss of the professorship at Edinburgh, see Mossner, *Life of David Hume*, 153–61, as well as Hume's letter to William Mure, where the cause is "Heresy, Deism, Skepticism, Atheism, &c &c &c" (*Letters*, 1:57–58), and the letter to Matthew Sharpe, where the cause is "Skepticism, Heterodoxy, & other hard Names" (*Letters*, 1:59). On the charge of infidelity, see Mossner, *Life of David Hume*, 336–55, and Sher, *Church and University*, 65–74. Phillipson, *David Hume*, 9–10, provides a helpful overview of both affairs.

140. Hume, *My Own Life*, 612–13.

141. Ibid., 615.

142. Ibid., 611, 615.

143. Ibid., 611.

144. Hume, *Letters*, 1:13. For background on this famous "Letter to a Physician," see Mossner, *Life of David Hume*, 65–74, and more recently, Harris, *Hume*, 35–37, 46–47. The difference between the tumult of Hume's epistolary autobiography and the considerably shorter and more serene autobiography in Hume's *My Own Life* was noted as early as Burton, *Life and Correspondence*, 1:39, published in 1846; the passage describing Hume's "new scene of thought" has continued to interest Hume scholars, as Johnson's *The Mind of David Hume*, 6–10, attests.

145. Hume, *My Own Life*, 613. Spacks, *Imagining a Self*, 13–14.

146. Hume, *My Own Life*, 615. A contemporary of Hume's, Sir John Pringle, refers to "the panegyric on himself which [Hume] calls his life" (Boswell, *Boswell for the Defence*, 136–37n1; Spacks, *Imagining a Self*, 13).

147. Later in the *Life* Gibbon achieves a similar effect by citing both the skeptical Bayle and Chillingworth, author of *The Religion of Protestants a Safe Way to Salvation*, as youthful converts to Catholicism. *A*, B:129, C:229, D:395, E:297.

148. *A*, C:231; compare B:137.

149. *L*, 3:211.

CHAPTER 2

1. *L*, 3:229; *A*, E:342.

2. *L*, 3:211. Jordan has noted Gibbon's adoption of this persona, "a pagan gentleman of the Roman empire" (*Gibbon and His Roman Empire*, 157). Cartledge says that Gibbon "placed himself squarely on the viewpoint of a conservative Roman senator" ("Enlightened Historiography," 71, 86).

3. In addition to Womersley, to whom we shall return, consider the report of Burke's friend Arthur Young, himself an influential reformer whom the French Revolution had moved right: Gibbon once admitted to Burke that he (Gibbon) "heartily repented of the anti-religious part of his work" (Young, *Autobiography*, 258–59; cited in Womersley, *Watchmen*, 227–28). Ghosh, "Gibbon's First Thoughts," 155, and Young, "'Scepticism in Excess,'" 197, by contrast, understand Gibbon (in Young's words) to have "favored paganism to Christianity on purely conservative grounds." Young adds that Gibbon's conservative attachment to paganism did not prevent his recognizing that its revival had become "hopeless" by the time of Julian.

4. News of Gibbon's youthful conversion to Catholicism had leaked prior to the controversy over the first volume of the *Decline and Fall*. See, for instance, *A*, F:88, where Gibbon says, "It was industriously whispered at Oxford that the historian had formerly 'turned Papist.'" Gibbon here seems to invoke a passage in Boswell's *Life of Samuel Johnson* recording a conversation of 1776 in which that phrase appears, and that continues: "I [Boswell] observed that as he had changed several times—from the church of England to the church of Rome,—from the church of Rome to infidelity,—I did not despair yet of seeing him a methodist preacher. JOHNSON. (laughing,) 'It is

said that his range has been more extensive, and that he has once been Mahometan. However, now that he had published his infidelity, he will probably persist in it.' BOSWELL. 'I am not quite sure of that, Sir'" (*Life of Samuel Johnson*, 503). James Chelsum also referred elliptically to Gibbon's conversion in the 1778 edition of his "Remarks." Turnbull, "Marionette Infidèle," 297–98, notes Chelsum's reference and remarks that Gibbon was understood to have been one of several authors whose faith journey included a layover in Rome before arriving at infidelity. Compare Gibbon's discussion of Bayle in the *Memoirs*, most fully at *A*, F:91–3.

5. We might be tempted to conclude that Gibbon found writing the history of Rome more congenial than writing his personal history, but Gibbon in fact revised sections of the *Decline and Fall* and its notorious discussion of Christianity, extensively and repeatedly. See, for instance, *A*, E:308–9: "Three times did I compose the first chapter, and twice the second and third, before I was tolerably satisfied with their effect. In the remainder of the way I advanced with a more equal and easy pace; but the fifteenth and sixteenth chapters have been reduced, by three successive revisals, from a large volume to their present size, and they might still be compressed without any loss of facts or sentiments." Womersley notes that Gibbon's revisions did not cease with the initial publication of his first volume ("Introduction to *Religious Scepticism*," ix–x, xiv–xx; *Watchmen*, 13–42). The effortless affect of the great work was hard-won. Had Gibbon lived to finish the *Memoirs* and destroy the drafts perhaps this work would seem the same to us.

6. Womersley's *Watchmen* gives the most compelling account of these discordant contexts and how they influenced the composition of the *Memoirs*. The *Memoirs* first appeared as a single text, thanks to the 1796 edition of Gibbon's friend Lord Sheffield; a number of other editions have appeared since that time. The six drafts as Gibbon left them are printed in John Murray's *The Autobiographies of Edward Gibbon*. I refer to this volume with a letter to indicate the draft and a number to indicate the page in Murray's edition.

7. Womersley, *Watchmen*, 236–40.

8. The ambivalence regarding whether the drafts would be published rests in Gibbon's having left his final attempt, Draft F, well short of completion. Gibbon's will entrusted publication of the *Memoirs* to his executor's discretion: "I will that all my Manuscript papers found at the time of my decease be delivered to my executors, and that if any shall appear sufficiently finished for the public eye, they do treat for the purchase of the same with a Bookseller" (*A*, 423). Gibbon's executor, Lord Sheffield, having noted Gibbon's dissatisfaction with the drafts, compiled them into a single text; "not long before his death," Sheffield wrote, Gibbon said he was eager to see the *Memoirs* published in his lifetime (*MW 1796*, 1:v, xi, 1n1).

9. *A*, A:356. Bonnard, xx–xxi; Craddock, *Luminous Historian*, 270–72.

10. *A*, Frag:417; compare *J3*, 16. Gibbon reflects on the significance of ancestry at greatest length in the first draft of his *Memoirs* (A:354–55). An independent and undated version of this section—"a double sheet of small size" (Bonnard, *Memoirs*, 3n1)—is included among Gibbon's drafts and seems to have been written in close proximity with the sections in A, since Gibbon omitted this section in B and subsequent drafts. Murray's edition presents the undated draft under the heading "Memoranda and Fragments"; I refer to it as "Frag:" followed by the page number in the Murray edition.

11. Ibid.

12. *A*, A:354, Frag:417.

13. In the second draft of the *Memoirs* Gibbon places his own autobiographical ambitions in an expansive and eclectic context by listing fifteen "ancients and moderns who, in various forms, have exhibited their own portraits" (*A*, B:104). The list runs from Pliny the Younger to contemporaries of Gibbon like the scholarly bishop Thomas Newton, and it testifies to the varied powers and purposes of a self-portrait. Pliny in antiquity and Petrarch and Erasmus during the Renaissance made public monuments of ostensibly private exchanges, while Cellini and Colley Cibber enable us to "smile without contempt" at passions and follies. Autobiography can also achieve the "faithful representation of men and manners." Indeed, in its highest form autobiography can surpass history narrowly conceived by disclosing the "secrets of the human heart." That is the purpose Gibbon assigns Rousseau and "St. Austin," the central figure in the list. Their self-portraits suggest how

personal narrative can approximate what Gibbon elsewhere calls "philosophical history."

14. *A*, A:354. In Draft A, the critic of ancestral pride is identified simply as "a philosopher" who "reasonably despise[s]" that sentiment. In the fragment, this character is split: "The Satirist may laugh, the Philosopher may preach" (Frag:418). In both cases, however, Gibbon uses the contemptuous and ostensibly "reasonable" critic as a foil for his own position. Womersley, *Transformation*, 257–60, is especially sensitive to Gibbon's use of characters (the philosopher, the satirist, etc.) to negate or revise, rather than reflect, his own positions; compare Ghosh, "Gibbon's Timeless Verity," 137–39, and Jordan, *Gibbon and His Roman Empire*, 76–77, who notes that Gibbon's "philosopher" is sometimes a *philosophe*.

15. *A*, A:354. Gibbon comments on one of his own female ancestors, Margaret Phillips: "If her marriage had preceded our alliance, I would not so confidently boast of my descent from the Whetnals of Pelham. Yet it is from this union that I claim the most illustrious of my ancestors" (A:361). See also Womersley's comments on the genealogies in Gibbon's late *Antiquities of the House of Brunswick* (*Transformation*, 184–86).

16. Gibbon's treatment and mistreatment of women in the *Decline and Fall* has been widely discussed. Richard Porson said in 1790 that Gibbon's humanity never slumbers "unless when women are ravished, or the Christians persecuted" (*Letters*, xxviii); more recently, see Brownley, "'The Purest and Most Gentle Portion,'" and Bremmer, *Rise of Christianity*, 16–17. Craddock detects a progressive softening of Gibbon's treatment of women, owing largely to the interventions of Gibbon's former fiancée Madame Necker, née Suzanne Churchod (*Edward Gibbon*, 52–53, 83–86, 169–70). For the history of their relationship, see *L*, 1:396–401, and Craddock, *Young Edward Gibbon*, 104–20.

17. *A*, Frag:418.

18. *A*, A:355, Frag:418.

19. *A*, A:354. Compare the corresponding passage in Gibbon's revision or early draft of A, which makes more explicit the political implications: "We wish to discover our ancestors . . . holding an eminent rank in the class of hereditary nobles, which has been maintained for the wisest and most beneficial purposes, in almost every climate of the Globe and in almost every form of political society" (*A*, Frag:417–18).

20. On inheritance, compare *DF*, 1:405 (1.14): "The ideas of inheritance and succession are so very familiar, that the generality of mankind consider them as founded, not only in reason, but in nature itself. Our imagination readily transfers the same principles from private property to public dominion: and whenever a virtuous father leaves behind him a son whose merit seems to justify the esteem, or even the hopes, of the people, the joint influence of prejudice and of affection operates with irresistible weight." Gibbon's thought on the importance of the nobility in "preserving a free constitution against enterprises of an aspiring prince" is extended in *DF*, 1:85 (1.3), 1:609 (2.17).

21. *A*, A:355, Frag:418–19.

22. *A*, A:358, 362; F:10.

23. Bonnard, "Preface," xx–xxxi, tells the story: In late 1786 or early 1787 the Duke of Brunswick's librarian sent Gibbon the work of Blue-mantle Poursuivant, which formed the basis for the *Memoirs*'s depiction of the Gibbon family history. Some five years later, in February 1792, Gibbon happened upon an article in the *Gentleman's Magazine* that cast doubt on his links to Blue-mantle's line. Gibbon wrote immediately to the magazine's editor requesting additional information (3:246–47); not receiving any, Gibbon asked Sheffield (3:263, 271, 285) and Cadell (3:273) to press the inquiry on his behalf. Gibbon's doubts remained unresolved, yet the final draft of his *Memoirs*, which Gibbon seems to have written from 1792 into early 1793, maintains the link to Blue-mantle: "To him I am indebted for almost the whole of my information concerning the Gibbon family" (F:9–10).

24. The quotation can be found in the final draft of the *Memoirs* (*A*, F:8), but the sentiment is present throughout the early drafts (e.g., *A*, A:370, B:108). Compare Pocock, "Clergy and Commerce," and Young, "Scepticism in Excess." Young argues that it is "behind an often conventional, if deeply ironic, presentation of the case for via media Anglicanism that the authentic tone of Gibbon is to be heard" ("Scepticism in Excess," 198). Consider, too, Turnbull's conclusion that "Gibbon considered the value of an established religion to be quite independent of its intellectual soundness," and Ghosh's that "there remains a correlation between the

sincerity of [Gibbon's] private belief in natural religion and his ostentatious public conformity to the national religion" (Turnbull, "Gibbon's Exchange," 153; Ghosh, "Gibbon's Timeless Verity," 153–54; Ghosh, "Gibbon's First Thoughts," 153).

25. *A*, A:355.

26. *A*, A:370.

27. *A*, A:355–56.

28. *A*, F:10–11. As the final draft of the *Memoirs* contains Gibbon's fullest account of his grandfather's character, we rely on it in this section. Much of the corresponding section of the first draft has been lost (*A*, A:378).

29. On the Gibbons' Jacobitism, see especially Turnbull's "'Buffeted for Ancestral Sins,'" and Pocock's *Barbarism and Religion*, 1:43.

30. *A*, F:3; compare A:363–64.

31. Gibbon's comments on heraldry suggest his skepticism on this point: "The armorial ensigns which in the times of Chivalry adorned the crest and shield of the soldier are now become an empty decoration, which every man who has money to build a carriage may paint, according to his fancy, on the panels" (*A*, F:3–4; A:359). Here is a measure of the distance between Blue-mantle's world and the one Gibbon inhabits, which goes some way to explain the tone of respectful mockery that Gibbon often employs in describing his assumed ancestor. Blue-mantle took quite seriously and based his hopes for literary immortality on a practice the significance of which we (Gibbon and his readers) have to make a great effort to comprehend. His world is not ours. And the sympathetic engagement with someone who assumed that world was going to last forever can generate a sense of both tragedy and comedy.

32. *A*, F:13. As in his discussion of genealogy, Gibbon juxtaposes his own sentiments to those of a "philosopher": "As a philosopher, I *should* mention without a sigh the irreparable loss of above ninety six thousand pounds of which, in a single moment and by an arbitrary vote I have been ultimately deprived." The stressed "should" and the precise accounting give us to understand that Gibbon is not that sort of a philosopher. A tally of Gibbon's personal finances runs throughout the *Memoirs*'s drafts, complementing and amplifying broader concerns about education and the transmission of ancestral virtues. Gibbon's thought, as opposed to that of his "philosopher," forgives attachment to one's own—as with family, so with property.

33. *A*, F:17. Mr. Francis Acton, a friend of the elder Gibbon, restores part of what had been lost. Gibbon notes that "the frequent imposition of oaths had enlarged and fortified the Jacobite conscience"—revealing a world more generous and less calculating than that in which everyone subordinated opinions to interest and Jacobites would ask the same rate of King William as King James.

34. *A*, F:17, 21.

35. *A*, F:17. In the first draft of this passage, Gibbon had described India as unfolding "her capacious bosom to the merit or fortune of every needy adventurer" (*A*, A:364). As so often in Gibbon, the conjunction—merit *or* fortune—expresses the essence of the problem.

36. Law, *Serious Call*, 8.

37. Ibid., 70.

38. Ibid., 84–85. Leslie Stephen offers an entertaining account of relations between the two sisters and Gibbon himself in *English Thought*, 2:390–92 (xii.69).

39. Law, *Serious Call*, 84.

40. Ibid., 136–37. Young, "Gibbon and Catholicism," 150, describes the Gibbons as "a family of religious contrasts": "High Church Anglican spirituality had fused with continental mysticism" in William Law and his devotee, Gibbon's Aunt Hester, but Gibbon's father "conspicuously led a life of religious indifference."

41. *A*, F:17.

42. *A*, F:17.

43. *A*, F:26; A:390.

44. *A*, F:21–22; compare A:383–84.

45. *A*, F:23; A:387.

46. See Pocock, *Barbarism and Religion*, 6:228, who links Gibbon's innuendo about Miranda to his discussion of clerical abuse of "devout females" at *DF*, 1:985–86 (2.25).

47. *A*, F:23; A:387.

48. I suggest below that this sort of paganism is more characteristic of Gibbon's *Decline and Fall* than is commonly understood.

49. Corp, *Stuarts in Italy*, 3–9, 213, 351–52.

50. Ibid., 1–2; Lewis, *Connoisseurs and Secret Agents*. The Prussian-born Baron von Stosch is an exemplary British agent of about the time of Gibbon's father's Tour; Stosch's intelligence-gathering grew increasingly difficult

throughout the 1720s, until he was exiled in 1731 and forced to rely on correspondents (Corp, *Stuarts in Italy*, 7–8; Lewis, *Connoisseurs and Secret Agents*, 84–92). Among these sources was the Catholic Cardinal Alessandro Albani, whom Lewis describes as being "'as staunch as a heretic' in favor of England" by the 1760s (*Connoisseurs and Secret Agents*, 214).

51. Not long after Gibbon's father had returned home, married, and his wife had given birth to the historian, Mann would establish himself in Florence and go on to report regularly on preparations for the invasion of 1745. Although, as Corp notes, "the Stuart court effectively ceased to function in 1763–4," Mann was still in Florence in 1764 to receive Edward Gibbon III, and he was still filing reports on the Pretenders, Old and Young (*Stuarts in Italy*, 344). Gibbon and Guise called on Mann (a by-then-famous host who happened also to be a relative of Guise's) immediately after arriving in Florence in June 1764 (*J4*, 119; *L*, 1:182). During the next three months they would dine together at least a half dozen times and visit on a number of other occasions as well. Their encounters became so regular, in fact, that Gibbon could record in his journal: "*Le soir nous somme allès comme à l'ordinaire chez le Chevalier Mann*" (*J4*, 209; also 219, 222). See also Craddock, *Young Edward Gibbon*, 209, 216–17.

52. *A*, F:18. Gibbon's description of his father's travels continues: "His excursions were neither long nor remote, and the slender knowledge which he had gained of the French language was gradually obliterated."

53. *A*, F:19; see also A:383, B:111, C:217.

54. Turnbull suggests that part of the rage of Gibbon's father at the son's conversion had to do with the son "having wrecked carefully laid plans to remove an old taint of disloyalty from the Gibbon dynasty in order to alleviate their growing impecuniosity" ("'Buffeted for Ancestral Sins,'" 26).

55. When the Gibbons hired Kirkby in April 1744, his novel, *Automathes*, and an English grammar, both of them plagiarized, had not yet been published. See *A*, F:41, for Gibbon's awareness of the novel's origins (Kirkby "is not entitled to the merit of invention"), and Tieken-Boon van Ostade, "Kirkby, John."

56. *A*, F:55–56.

57. *A*, F:68.

58. Ibid.

59. Womersley's *Watchmen* helpfully sets Gibbon's critique of Oxford among contemporary debates over higher education. He notes, for instance, that eighteenth-century critics of Oxford had created an idiom "in which the fellows were monks, the college monasteries or convents, and in which the traditional customs and practices of a university . . . were stigmatized as monkish" (*Watchmen*, 279).

60. *A*, F:63.

61. *A*, F:73–74. Gibbon's distaste for the monastery (*DF*, 2:411–50 [3.37]) did not preclude appreciation of the Benedictines' scholarship (see Trevor-Roper, "Historiography I," 99; compare Momigliano, "Gibbon's Contribution," 54–55).

62. *A*, F:74, 95.

63. The first volume of the *Decline and Fall* appeared on February 17, 1776; the *Wealth of Nations*, less than a month later on March 9, 1776. Gibbon immediately recognized its significance. In a letter to Adam Ferguson of April 1, 1776, Gibbon exclaims: "What an excellent work is that which our common friend, Mr. Adam Smith, has enriched the public!—an extensive science in a single book, and the most profound ideas expressed in the most perspicuous language" (*Letters*, 2:101). For Smith's analysis of university finances, see Smith, *Wealth of Nations*, 760–61. Gibbon's indictment of Oxford also borrows from Smith's analysis of monopoly (F:68, attributed to Smith in E:296n9).

64. The situation of English Catholics prior to the Relief Act of 1778 is most eloquently described in Edmund Burke's "Speech at Bristol Guildhall" (with Bromwich, *Intellectual Life*, 406–14); see also the interested Amherst's *History of Catholic Emancipation*, 1:76–90; Rosman's *Evolution of the English Churches*, 130–36; Turnbull, "'Supposed Infidelity,'" 25; and Turnbull, "'Buffeted for Ancestral Sins,'" 25–26. A scene from Gibbon's travels in Italy provides a useful illustration. In September 1764 Gibbon visited his relatives, the Actons (see *A*, A:372–74), among them a John Acton who served in the Tuscan navy and embraced the Catholic religion. Of the meeting, Gibbon wrote to his father: "The poor old Commodore is in a most melancholy situation. Last winter he had a most violent attack of the Apoplexy; whilst in that situation he was persuaded either from

motives of interest or devotion to change his religion in which he had been till then very steady. The immediate consequence of which imprudent step was the total neglect of all his English friends who from being very intimate with him have taken the unanimous resolution of not holding the smallest connection with him. I most sincerely pity him. . . . I think from his manner and conversation that I never saw a more lively picture of an unhappy man" (*L*, 1:184; *J4*, 230).

65. *A*, B:128.

66. *A*, B:129.

67. *A*, B:130.

68. *A*, D:395.

69. *A*, E:296–97. EG "believed that he believed," also at C:227 and D:395.

70. *A*, E:296, D:395.

71. Womersley suggests that in this draft, written in 1791 immediately after Gibbon had read and virtually endorsed Burke's *Reflections*, Gibbon was concerned to minimize his critique of ancient English institutions and so muted his hostility toward Oxford. It is notable that the invocation of Smith's critique of the university and Gibbon's hints regarding the significance of using Chillingworth and Bayle to frame his conversion (constants across the other drafts that touch on Oxford) are both relegated to footnotes in Draft E.

72. *A*, F:87, 89.

73. *A*, F:87. Burrow nicely restates this account: Gibbon's conversion was "characteristically bookish; he knew no Catholic; he read himself into the Catholic Church" (*Gibbon*, 7).

74. The books are described variously as "some books of controversy" (B:128), "some Popish books" (C:227), "some Popish Treatises of Controversy" (D:395), and as we have seen, "some books of Popish controversy" (E:296).

75. *A*, F:86.

76. Womersley, *Watchmen*, especially 311n148, questions the historicity of Middleton's role in Gibbon's conversion: "The allegation that the conversion to Catholicism was due to a reading of Middleton is a fiction of 1791, calculated to meet the needs of the moment of its composition." Although, as Womersley argues, we have no contemporaneous testimony to Gibbon's engagement with the *Free Inquiry* prior to the 1760s, Gibbon does mention reading Middleton in the mid-1750s in the first draft of his *Memoirs* (specifically his *Life of Cicero* at *A*, C:232). Gibbon's commonplace book, which he kept between 1755 and 1757, notes Matthieu Maty's opinions of Middleton's faith (*E*, 13–14n36, 293). In the *Essai* of 1761 Gibbon praises the *Free Inquiry*, alongside Beausobre's *Histoire du Manichéisme*, as a "handsome monument of an enlightened age" (*E*, 128 (LVI[I]). These brief mentions, along with the curious and spirited persona Gibbon casts for his younger self across all drafts of his *Memoirs* (see especially B:128, where Gibbon reports that as a boy he "puzzled [his] aunt by [his] questions and objections on the mysteries of religion"), make plausible, at least, the claim that Middleton's notoriety attracted Gibbon to his works prior to his conversion.

77. Trevor-Roper, *History and the Enlightenment*, 102; Pocock, *Barbarism and Religion*, 1:36, 45–48; Stuart-Buttle, "Gibbon and Enlightenment History," 120–23. See Middleton's discussion of prevailing opinions among Protestants (*Free Inquiry*, xlvi–lii). Middleton notes that some theologians would extend miraculous powers down to the final suppression of Arianism in the fifth century (l–li). In the fifteenth chapter of the *Decline and Fall*, Gibbon praises and distances himself from Middleton's "very free and ingenious inquiry" (*DF*, 1:472n73, 473 [1.15]). Gibbon restates Middleton's question with great clarity: "Since every friend to revelation is persuaded of the reality, and every reasonable man is convinced of the cessation, of miraculous powers, it is evident that there must have been *some period* in which they were either suddenly or gradually withdrawn from the Christian church" (1:474 [1.15]). Gibbon also follows Middleton's review of the scholarly literature on the topic: miracles could have ceased with the death of the apostles, the conversion of the Empire, or the suppression of Arianism (ibid.). In the sequel, however, Gibbon seems to extend Middletonian skepticism to miracles that Middleton himself had been careful to affirm (1:511–12 [1.15]; compare Middleton, *Free Inquiry*, vi).

78. Middleton does not draw a definite end point, though he suggests that miracles had likely ceased before the death of John in 100 (*Free Inquiry*, xxvi, xxix–xxx). By that point the purpose for which miraculous powers had been conferred—to enable the apostles "more easily

to overrule the inveterate prejudices both of Jews and Gentiles" in establishing Christianity throughout the known world—had been achieved (xxvii–xxviii). In the *Vindication*, Gibbon says that Middleton "rose to the highest pitch of skepticism, in any wise consistent with religion" (277).

79. Womersley, "Gibbon's Apostasy," 55–58. For studies of the controversy, see especially Trevor-Roper, *History and the Enlightenment*, 101–9.

80. Middleton, *Free Inquiry*, xl–xli.

81. *A*, F:85. Gibbon here makes himself resemble the early Christians of the *Decline and Fall* (especially 1:471–75 [1.15]): a secure faith in the possibility of miracles grounds assent to the Catholic doctrines with which miracles are associated.

82. Haydon, *Anti-Catholicism*, 7–8. In a letter to Gibbon's father in August 1753, while Gibbon was still a Catholic, his tutor Pavillard reports that Gibbon had declared himself also a Jacobite (Bonnard, *Memoirs*, 217). See Turnbull, "'Buffeted for Ancestral Sins,'" 25; Baridon, *Edward Gibbon et le mythe de Rome*, 45.

83. Turnbull, "Supposed Infidelity," 41, helpfully links Gibbon's ambivalence regarding his own conversion in the *Memoirs* to the overdetermined account of Constantine's conversion in the *Decline and Fall*'s second volume. Although Gibbon allows that Constantine may have acted on interest, he is reluctant to leave it at that. "A conclusion so harsh and so absolute is not . . . warranted by our knowledge of human nature, of Constantine, or of Christianity." Gibbon continues in terms that also anticipate *Memoirs*: "Nor can it be deemed incredible that the mind of an unlettered soldier should have yielded to the weight of evidence, which, in a more enlightened age, has satisfied or subdued the reason of a Grotius, a Pascal, or a Locke" (*DF*, 1:742–44 [2.20]; compare, e.g., *A*, B:143, C:249–50, F:89–93).

84. *A*, B:130, C:228, F:88. The second draft of the *Memoirs*, written late in the spring of 1789, is the first to describe Gibbon's Swiss exile. The initial draft had ended with Gibbon's portrait of Law, before reaching the memoirist's own birth.

85. *A*, B:130.

86. *A*, C:228. On the dating of Gibbon's initial conversion, see Craddock, *Young Edward Gibbon*, 50.

87. *A*, D:397.

88. *A*, E:297.

89. *A*, B:132–33.

90. *A*, B:133. The phrase "pleasure and profit" links Gibbon's accounts of Lausanne and Oxford, the latter of which includes lessons that "were equally devoid of profit and pleasure" (B:125; F:78). In subsequent drafts Oxford will consume "fourteen months, the most barren and unprofitable of my whole life" (D:394; F:67).

91. *A*, B:152. "Such as I am, in Genius or learning or manners, I owe my creation to Lausanne."

92. *A*, B:135. Womersley, "Gibbon's Apostasy," 63.

93. *A*, B:135, 137.

94. *A*, B:135.

95. *A*, B:135–36; compare D:397.

96. *A*, B:136. Baridon, *Gibbon et le mythe de Rome*, 47–59.

97. *A*, B:135–36; C:234, D:397. Gibbon's wide reading as a young man and the influence of his aunt had brought him into contact with "works of philosophy and divinity" that could conceivably have included Locke's *Essay* and certainly did include devotees of Lockean empiricism like Shaftesbury, but Gibbon describes these works as "least adapted to the capacity of a child" (B:118–19). As opposed to the works of history that he devoured in English translation ("Before the age of sixteen I was master of all the *English* materials, which I have since employed in the chapters of the Persians and Arabians, the Tartars and the Turks"), Gibbon did not consider these works of philosophy to have made a lasting impact (B:119, 121).

98. *A*, B:136.

99. *A*, B:136.

100. *A*, F:86.

101. *A*, B:137.

102. Pavillard's letters to Gibbon's father are printed in Bonnard's edition of Gibbon's, *Memoirs*, 214–27. The tutor notes the student's *caractère sérieux* early in their relationship (*Memoirs*, 216).

103. *A*, B:136–37.

104. *A*, B:130.

105. *A*, B:137. Pocock notes the irony of this passage: if belief "was not explicit [it] could not be unreserved" (*Barbarism and Religion*, 1:73).

106. B. W. Young, "'Scepticism in Excess,'" 181, 199, nicely captures the direction of Gibbon's development: "Scholarship could well be described as acting as Gibbon's religion, or substitute religion."
107. *A*, C:231; compare B:137.
108. *A*, B:138.
109. Gibbon credits Pascal's *Provincial Letters* with teaching him how "to manage the weapon of grave and temperate irony, even on subjects of Ecclesiastical solemnity" (*A*, B:143; C:235). Craddock notes that Pascal does not appear in the commonplace book Gibbon kept during this period (*Young Edward Gibbon*, 76), though a journal entry in October 1762 corroborates the *Memoirs*'s account of Pascal's influence (*J1*, 151; see also *EE*, 114). In the *Decline and Fall* Gibbon admires Pascal, "that superior genius," but casts him as a man of faith rather than a master of irony (*DF*, 3:721n53 [6.61], 1:744 [2.20]). Young, "Gibbon and Catholicism," 154–59, offers a helpful assessment of Pascal's influence on Gibbon.
110. *Voyage*, 28. Turnbull notes the combination of astonishment and fascination with religion in Gibbon's reaction ("'Supposed Infidelity,'" 28). On the basis of this passage Craddock, *Young Edward Gibbon*, 81, judges Gibbon a "reluctant or *manqué* romantic." Kapossy and Whatmore stress correctly that Gibbon's "awe" does not prevent his interpreting the scene in a quite Protestant fashion; it is "a masterpiece of ecclesiastical politics" ("Gibbon and Republicanism," 134).
111. *Voyage*, 28. Gibbon links the sentiment of awe, for instance, to the placement of the abbey amid caverns and woods. Already in 1755, then, Gibbon can link religious sentiments and manipulative priestcraft (compare *DF*, 1:245 [1.9]). The conclusion to his account of Einsiedeln strengthens the skeptical or reformed tone: "These places are at once the height of superstition, the masterpiece of Ecclesiastical politics, and the shame of humanity" (*Voyage*, 33). One must keep in mind that Gibbon's father, who had hardly forgotten the son's conversion (see his letter of December 24, 1755, in Low, *Edward Gibbon*, 60), was the intended audience of Gibbon's travelogue. Gibbon had different but equally powerful reasons for deemphasizing his youthful Catholicism in the *Memoirs*, where an account of the trip to Einsiedeln allows him to report that "the lively naked image of superstition suggested to me, as in the same place it had done Zuinglius, the most pressing argument for the reformation of the Church" (*A*, B:145).
112. *A*, B:145–48, C:235, D:398, E:298. Middleton reappears during this period, now through his *Life of Cicero* rather than the *Free Inquiry*.
113. *A*, B:166, C:251. On Gibbon's fluency in French, see Introduction, note 6.
114. *L*, 1:12. "At present there is [no Latin author] I do not read fluently. Recently I have read several, including the greater part of Cicero's works, Virgil, Sallust, Pliny's epistles twice, the comedies of Terence as often, Velleius Paterculus, and I plan in time to read all of them."
115. *A*, B:141. After returning to England Gibbon would make a habit of bringing his Greek Bible with him to Church to follow the readings and compare translations (*J1*, 94; for comment, see Smith, "Gibbon in Church," 454–58).
116. Nevertheless, Gibbon's reading during this period was not limited to ancient texts. In the *Memoirs* Gibbon would specify three modern texts that "may have remotely contributed to form the historian of the Roman Empire": Pascal's *Provincial Letters*, the Abbé de la Bleterie's *Life of Julian*, and Giannone's *Civil History of Naples* (*A*, B:143).
117. Smith, "Gibbon in Church," describes Gibbon's religious practice.
118. See, for instance, *A*, B:199, C:263.
119. [Suard], "Article VIII"; [Suard], "Article VIII . . . *Second Extrait*"; [Suard], "Article III."
120. [Suard], "Article VIII . . . *Second Extrait*," 201; "Article III," 85. Gibbon identified Suard as the anonymous reviewer in the fifth draft of his *Memoirs*: "The copious extracts which were given in the *Journal étranger* by Mr. Suard, a judicious critic, must satisfy both the author and the public" (*A*, E:300n18). Gibbon and Suard seem to have first met in May 1776 (see Craddock, *Luminous Historian*, 75); a few months later Gibbon would attempt without success to recruit Suard as the French translator of the *Decline and Fall* (*L*, 121–24; *MW 1814*, 2:183–86).
121. [Suard], "Article III," 76. In the third part of the review, Suard transcribes portions of *E*, 128–29 (LVI[I]), 134–35 (LXV[I]–LX[IX]), and

136 (LX[X]), and he paraphrases much of what he does not quote directly.

122. Bonnard, "Gibbon's '*Essai*,'" 149, notes that the review in the *Bibliothèque des sciences* also praised the *Essai*'s treatment of polytheism.

123. Norton, *Bibliography*, 7. In the *Memoirs* Gibbon tentatively recorded the place of publication as Geneva (*A*, B:171, C:256, D:402).

124. *J2*, 105. Bonnard, "Gibbon's '*Essai*,'" 145–46, notes that Gibbon's first report of the *Essai*'s favorable reception on the Continent seems to have reached him by way of David Mallet. In his *Memoirs*, Gibbon would recall "the copious extracts, the warm commendations, and the flattering predictions of the Journals of France and Holland" (*A*, B:171; compare C:256, D:402, E:300). Suard's is the only review that Gibbon cites; it offers an occasion to lament the poor quality of reviews of his *Decline and Fall*. "The manufacture of journals, at least on the Continent, is miserably debased" (E:300n18).

125. *L*, 1:136.

126. Several years later Gibbon would offer this ringing endorsement of literary ambition:

> I am disgusted with the affectation of men of letters, who complain that they have renounced a substance for a shadow, and that their fame (which sometimes is no insupportable weight) affords a poor compensation for envy, censure, and persecution. My own experience, at least, has taught me a very different lesson: twenty happy years have been animated by the labour of my history; and its success has given me a name, a rank, a character, in the World, to which I should not otherwise have been entitled.... The rational pride of an author may be offended rather than flattered by vague indiscriminate praise; but he cannot, he should not, be indifferent to the fair testimonies of private and public esteem. Even his social sympathy may be gratified by the idea that, now in the present hour, he is imparting some degree of amusement or knowledge to *his friends* in a distant land; that one day his mind will be familiar to the grandchildren of those who are yet unborn. (*A*, E:346–47; compare *Vindication*, 232, and Hume's "love of literary fame, my ruling passion," from Hume, *My Own Life*, 615)

Womersley has provocatively suggested that after Gibbon's return to Protestantism in 1754, his religious personae were "shaped by the imperative of that much more fundamental element in his identify... his hunger for literary fame, and his attempts to control that fame once he had acquired it" ("Gibbon's Religious Characters," 88; compare Pocock, *Barbarism and Religion*, 1:66: "In [Gibbon's] mind critical freedom, and the freedom to write history, at some point substituted themselves for belief altogether").

127. *J2*, 105: "I have been received as a man of letters." As Craddock, *Young Edward Gibbon*, 165, 337n2, and Womersley, *Watchmen*, 92–93n160, note, Gibbon was not eager for his literary reputation entirely to supplant his status as gentleman (*l'homme de qualité*).

128. *A*, B:204. Gibbon finds fault with "the philosophers and Encyclopedists the friends of d'Holbach and Helvetius."

129. *A*, B:201, C:261.

130. *A*, B:204, C:262.

131. *A*, B:130.

132. *L*, 1:133. Gibbon goes on to say that "the only thing I dislike in [Helvetius]" is his fondness for Hans Stanley, an Englishman with whom Gibbon had tussled while serving in the militia and who was then in Paris as *charge d'affaires* in negotiations with France. See *J1*, 18, and Low, "Introduction," cix.

133. *L*, 1:136.

134. *J2*, 96–99; *L*, 1:135. Writing to his father, Gibbon stresses that his lodgings are located "up two pair of stairs" before describing the lease of a coach for nearly three times his monthly rent. See Craddock, *Young Edward Gibbon*, 167, and Black, *British Abroad*, 96–99, whose survey of prices on the Continent suggests Gibbon's spending was not unusual.

135. Womersley, *Watchmen*, 87n139, provides an illuminating survey of seventeenth- and eighteenth-century British writers who linked Catholicism and freethinking. Shame at excessive credulity was thought to generate excessive skepticism; the biographies of Tindal and Gibbon illustrated the point. I am suggesting here, however, that, once Gibbon's skepticism was secure and his flirtation with Catholic faith was long past, he was able to approach Catholicism with more generosity of spirit than, say, a Tindal. Gibbon's skepticism and a certain

warm curiosity about Catholicism were surprisingly synchronous.

136. *A*, B:199.

137. *A*, C:263.

138. *L*, 1:140.

139. *L*, 1:190–91.

140. *L*, 1:197. This description of Naples occurs in Gibbon's letter to his uncle, Stanier Porten, on July 21, 1765.

141. *J2*, 95. Bonnard identifies the Church as *la chapelle de la Madeleine de l'église des Carmélites du faubourg St-Jacques* (95n2).

142. Although Louise de La Vallière was about six years old when le Brun painted *Sainte Madeleine repentante* and resided far from court, she was commonly thought to have been le Brun's model when Gibbon viewed the painting. For discussion, see *J2*, 96n1, and Peacocke's *Romanticism and the Museum*, 42–43.

143. *J2*, 95–96.

144. "Close friend" is perhaps a pale reflection of this complicated and close relationship, as we shall see. For additional detail, see Craddock, *Young Edward Gibbon*, 167–71. Womersley, *Watchmen*, 351–52, notes the "uncanny prolepsis of twentieth-century idiom" in the name of Gibbon's companion.

145. *J2*, 97.

146. *A*, B:204; at C:263 Mme. Bontems is more simply a "devotee without gall."

147. *J2*, 107.

148. *A*, B:137.

149. Junod, "Preface," 116–21, gives compelling arguments for dating the "Letter" to Gibbon's second stay in Lausanne rather than the stay that ended in April 1758 (compare Giarrizzo, *Edward Gibbon*, 35n67; Low, *Edward Gibbon*, 66n1; and *MW 1814*, 2:1). Craddock, *Young Edward Gibbon*, 187–89, and Pocock, *Barbarism and Religion*, 1:85, 89–93, provide further support for the later dating. On the historical context surrounding the "Letter" and its place among Gibbon's Swiss writings, Kapossy and Whatmore's "Gibbon and Republicanism" is particularly helpful.

150. Baridon attributes the politics of the "Letter" to the influence of the *philosophes* whom Gibbon met in Paris ("Edward Gibbon en Italie," 132).

151. *Lettre*, 123: The author's taste, reason, and mores were formed there. Compare *A*, B:152, where Gibbon writes in his own name: "Such as I am, in genius or learning or manners, I owe my creation to Lausanne."

152. *Lettre*, 123.

153. Ibid., 124–25.

154. Ibid., 132.

155. Ibid., 133–34.

156. Ibid., 134.

157. As we shall see in the following chapter, Gibbon is impressed by the degree to which, in the Empire of the Antonines, imperial centralization coincided with religious pluralism (*DF*, 1:56–61 [1.2]). The subsequent development of the Empire, however, tends in the direction indicated here (*DF*, 1:220–21 [1.8], 1:730–32 [2.20], 1:766–67 [2.21]).

158. *Lettre*, 141.

159. Ibid.

160. Craddock, *Young Edward Gibbon*, 188.

161. *Lettre*, 135.

162. *J3*, 161.

163. Smith says of this episode: "Perhaps this was Gibbon's ideal of a sermon, at least of a civic sermon: namely eloquence directed to a moral purpose" ("Gibbon in Church," 462–63).

164. *A*, C:265.

165. On the *Recueil*, see especially Mayhew, "Gibbon's Geographies," 47–51, and Pocock, *Barbarism and Religion*, 1:270–72.

166. *J3*, 169. Where possible, I follow here Lord Sheffield's translations of Gibbon's journal found in the fifth volume of *MW 1814*.

167. *J3*, 169. Gibbon abandoned the *Recueil* only in the most superficial sense, as this work contained many seeds of the *Decline and Fall* (e.g., *DF*, 1:47–55 [1.1]).

168. *J3*, 20, 25, 38.

169. Ibid., 179.

170. Ibid., 182–83.

171. Ibid., 246.

172. Ibid., 195–96.

173. Ibid., 239.

174. Ibid., 131.

175. Ibid. Gibbon here applies to humanity a principle (*le Coeur corrige les erreurs de l'Esprit*) he had used to account for Mdme. Bontems's goodness and gaiety (*son Coeur redressoit son Esprit*) (*J2*, 107).

176. *J3*, 132.

177. Ibid.

178. Ibid., 133: . . . *Calvin avoit l'ame atroce et l'Esprit eclairé.* When Gibbon later encounters Calvin's letters in the *Bibliothèque Raisonnée* he

exclaims: "Here we find you, harsh and intractable spirit (*Te voila Esprit dur et farouche*)" (*J3*, 158).

179. *L*, 1:165. In a journal entry on April 6, 1764, Gibbon judges Guise "brave, true, and sensible, but possessing an impetuosity which is all the more dangerous for usually being suppressed" (*J3*, 259). Craddock, *Young Edward Gibbon*, 196, notes that Guise "almost celebrated their departure from Lausanne with a duel."

180. This account of Guise's motives is Bonnard's plausible interpretation of Gibbon's remarks at *J3*, 18 ("I had supper with Holroyd and Guise, whose sadness begins to give way to its only consoler, time"). See Bonnard, "Preface," vii.

181. *J4*, 210n1. Compare Tobias Smollett's remarks while traveling in Boulogne: "Their [Catholicism] affords a perpetual comedy. Their high masses, their feasts, their processions, their pilgrimages, confessions, images, tapers, robes, incense, benedictions, spectacles, representations, and innumerable ceremonies, which revolve almost incessantly, furnish a variety of entertainment from one end of the year to the other. If superstition implies fear, never was a word more misapplied than it is to the mummery of the religion of Rome" (*Travels*, 28–29 [Letter 4]).

182. *J4*, 18.

183. Ibid., 115, 244; compare Baridon, "Edward Gibbon en Italie," 136. Gibbon would go on to consider trinitarian theology extensively, if skeptically, in the *Decline and Fall*. See especially *DF*, 1:780–82 (2.21), 3:176–78 (5.50), and for comment, see Young, "'Scepticism in Excess,'" 190–92, and Pocock, 5:375–83, 6:87–92.

184. *A*, B:199.

185. See, for instance, *DF*, 1:451 (1.15): "The painful and even dangerous rite of circumcision was alone capable of repelling a willing proselyte from the door of the synagogue." And on exorcism, see *DF*, 1:472 (1.15).

186. *J4*, 85.

187. Ibid., 97. Craddock, *Young Edward Gibbon*, 207–8, discusses many of these passages. The quotation here is her translation.

188. *A*, B:145. Note that this description was written some thirty years after the event. We have discussed above Gibbon's awe in Einsiedeln and his account of its sources. We might add, in connection to this specific passage in the *Memoirs*, Gibbon's description of a *tres beau tableau* he encountered during this youthful Tour of Switzerland: "A lady on her knees before Our Lady who appears in the clouds holding J. C. in her arms. I ignore the subject of the piece" (*Voyage*, 18).

189. *J4*, 179.

190. Ibid., 186.

191. *A*, C:267.

192. See Corp, *Stuarts in Italy*, 231–34.

193. *J4*, 159n2.

194. Ibid., 211.

195. Ibid., 159.

196. Sismondi, *De la vie*, 13.

197. Consider Mallet's description of how his history departs from the works of his predecessors: "To run cursorily over a number of events, unconnected and void of circumstances, without being able to penetrate into their true causes; to see a people, princes, conquerors and legislators succeed one another rapidly upon the stage, without knowing anything of their real character, manner of thinking, or of the spirit which animated them, this is to have only the skeleton of History. . . . For this reason I have all along resolved not to meddle with the body of the Danish History, till I have presented my Readers with a sketch of the manners and genius of the first inhabitants of Denmark" (*Northern Antiquities*, l).

198. Mallet, *Northern Antiquities*, l. See in addition li, where Mallet argues that the "history of our own manners and institutions ought necessarily to ascend back . . . [to] a period, which discovers to us their chief origin and source." Compare *Northern Antiquities*, 55: "For why should history be only a recital of battles, sieges, intrigues, and negotiations? And why should it contain merely a heap of petty facts and dates, rather than a just picture of the opinions, customs and even inclinations of a people?"

199. Ibid., 1:58, 1:414. In this last passage, communication between north and south, "formed . . . by commerce and religion," is one of three causes that account for the spread of "arts, sciences, industry, and politeness" in Europe. The other two causes are natural restlessness—the desire to improve one's present condition—and climate change. Mallet, relying mainly on a source that Gibbon, too, will use (Pelloutier's *Histoire des Celtes*) anticipates Gibbon's argument in chapter 9 of the *Decline*

and Fall, that "Europe was much colder formerly than it is at present" (1:231 [1.9]). Gibbon credits this insight not only to Pelloutier but to Hume ("Of National Characters," though Gibbon does not name the work) and the Abbé du Bos, both of whose works preceded Mallet (1:231n2 [1.9]).

200. *J4*, 159. Mallet, the tutor to Lord Montstuart, was traveling through Italy at the same time as Gibbon and Guise. See *J4*, 159n3, 234n2, 257.

201. Ibid., 160. Gibbon continues: "A religion inculcating the fear of death would have met with a very unfavorable reception among the Celts. The genius of Odin's superstition and moral prevailed among the Cimbri, who were long anterior to that legislator; and among the Celtiberians, who probably never heard of his name."

202. It is not entirely clear whether Gibbon intended this insight as an epitome or a criticism of Mallet's argument. Mallet's text at different points seems to justify either approach: Mallet draws a strong contrast, for instance, between an old, monolatrous, doctrinally simple religion and a new polytheism "corrupted by an intermixture of ceremonies, some of them ridiculous and others cruel" (*Northern Antiquities*, 77, 84); elsewhere Odin does not transform but merely intensifies the Northerners' "natural ferocity, by infusing into minds so prepared the sanguinary doctrines of his religion" (*Northern Antiquities*, 89).

203. *J4*, 162.

204. See note 83 above on Gibbon's surprisingly sympathetic account of Constantine's conversion.

205. *J4*, 162–63. Gibbon adds that policy would hardly have led Vandal and Burgundian leaders to embrace Arianism.

206. Ibid., 163.

207. Ibid.

208. Ibid.

209. Ibid., 164.

210. Ibid.

211. Ibid., 164–65. Compare Gibbon's account of the barbarians' conversion in the third volume of the *Decline and Fall* (*DF*, 2:429–50 [3.37]). As in his comments on Mallet, Gibbon here allows that material motives and fear (see especially *DF*, 2:440) inform conversion, but his account ultimately comes to rest on nobler sentiments: "The direct authority of religion was less effectual, than the holy communion which united [the barbarians] with their Christian brethren in spiritual friendship" (*DF*, 2:433). Woudhuysen's comments on these passages are valuable ("Gibbon among the Barbarians," 105–8).

212. *L*, 1:190–91.

213. *J4*, 163.

214. Ibid., 235.

215. *L*, 1:184.

216. *J4*, 235.

217. Ibid.

218. *L*, 1:190.

219. Ibid., 1:184.

220. Ibid.

221. Lassels, *Voyage*, part 2, 4. Lassels was sufficiently broad-minded to appreciate the ruins of pagan antiquity on their own terms, of course, but even when he is most appreciative of pagan remains his concern to construct an identifiably Christian history is evident. He considers the Colosseum, for instance, "one of the rarest pieces of antiquity in Rome, and though Rome be grown again, by her new palaces, one of the finest cities of Europe, yet her very ruins are finer than her new buildings" (*Voyage*, part 2, 120–21). Yet when he proceeds to discuss the Colosseum's interior he notes the caves, "out of which they turned [wild beasts] loose to fight, sometimes against condemned men, sometimes against innocent Christians. Nero made the Christians be clad in the skins of beasts, and so to be exposed to lions and bears" (*Voyage*, part 2, 122). In this way a pagan "wonder of the world" is incorporated into a history that belongs at bottom to the Church.

222. For a modern translation of the relevant passage, see Voragine, *Golden Legend*, 40–41. Reames's *The Legenda Aurea* contains helpful overviews of the work's reception history.

223. On Augustus's preservation of the republic, see *DF*, 1:93 (1.3), and compare *DF*, 1:87 (1.2) and *DF*, 1:389 (1.13). On Augustus's character, see *DF*, 1:96 (1.3); Augustus is at various points also characterized as artful (1:92 [1.3]), prudent (1:99 [1.3]), and crafty (1:87 [1.3]).

224. *A*, C:270.

225. For assessments of the significance of Gibbon's editing of this scene, compare the account given here to Rawson, "Musing on the Capitol"; Kennedy, "Sense of Place"; Spacks, *Imagining a Self*, 111–12; and Jordan, *Gibbon and His Roman Empire*, 17–23.

226. *A*, D:405–6.
227. Ibid., E:302.

CHAPTER 3

1. D'Alembert, *Discours préliminaire*, 61–62.
2. Ibid., 56. The original source is a footnote in Voltaire's *Le temple du goût* (1731). See Mankin, *Edward Gibbon* Essai, 197–98, for discussion. Rousseau also adapted the phrase in a reply to criticism of his *First Discourse* ("Observations," 48).
3. Pocock points out that Gibbon would have been well aware of the *philosophes'* contempt for *érudits* prior to reading the *Encyclopédie*; d'Alembert's opening discourse was "the last straw" (*Barbarism and Religion*, 1:153).
4. *A*, C:250; B:167.
5. Ibid., B:171.
6. Ibid., B:171–72, C:256, D:403 E:311. Womersley notes that Gibbon's clerical critics were particularly eager to locate *Essai* in order to trace the roots of his apostasy (*Watchmen*, 54n41).
7. *A*, D:403.
8. Ibid., C:256; at D:403 the seeds deserve "cultivation."
9. Ibid., B:169.
10. Ghosh's "Gibbon's First Thoughts" and Mankin's critical edition of the *Essai* are indispensable guides to Gibbon's revisions.
11. A similar analogy between war and literary polemic will pervade Gibbon's *Vindication* of the concluding chapters of the *Decline and Fall* against Davis's "Examination": "His title-page is a declaration of war," Gibbon writes, "and in the prosecution of his religious crusade, he assumes a privilege of disregarding the ordinary laws which are respected in the most hostile transactions between civilized men or civilized nations" (*Vindication* 231; see also 233–34, 267, 276).
12. *E*, 93 (I). Compare *DF*, 1:102 (1.3), where history is "little more than the register of the crimes, follies, and misfortunes of mankind."
13. *E*, 94 (II). Later in the *Essai* Gibbon will refer to geometry as "that imperious Queen, for whom it is not enough to reign: she must also banish her sisters, declaring all reasoning that does not make use of line and number unworthy of that name" (*E*, 120 [XLV]).
14. Ibid., 120 (XLV), 127–28 (LIV–LV).
15. Ibid., 127 (LIV).
16. Ibid., 108–9 (XXV, XXVII), 120 (XLV), 127 (LIV).
17. Ibid., 98 (VIII), 126 (LII).
18. "Geometry," Gibbon says, "deals with demonstrations that do not exist outside of itself, whereas criticism weighs different degrees of probability. Comparing these enables us to regulate our everyday actions and often to take fateful decisions" (*E*, 108 [XXVI]). Just before this passage Gibbon says of the "true critic" that "he never presents his conjectures as truths, his inductions as facts, his probabilities as demonstrations" (*E*, 108 [XXV]).
19. *E*, 107–8 (XXIII–XXIV).
20. Ibid., 108 (XXV).
21. Compare Gibbon's description of criticism in this passage to his later discussion of autobiography: "The confessions of St. Austin and Rousseau disclose the secrets of the human heart" (*A*, B:105).
22. *E*, 123 (XLVIII).
23. Ibid., 141 (LXXX).
24. Ibid., 142 (LXXX[I]).
25. The narrative of Roman history developed here will continue to be central to Gibbon's thought, as Ghosh, "Conception," 271; Ghosh, "Gibbon Observed," 142, 146; Trevor-Roper (in *History and the Enlightenment*, 6, the *Essai* is Gibbon's "historical *credo*"); Momigliano ("Gibbon's Contribution"); and Pocock, above all, have emphasized. (For a dissenting view, see Womersley, *Transformation*, especially 136–42.) In the third volume of *Barbarism and Religion*, Pocock restates the theory succinctly: "The *imperium* won by *libertas* is seen subverting the *virtus* on which the *libertas* depends" (3:203). Restated, "Liberty achieves empire, but is corrupted by it, and empire cannot be retained once it has destroyed the liberty that once conquered and no longer defends it" (3:419; see also 6:311–14, and "the familiar grand narrative," 6:432). We examine this theory as it appears in the *Decline and Fall* in chapter 5. After the publication of the *Decline and Fall*'s concluding volumes Gibbon returned to Herodotus and wrote in the margins of the account of Persian history in book 1: "In this doubtful history of the Medes we may trace the progress of civil society. They renounced their freedom to escape the evils of anarchy; their slavery was confirmed and

alleviated by the selfish arts, and specious virtues of their first King; but his son was a conqueror, and his great-grandson a tyrant" (*EE*, 367).

26. *E*, 128 (LV).

27. Trevor-Roper glosses "philosophical history" as "history related to and explained by the social institutions in which it is contained" (*History and the Enlightenment*, 6; see also "Historiography I," 98), which allows for some degree of variance across time. Womersley, by contrast, stresses uniformity: "The central tenet of the philosophic historian" holds "that mankind is everywhere and at all times the same" (*Transformation*, 146). Ghosh's analysis of a passage from one of Gibbon's early essays best captures the manner in which Gibbon's notion of philosophical history joins variation and constancy: "With regard only to human manners, the great sources of character passion, and situation may be combined, in such a variety of ways as no Algebra would reach. . . . Consult the annals of any nation, observe the various effects, of the modifications of those three principles, upon their history; and then say whether the operations of human nature, are easily classed or circumscribed" (*EE*, 50; "Gibbon's Timeless Verity," 136–37; compare Pocock, *Barbarism and Religion*, 2:23–24, 207–8, 4:7, 6:257–58; Bowersock, "Gibbon's Historical Imagination," 12–15, 26–27; and Momigliano's influential praise of Gibbon for forming a "new type of philosophical history" from philosophy and erudition in "Gibbon's Contribution," 50–51).

28. History and poetry were the ruling disciplines in the age of Augustus; Tacitus, "the only historian I know who satisfies my idea of the philosophical historian," straddled that age and the Age of the Antonines (*E*, 126 [LII]). Compare Pocock, *Barbarism and Religion*, 1:216.

29. *E*, 152–53 (62).

30. Ibid., 152 (60).

31. Ibid., 153 (63).

32. Ibid., 154 (65).

33. Ibid.

34. Ibid., 155 (66). Compare *DF*, 1:498–99 (1.15), and see our discussion in chapter 5.

35. *E*, 143 (LXXXII[I]).

36. Ibid.

37. Ibid., 155 (67). Pocock rightly notes how "orthodox" this sentiment is, compared to what would follow eventually in the *Decline and Fall* and immediately in the final draft of the *Essai* (*Barbarism and Religion*, 1:211–13). Edwards, however, notes the resonance between this passage and the opening of the *Decline and Fall's* fifteenth chapter, where a "pure and humble religion . . . finally erected the triumphant banner of the cross on the ruins of the Capitol" ("Gibbon and the City of Rome," 66–67; *DF*, 1:446 [1.15]).

38. *E*, 152 (60).

39. Womersley summarizes this theory in *Transformation*, 15, and discovers expressions of it in two sources contemporary to Gibbon: John Leland's *Reflections on the late Lord Bolingbroke's Letters on the Study and Use of History*, published in 1753, and a collection of Joseph White's sermons published in 1784. We might compare Augustine's argument in the *Confessions* that God's joy in a conversion correlates to the prior sinfulness of the convert (8.3–4).

40. *A*, C:251; B:169, D:402.

41. See especially Gibbon's entry for January 11, 1761: "In these seven or eight months of a most disagreeably active life, I have had no studies to set down, indeed, I hardly took a book in my hand the whole time. . . . The charm was over, I was sick of so hateful a service, tired of companions who had neither the knowledge of scholars nor the manners of gentlemen" (*J1*, 21–22). Gibbon also discusses his militia service in the *Memoirs*, most extensively in the second draft (*A*, B:177–90), where self-mockery and earnestness combine for singular effect. Gibbon proposes to "amuse [himself] with the recollection of a scene which bears no affinity to any other period of [his] studious and social life"; in the course of the recollection, he compares himself to Major Sturgeon of Samuel Foote's farce, "The Mayor of Garratt" (*A*, B:177, 184). And yet he acknowledges his debt to the militia for "making [him] an Englishman and a soldier" (*A*, B:190). The two tones, silly and serious, combine in the section's concluding sentence, which Gibbon would use in subsequent drafts as well: "The Captain of the Hampshire grenadiers (the reader may smile) has not been useless to the historian of the Roman Empire" (*A*, B:190, C:258, D:401–2).

42. *A*, C:249. Smith, "Gibbon in Church," 454–58.

43. Ibid.

44. See Womersley, *Watchmen*, 77–82, and Turnbull, "Marionette Infidèle," 298–303, for background on this exchange.

45. *L*, 1:328–29.

46. Ibid., 1:338.

47. *MW 1814*, 2:86.

48. Ibid., 2:94–95.

49. *A*, C:249–50. On this episode, see especially Giarrizzo, *Edward Gibbon*, 42–49.

50. Ibid., C:249.

51. Ibid., C:249.

52. Ghosh notes the significance of this "final reduction of [Gibbon's] religious views to fixity, and the end of the pilgrimage begun in 1753" ("Gibbon's First Thoughts," 153). Craddock, *Young Edward Gibbon*, 169, argues nevertheless that Gibbon "had not yet become a complete skeptic, much less a convinced atheist," on the basis of Gibbon's reactions to a sermon in Paris, in 1763.

53. *A*, C:255.

54. *J1*, 24–25.

55. Ibid., 28; compare *A*, C:255.

56. Religion—the "system of paganism"—is the focus of "the chapters from 57–78" of the *Essai* (*J1*, 25). Earlier Gibbon recorded how this section was composed: "Recollecting some thoughts I had formerly had in relation to the System of Paganism, which I intended to make use of in my Essai, I resolved to ready Tully de Nature Deorum, and finished it in about a month" (*J1*, 22).

57. *E*, 128 (LVI); compare Gibbon's comments on Dangeau's system at *E*, 123 (XLVIII).

58. Ibid., 128 (LVI[I]).

59. *DF*, 59–61 (1.2).

60. *E*, 128–29 (LVI[I]).

61. Recall how Gibbon deployed Crousaz's *Logic* against the doctrine of transubstantiation during his reconversion to Protestantism (*A*, B:136–37), discussed in chapter 2.

62. *E*, 130–31 (LX[I]).

63. Ibid., 132 (LXII[I]).

64. Ibid., 133 (LXV).

65. Ibid., 134 (LXV[I]).

66. Ibid.

67. Mankin notes that this section of Gibbon's *Essai* resembles, but does not simply copy, Hume's *Natural History of Religion*: "[Gibbon's] account mixes Hume's naturalistic, historical and degrading view of man with a more abstract position derived, I suggest, from basic elements of Lockean philosophy" (*E*, 71).

68. There is no definitive evidence that Gibbon had read Rousseau's *Discourses* at this point, though Gibbon was so engaged with French intellectual culture at the time of the publication of the "Second Discourse" in 1755 that it is hard to imagine him being unfamiliar with its arguments (*E*, 179). Despite several points of similarity in content and style (as Mankin repeatedly notes at *E*, 72, 208, 244, 314, 316), Gibbon's *Essai* does not cite the "Second Discourse," a practice he would follow in the *Decline and Fall* (see especially Goguet's replacement of Rousseau in Gibbon's "General Observations" [*DF*, 2:515]). The *Emile*, by contrast, appears relatively frequently and often quite favorably in Gibbon's work (*DF*, 1:1026n9 [2.26], 2:922n96 [4.46], 2:939n16 [4.47]; *EE*, 367; *A*, F:44; and compare *A*, B:105). It is difficult to suppress the suspicion that Gibbon's relative neglect of Rousseau stemmed from personal antipathy. The two thinkers differed in their judgments of the English (*DF*, 1:1026n9 [2.26]; *L*, 1:212) and the Swiss (*J3*, 209; *L*, 2:328), and Gibbon's broken engagement with Suzanne Churchod brought them into a distant, tense contact with one another when Rousseau was asked to intervene (*L*, 1:149; *J3*, 299–301; Craddock, *Young Edward Gibbon*, 173). By the time Gibbon composed his *Memoirs*, however, Rousseau's harsh judgment of the *Essai* and its author (*"M. G— n'est point mon homme . . . est un homme à mépriser"*), which the fifth draft of the *Memoirs* would have published, seems the deepest wound. "As an author," Gibbon replied, "I shall not appeal from the judgment, or taste, or caprice of *Jean Jacques*; but that extraordinary man, whom I admire and pity, should have been less precipitate in condemning the moral character and conduct of a stranger" (*A*, E:298n13).

69. *E*, 134–35 (LXV[I]–LXVI[I]); compare *DF*, 1:245 (1.9). Rousseau's natural man, by contrast, satiates himself (presumably with acorns) and sleeps under an oak, but does not spend any time admiring it ("Second Discourse," 134 (1.2); compare "Second Discourse," 161 (2.3) where the height of trees prevents man from reaching their fruits and inspires him to learn to climb).

70. *E*, 134–35 (LXVII[I]).

71. Ibid., 138 (LXXIV).

72. Ibid., 140 (LXXVI[I]). The gods assumed human form long after majestic oak trees made man feel contempt for himself (ibid., 134–35 (LXV[I]–LXVI[I]).

73. Ibid., 140 (LXXVII[I]).

74. As Womersley, *Transformation*, 9–19, Pocock, *Barbarism and Religion*, 1:85–93, and many others have noted, the young Gibbon's debts to Montesquieu were not limited to style. By the time Gibbon wrote the *Decline and Fall*'s first volume, however, his admiration for Montesquieu's style (as in *DF*, 1:202n33 [1.7]) had already outlived his estimation of Montesquieu as a historian (see, for instance, *DF*, 1:210 [1.7], 243n54 [1.9], and 262n37 [1.10], where Gibbon notes the "uncommon precision" of a passage in the *Considérations*). The concluding words of the *Decline and Fall*'s sixty-sixth chapter characterize Gibbon's growth: "Nor may the artist hope to equal or surpass, till he has learned to imitate, the works of his predecessors" (*DF*, 3:909 [6.66]).

75. And we might think toward becoming "Gods [man] would blush to resemble" (*E*, 134 (LXV[I]). But note how different the rhetoric of this section's conclusion is from its introduction. Does man "blush to resemble" gods who "live in temples, enjoy human distractions, take part in the hunt or the dance, and sometimes even be charmed by a mortal beauty, [giving] birth to a race of Heroes" (*E*, 140 [LXXVII[I]])?

76. Compare *DF*, 1:447 (1.15).

77. Gibbon would return to the theology of the incarnation in a magisterial survey, stretching from Christ's birth to the seventeenth century, that concludes the *Decline and Fall*'s forty-seventh chapter (2:932–1002 [4.47]).

78. *E*, 131 (LX[I]).

79. Ibid., 134 (LXVI[I]).

80. Ibid., 155 (66).

81. *DF*, 1:498–99 (1.15).

CHAPTER 4

1. *DF*, 1:31 (1.1).

2. On the occasion of the Roman consuls ceasing to lend their names to years, Gibbon expresses his own preference for counting years from the creation of the world over "our double and perplexed method of counting backwards and forwards the years before and after the Christian aera" (*DF*, 2:617n160 [4.40]).

3. *DF*, 1:31 (1.1).

4. Christianity marking time: *DF*, 1:33 (1.1), 1:53n83 (1.1), 1:214 (1.8), 1:221n31 (1.8), 1:257 (1.10); space: *DF*, 1:51 (1.1); linked to a source: *DF*, 1:283n135 (1.10), 1:286n150 (1.10).

5. *DF*, 1:427 (1.14); 1:735–42 (2.20). See also Pocock, *Barbarism and Religion*, 3:495, 6:73–74.

6. Scholars divide sharply over what to make of Gibbon's delayed treatment of Christianity in the *Decline and Fall*'s first volume. Womersley understands Gibbon to have kept the "real villain of the fall of the Roman Empire" off stage until chapters 15–16; the delay demonstrated that Rome's decline could not be explained without Christianity (see especially Womersley, *Transformation*, 17, 102, 209; compare Bremmer, *Rise of Christianity*, 6). Pocock provides the counterpoint: "The first fourteen chapters of the *Decline and Fall* narrated the decline of the Antonine monarchy . . . as the effect of causes among which Christianity had yet to appear." Pocock continues, "If [Gibbon] had thought the church the principal cause of the empire's fall, he would have given it a higher priority than he does" (*Barbarism and Religion*, 6:43; for restatements and variations of the case, see *Barbarism and Religion*, 3:497–98, 6:36, 493). My own reading follows Womersley in viewing chapters 1–14 as in a sense preparatory for chapters 15–16, and Pocock in considering the "basic narrative" (the secular theory, discussed in chapter 3, according to which empire itself erodes virtue) sufficient to account for the decline Gibbon traces before introducing Christianity. I do not, for instance, think Gibbon understood Diocletian (the protagonist of the chapters immediately preceding 15–16) to be the "restorer" of the Empire Augustus established, with its hypocritical but not meaningless homage to the Republic; Diocletian was instead a founder of a new, more despotic, and ultimately weaker empire (*Transformation*, 132; *DF*, 1:359, 387–92 [1.13]). We consider the important question of whether Gibbon understood Christianity as a cause of imperial decline at greater length in the concluding chapter.

7. *DF*, 1:245 (1.9). Following Gibbon, we refer to the empire established by Artaxerxes (or Ardshir I) as "Persia," while "Parthia" shall be

reserved for the eastern empire that Tacitus described and Artaxerxes subverted (*DF*, 1:214 [1.8]).

8. Druid priests: *DF*, 1:60 (1.2); Elegabalus's cult: *DF*, 1:166 (1.6); Odin: *DF*, 1:256 (1.10).

9. *A*, B:137.

10. See our discussion of these developments in chapter 3.

11. Richard Porson's quip that Gibbon hated Christianity "so cordially, that he might seem to revenge some personal injury" represents a more common way of relating the *Decline and Fall* to the author's own religious history (*Letters*, xxix). Compare Turnbull, "Marionette Infidèle," 286; Womersley, "Gibbon's Apostasy," 67; and Jacob Bernays's claim that Gibbon's concern with Christian theology "can only be ascribed to an interest that had cooled down after a period of heat; it could not possibly be the mark of a radical indifference" (as quoted in Young, "Gibbon and Catholicism," 147).

12. Compare Gibbon's analysis of the "system of paganism" fifteen years before the first volume of the *Decline and Fall* (*E*, 128–43 [LVI–LXXXII[I]]); see our analysis of this passage in chapter 3.

13. *DF*, 1:56 (1.2).

14. Ibid., 1:230 (1.9), 1:237 (1.9), 1:329 (1.12). For scholarly assessments of Gibbon's considerable debts to Tacitus, see especially Cartledge, "'Tacitism' of Edward Gibbon"; Bowersock, "Gibbon on Civil War"; Ghosh, "Gibbon's Dark Ages," 5; Womersley, *Transformation*, 80–88; Pocock, *Barbarism and Religion*, 1:232–34, 287, 3:11–14, 17–31. I consider several of Gibbon's departures from Tacitus below.

15. *DF*, 15.486n114 (1.15). On Gibbon's view of the constancy of human passions, see Ghosh's "Gibbon's Timeless Verity" and Cartledge's "Enlightened Historiography," 80n66; contrast Womersley's claim that Gibbon moves toward historicism as the *Decline and Fall* progresses (*Transformation*, 1–5, 44–45, 232–33; compare Womersley, "Historical Writings," 505–6). On Gibbon's adaptation of Hume's distinction between enthusiasm and superstition, see especially Pocock, "Superstition and Enthusiasm," and Pocock, "Enthusiasm."

16. *DF*, 1:372 (1.13), 1:451 (1.15), 1:459 (1.15).

17. Ibid., 1:447 (1.15).

18. Ibid., 1:23 (1.11); compare 1:245 (1.9).

19. Ibid., 1:46n66 (1.1), 1:136–37 (1.5), 1:204 (1.7), 1:211 (1.7).

20. Ibid., 1:39 (1.1), 1:85 (1.3), 1:155n22 (1.6).

21. Ibid., 1:36 (1.1), 1:59 (1.2), 1:135 (1.5), 1:203 (1.7).

22. *E*, 134–35 (LXV[I]–LXVI[I]). See our discussion above in chapter 3.

23. *DF*, 1:57 (1.2), 1:499 (1.15).

24. Ibid., 1:218 (1.8).

25. Ibid., 1:486n114 (1.15), 1:218 (1.8).

26. Ibid., 1:193 (1.7). On facts and theories in "philosophical history," see our discussion of the *Essai*'s "system of paganism" in chapter 3. One might compare the relationship between historical narrative and theory in Gibbon's history to that of dramatic action and philosophical argument in Plato's dialogues.

27. Ibid., 1:57 (1.2).

28. Ibid.

29. After appearing as a cause of theological change, "flattery" quickly assumes a prominent role in Gibbon's (following Tacitus's) account of the imperial regime. See, e.g., *DF*, 1:85, 90, 94, etc. (1.3).

30. *DF*, 1:89 (1.3), 1:93 (1.3).

31. Ibid., 1:58 (1.2).

32. Ibid.

33. Ibid.

34. Ibid., 1:58–59 (1.2).

35. Ibid., 1:59 (1.2).

36. Ibid.

37. Ibid. This passage reflects Gibbon's understanding of the Roman elites' theory of religious difference: these differences had to do not with the ends of religious belief, which were everywhere the same, but with variations in the matter, such as the climate and character of the believers.

38. *DF*, 1:56 (1.2).

39. Ibid., 1:59 (1.2).

40. Ibid., 1:56 (1.2). Compare Gibbon's comment on Trajan's martial ambition: "As long as mankind shall continue to bestow more liberal applause on their destroyers than on their benefactors, the thirst of military glory will ever be the vice of the most exalted characters" (*DF*, 1:35 [1.1]).

41. *DF*, 1:57n3 (1.2). The parallel Gibbon draws in this note between Bossuet and Hume—"the best commentary [on the true genius of polytheism] may be found in Mr. Hume's Natural History of Religion; and the best contrast in

Bossuet's Universal History"—might be read in light of Gibbon's own conversion narrative, described in chapter 2. Recall that Gibbon attributed his conversion to Catholicism in large part to Bossuet, a "master of all the weapons of controversy" (*A*, F:86). Recall, too, Gibbon's practice in the *Memoirs*, discussed in chapter 1 above, of pairing believers and skeptics for rhetorical effect: de Thou and Hume, Bayle and Chillingworth, etc.

42. Juvenal, *Satires*, 490–91 (15.35–38). Compare Gibbon's first reactions to this passage on September 16–17, 1763, in *J3* and *MW 1814*, 5:306–9.

43. *DF*, 1:59 (1.2).

44. Ibid., 1:60 (1.2); compare 1:33 (1.1), 1:465n56 (1.15), 2:504 (3.38). As Craddock has noted (*Young Edward Gibbon*, 92), Gibbon remarked on the resemblance of Druid and Catholic priests as early as 1756. Among his notes to Caesar's *Gallic Wars* from that year, Gibbon says the two sets of priests resembled one another *si parfaitement* that he would suspect the Catholics to have modeled themselves on the Druids if that were historically tenable. "We must be content to say," Gibbon continues, "that the clergy of all ages and the people of all ages resemble one another" (*MW 1814*, 4:413–14). See also Gibbon's "Index Expurgatorius" from the late 1760s (*EE*, 126–27), and Womersley's remarks on *DF*, 1:456n56 (1.15) in his "Introduction to *The History of the Decline and Fall*," xv–xvi.

45. *Divus Claudius* in Suetonius, *Lives*, 2:50–51 (5.25.4). Pliny the Elder, *Natural History*, 8:286–87 (30.1).

46. *DF*, 1:57n3 (1.2); compare 1:516n1 (1.16). The passage Gibbon cites in Suetonius also helps us to link the case of the Druids to those of the Jews and Christians. While discussing Claudius's religious policy just prior to the passage quoted above, Suetonius comments: "Since the Jews constantly made disturbances at the instigation of Chrestus, he expelled them from Rome" (*Divus Claudius* in Suetonius, *Lives*, 2:50–51 [5.25.4]).

47. *DF*, 1:59 (1.2).

48. Ibid., 1:60 (1.2).

49. Ibid., 1:60 (1.2). The Temple of Serapis in Alexandria will later feature in Caracalla's massacres (1:155n21, 158 [1.6]) and in a stunning set piece in Gibbon's chapter on the "ruin of paganism" (2:71, 81–85).

50. Ibid., 1:60–61 (1.2).

51. In the concluding chapter of the first volume of the *Decline and Fall*, Gibbon links the Roman magistrates' polished manners and their aversion to religious persecution. The "magistrates who exercised in the provinces the authority of the emperor, or of the senate, and to whom the jurisdiction of life and death was entrusted," Gibbon writes, "behaved like men of polished manners and liberal educations. . . . They frequently declined the odious task of persecution, dismissed the charge with contempt, or suggested to the accused Christian some legal evasion, by which he might elude the severity of the law" (*DF*, 1:539 [1.16]).

52. On the blurry line between mass and elite, see *DF*, 1:85–86 (1.3), 498 (1.15), 501 (1.15); see also *E*, 154–55 (65–67).

53. *DF*, 1:213 (1.8). Compare *DF*, 1:218 (1.8), where Gibbon speaks of "*every* mode of religion" (our emphasis).

54. *E*, 128 (LV). On digressions from narrative as revelations of authorial intent, see Nichols, *Thucydides*, 21, 180.

55. For the dating of Tacitus's death, see Syme, *Tacitus*, 473.

56. Gibbon's invocation of Tacitus refers specifically to Tacitus, *Annals*, 4:220–21 (6.38): "I have conjoined the events of two summers, in order to allow the mind some respite from domestic horrors (*domesticis malis*)." The preceding section includes several fleeting invocations of national differences (e.g., "among barbarians [being a eunuch] brings with it not contempt but actual power," Tacitus, *Annals*, 4:208–9 [6.31]) and a brief glance at the customs of Iberia and Albania (Tacitus, *Annals*, 4:212–13 [6.34]), but Tacitus is otherwise occupied with narrative of a military campaign. Closer analogues for the sort of ethnographical digressions Gibbon launches in chapter 8 can be found in Herodotus or in the sixth book of Polybius's *History*.

57. Apart from passing characterizations of entire peoples (e.g., "Germans delight in war" (Tacitus, *Histories*, 3:30–31 [4.16] and others discussed above) important exceptions in Tacitus's historical works include the discussion of Vespasian's inquiry into Serapis (Tacitus, *Histories*, 3:158–67 [4.81–84]) and the extensive discussion of the Jews in the fifth book of the *Histories*.

58. The words Tacitus puts into the mouth of the Batavian leader, Civilis, are representative: "Let Syria, Asia, and the East, which is accustomed to kings, play the slave; there are many still alive in Gaul who were born before tribute was known" (*Histories*, 3:32–33 [4.17]; compare Tacitus, *Annals*, 3:248–49 [1.3], 4:226–29 [6.42]). The stretch on Parthia that Tacitus offers up to relieve the reader's mind from "domestic horrors" describes the tyranny of Artabanus, several cases of bribery and double-dealing, including a poisoning under the pretense of friendship, and various other forms of deceit (Tacitus, *Annals*, 4:206–21, 6.31–37). The Eastern courts, in short, bear little resemblance to the German banquets, where "people are without craft or cunning, and expose in the freedom of the occasion the heart's previous secrets" (Tacitus, *Germania*, 1:164–67 [22.4]). Pocock, *Barbarism and Religion*, 3:465–66, 4:19–23, remarks on the distinction between northern and eastern "barbarians"; see also Woudhuysen, "Gibbon among the Barbarians," 94–95.

59. "State" is to be read here, though not everywhere (e.g., "whole force of the state" at *DF*, 1:35 [1.1]) as "status."

60. *DF*, 1:251 (1.9).

61. Ibid., 1:213 (1.8).

62. Ibid., 1:213 (1.8).

63. See our discussion of this fundamental historical cycle in chapter 3, especially note 25.

64. *DF*, 1:214 (1.9).

65. See, for instance, *DF*, 1:33 (1.1), 1:89n10 (1.3).

66. Tacitus, *Histories*, 2:8–9 (1.4).

67. *DF*, 1:215 (1.8), emphasis added.

68. Syme, *Tacitus*, 466–70. Tacitus makes a passing allusion to the Magi in *Annals*, 5:252–53 (15.24) and notices the Jewish priests' political power (*Histories*, 3:188–89 [5.8], 3:198–99 [5.13]).

69. *DF*, 1:59 (1.2).

70. Ibid., 1:215 (1.8).

71. Ibid. See also Pocock, *Barbarism and Religion*, 4:32–36.

72. *DF*, 1:57–59 (1.2), 1:215 (1.8).

73. Ibid., 1:59 (1.2), 1:215 (1.8), 1:221–22 (1.8). The Arsacides "practised the worship of the Magi," Gibbon says with a deviously ambivalent genitive.

74. *DF*, 1:59 (1.2).

75. Ibid., 1:215 (1.8). Womersley, *Watchmen*, 18–19, notes that for the second edition of the *Decline and Fall* Gibbon revised his depiction of Persian priestcraft so that it was less reminiscent of freethinkers' critiques of Christian priests.

76. Ibid., 1:216, 220 (1.8).

77. Ibid., 1:220–21 (1.8). Note that eighty thousand is an "inconsiderable number" of schismatics, but an "extremely numerous" body of priests (1:216, 219, 221 [1.8]).

78. Ibid., 1:56, 59 (1.2).

79. Ibid., 1:59 (1.2).

80. Ibid., 1:220 (1.8).

81. Ibid., 1:220n24 (1.8).

82. Ibid., 1:580 (1.16).

83. Ibid., 1:221 (1.8).

84. Later the heirs of Artaxerxes will reenact the Jews and Christians' resistance to Roman religious policy (*DF*, 1:284 [1.10]).

85. *DF*, 1:218 (1.8).

86. Ibid., see also 1:117 (1.4).

87. Ibid., 1:218 (1.8).

88. Ibid., 1:219 (1.8): "Their [the Magi's] forces were multiplied by discipline."

89. Civilis encourages the Gauls to join his revolt, for instance, by reminding them that they are not divided "and we have gained besides all the strength that *disciplina* the Roman camps can give" (Tacitus, *Histories*, 3:32–33 [4.17]; compare Tacitus, *Annals*, 3:588–89 [3.42]). On one occasion Tacitus has Claudius refer to divination as the *vetustissima disciplina* (Tacitus, *Annals*, 4:270–71 [11.15]).

90. *DF*, 1:40 (1.1).

91. Ibid., 1:125 (1.4), 1:145 (1.5), 1:206–7 (1.7).

92. Ibid., 1:212 (1.7).

93. Tacitus, *Histories*, 2:10–11 (1.5).

94. *DF*, 1:220 (1.8).

95. Compare Cartledge, "'Tacitism' of Edward Gibbon," 261–62, and see the sources cited above in note 14.

96. *DF*, 1:230 (1.9).

97. Ibid.

98. Ibid., 1:234 (1.9). Compare Mallet's account of Rudbeck in *Northern Antiquities*, 1:42–43: "As this author joined to the most extensive learning an imagination eminently fruitful, he wanted none of the materials for erecting plausible and frivolous systems."

99. *DF*, 1:33n8 (1.1), 1:233n13, 247n71 (1.9), 1:342n46 (1.12), 1:366n28 (1.13), 1:403n10 (1.14).

100. Gibbon could read the *Germania* in this way. In discussing Tacitus on the mores of German women, for instance, Gibbon says that "We may easily discover that Tacitus indulges an honest pleasure in the contrast of barbarian virtue with the dissolute conduct of the Roman ladies." Gibbon's explanation of German chastity serves to demote it from a virtue to a necessity (*DF*, 1:244 [1.9]).
101. Tacitus, *Germania*, 1:166–69 (23–24), 170–71 (27.1), 208–11 (45.4–8).
102. Ibid., 1:140–41 (7.1–2), 152–53 (14.1), 160–63 (20.2), 168–69 (25).
103. Ibid., 1:168–71 (26.1–2).
104. Ibid., 1:160–61 (19.3).
105. Ibid., 1:188–89 (37.3).
106. *DF*, 1:151–52 (1.6). Note that this is all premised on the dubious but "pleasing supposition that that Fingal lived, and that Ossian sung" (1:152 [1.6]; see also *L*, 2:90–91).
107. See, for instance, Tacitus's digression on ancient and modern mores in the *Histories*, 2:222–23 (2.38); compare 3:124–25 (4.64), the preface to Tacitus, *Annals*, 3:242–51 (1.1–4), and the retrospective occasioned by Augustus's *Lex Papia Poppaea*, 3:562–69 (3.25–28).
108. *DF*, 1:212 (1.7).
109. See chapter 3, especially note 25.
110. Womersley, *Transformation*, 84–88.
111. *DF*, 1:233 (1.9).
112. Ibid., 1:244n59 (1.9). See chapter 2 above, note 16. Compare Pocock, *Barbarism and Religion*, 4:79, 87–88.
113. *DF*, 1:241n45 (1.9); see also 1:244n60, 250n79 (1.9). The correction of Tacitus belongs to Grotius, whom Gibbon generally admired while considering him perhaps too mild in his pieties and support of established powers (1:731 [2.20]; compare *A*, C:249 and *DF*, 1:580 [1.16]).
114. *DF*, 1:248n74 (1.9).
115. Ibid., 1:235 (1.9). Cartledge, "'Tacitism' of Edward Gibbon," 261–62.
116. On German virtue, see, for instance, Tactitus, *Germania*, 1:140–41 (7.1), 152–53 (14.1); on German simplicity, Tactitus, *Germania*, 144–45 (10.1), 166–67 (23.1). See also Pocock, *Barbarism and Religion*, 3:262–64.
117. Tacitus, *Germania*, 1:164–67 (22); Herodotus, *Histories*, 96 (1.133).
118. *DF*, 1:234–35 (1.9).
119. Ibid., 1:235 (1.9). Compare Tacitus, *Germania*, 1:214–15 (46.6).
120. *DF*, 1:237 (1.9).
121. Gibbon first uses the term "industry" in the survey of the Empire's economy in his second chapter: "The coasts of Italy are, in general, destitute of safe harbors; but human industry had corrected the deficiencies of nature" (*DF*, 1:78 (1.2); compare *DF*, 260 (1.10) where "the liberality of Nature . . . tempted the industry of man"). From that point forward "industry" suggests cleverness combined with hard work (as, for instance, at *DF*, 1:139 [1.5]); it is a virtue discouraged by excessive taxation (*DF*, 1:173 [1.6], 219 [1.8]) and oppressive government (*DF*, 1:212 [1.7], 260 [1.10]). Though present in the ancient world, as these examples attest, industry as a source of wealth Gibbon considers more characteristic of modernity (*DF*, 1:372–73 [1.13]; compare *DF*, 446, 452 [1.15]). On the Germans as preagricultural—"a people whose swords are not yet beaten into ploughshares"—see Pocock, *Barbarism and Religion*, 4:80.
122. See *DF*, 1:237 (1.9), where Gibbon links money and letters: "The value of money has been settled by general consent to express our wants and our property, as letters were invented to express our ideas; and both these institutions, by giving a more active energy to the powers and passions of human nature, have contributed to multiply the objects they were designed to represent."
123. *DF*, 1:245 (1.9).
124. Tacitus, *Germania*, 144–45 (9.3).
125. *DF*, 1:245 (1.9), compare 1:57 (1.2).
126. Tacitus, *Germania*, 148–49 (11.3–6). The priests' ability to impose capital punishment whenever god wills suggests greater autonomy from civil magistrates (140–41 [7.2]).
127. *DF*, 1:245 (1.9).
128. Ibid.
129. Pocock, *Barbarism and Religion*, 4:82.
130. Ibid. Compare Gibbon's description of his conversion in the last draft of his *Memoirs*: "The blind activity of idleness urged me to advance without armour into the dangerous mazes of controversy, and at the age of sixteen I bewildered myself in the errors of the Church of Rome" (*A*, F:84).
131. Tacitus, *Germania*, 1:136–37 (4.2), 170–71 (27.3), 182–83 (33.2). Gibbon's comment at *DF*, 1:250 (1.9).
132. Tacitus, *Annals*, 3:300–301 (1.33).
133. Tacitus, *Germania*, 1:188–93 (37.2–6).

134. Tacitus, *Annals*, 3:342–49 (1.59–62), 3:384–87 (2.2).
135. On number, see *DF*, 1:222 (1.8), 1:239 (1.9); on discipline, *DF*, 1:228–29 (1.8), 1:246–47 (1.9).
136. *DF*, 1:228 (1.8).
137. Ibid., 1:248 (1.9).
138. Ibid., 1:226–27 (1.8), 1:248–49 (1.9).
139. Womersley, *Transformation*, 80–81.
140. *DF*, 1:213 (1.8).
141. For Gibbon feigning surprise, see *A*, E:311, 316–19. For his anticipation of controversy, see *Vindication*, 232; *L*, 2:100; *A*, E:311–13n30. Womersley discusses these and other passages; he also analyzes Gibbon's revisions to the first edition: "In anticipation of the attack about to be launched against him, [Gibbon] minimizes the target he presents to the spokesmen for outraged religious orthodoxy" ("Introduction to *Religious Scepticism*," xv).
142. *DF*, 1:513 (1.15).
143. Ibid., 1:580 (1.16); see also 1:524 (1.15).
144. Ibid., 1:56 (1.2).
145. Ibid., 1:498–99 (1.15). See our discussion at the end of chapter 3 of *E*, 155 (66). Turnbull, "Gibbon's Exchange," 140, 149–51, and Pocock, "Superstition and Enthusiasm," 93, link Gibbon's depictions of the Roman and the English religious establishments.
146. *DF*, 1:510 (1.15); in the following chapter, Gibbon notes "the careless indifference which the most copious and the most minute of the Pagan writers have shewn to the affairs of the Christians" (1:524–25 [1.16]). On the analogy between the early Christians and a republic, see especially Womersley's observation that "amongst the more devout Christians the dignified aspects of the Roman republic enjoy an afterlife" (*Watchmen*, 134). Pocock notes that Gibbon seems intentionally to delay his account of the bishops' accruing authority for themselves "apparently in order to use the image of the republic to emphasize that new forms of freedom as well as power were arising over which the emperor had little control" (*Barbarism and Religion*, 6:76; see also 2:94–95, where Pocock notes a Voltairean antecedent for Gibbon's analogy).
147. *DF*, 1:510 (1.15).
148. Polybius, *Histories*, 1:2–5 (1.1.5), 3:292–93 (6.2.3).
149. *DF*, 1:446–47 (1.15). In the following chapter the Christian Pontiffs extend "their spiritual jurisdiction from the coast of the Baltic to the shores of the Pacific Ocean" (1:528 [1.16]).
150. Ibid., 1:447 (1.15).
151. For Gibbon's use of "republic" to describe pre-imperial Rome and the old Greek regimes, see, for instance, *DF*, 1:31 (1.1), 1:52 (1.1), 1:441 (1.14). For the restoration of the "republic" under Augustus, *DF*, 1:87–93 (1.3); for the imperial regime as "republic," 1:184 (1.6), 1:207 (1.7); for Augustus's government by names, *DF*, 1:96 (1.3).
152. *DF*, 1:497 (1.15).
153. Ibid., 1:55 (1.1), 1:500 (1.15).
154. See above, chapter 3, note 25.
155. *DF*, 1:38–39 (1.1). Note that by referring to "the ancients" (not only the Romans), Gibbon extends his analysis of patriotism to include the Greek republics.
156. Ibid., 1:39–40 (1.1).
157. Ibid. Gibbon's deflationary account of the Empire's persecution of Christians in the sixteenth chapter similarly begins from the obstinate Jews, who were largely tolerated and granted "free exercise of their unsocial religion" (1:515–17 [1.16]).
158. Ibid., 1:447–48 (1.15).
159. Ibid., 1:448 (1.15). Compare Montesquieu, *Spirit of the Laws*, 42–43 (1.5.2)
160. Gibbon presents the zeal of the Jews in striking terms: "Under the pressure of every calamity, the belief of those miracles has preserved the Jews of a later period from the universal contagion of idolatry; and in contradiction to every known principle of the human mind, that singular people seems to have yielded a stronger and more ready assent to the traditions of their remote ancestors, than to the evidence of their own senses" (*DF*, 1:449 [1.15]). In light of the passage from Montesquieu cited above, we should read "every known principle of the human mind" to refer to the principles known to Gibbon's ancient guides, not to the moderns. See Manent's analysis of this passage from Montesquieu (*Metamorphoses*, 74–76), and compare Hobbes, *Leviathan*, 70 (1.12.21). Gibbon's abuse of the Jews was noted by contemporaries such as John Whitaker, who speculated that Gibbon's "mean and vulgar spite" stemmed from personal encounters with "the usurious part of the modern Israelites" having worked him into "a frenzy of illiterate fanaticism against the whole race" (*Gibbon's History*, 240). See, more recently, Lerner's "Gibbon's 'Jewish

Problem'" and Aston, "'Disorderly Squadron,'" 271–72.

161. *DF*, 1:449 (1.15).

162. Ibid., 1:450 (1.15).

163. Ibid., 1:61 (1.2), 1:451 (1.15), 1:459 (1.15).

164. Ibid., 1:61 (1.2), 1:65 (1.2).

165. Ibid., 1:462 (1.15).

166. Ibid., 1:39 (1.1), 497 (1.15). Odin, "the Mahomet of the North," like the Christians demonstrates "invincible valor" (1:256 [1.10]). Prior to the fifteenth chapter, Gibbon regularly uses "obstinate" to characterize military forces, particularly when they are besieged (e.g., *DF*, 1:203 [1.7]). As the *Decline and Fall*'s first volume concludes, Maximin's praetorian prefect is forced to acknowledge the "invincible obstinacy" of the Christians (1:575 [1.16]).

167. See, for instance, *DF*, 1:38–39, 70, 78, 82 (1.1–2).

168. *DF*, 1:466–67 (1.15).

169. Ibid., 1:474–75 (1.15).

170. Ibid., 1:477–78 (1.15). Compare 1:104 (1.3).

171. It is important to stress, in light of Womersley's argument that Gibbon progressed in historicism and a willingness to express the incomprehensibility of the past as the *Decline and Fall* proceeded (for sources, see note 15 above), and that Gibbon was already in the first volume calling his readers' attention to areas where he expected their imagination, formed in their own times, to fall short. In addition to the passages cited here, consider Gibbon's description of the German bards: "We cannot so easily express, or even conceive, the enthusiasm of arms and glory which they kindled in the breast of their audience. Among a polished people, a taste for poetry is rather an amusement of the fancy, than a passion of the soul. And yet, when in calm retirement we peruse the combats described by Homer or Tasso, we are insensibly seduced by the fiction, and feel a momentary glow of martial ardor. But how faint, how cold is the sensation which a peaceful mind can receive from solitary study! It was in the hour of battle, or in the feast of victory, that the bards celebrated the glory of the heroes of ancient days, the ancestors of those warlike chieftains, who listened with transport to their artless but animated strains" (*DF*, 1:247 [1.9]; compare 1:539 [1.16] and 1:546 [1.16], where Gibbon notes that "the sober discretion of the present age will more readily censure than admire, but can more easily admire than imitate, the fervor of the first Christians").

172. *DF*, 1:468–71 (1.15). When Gibbon speaks of "liquefying in fiercer fires," he quotes Tertullian, *De Spectaculis*, 298–99.

173. *DF*, 1:473 (1.15).

174. Ibid., 1:475 (1.15). Compare Gibbon's comments on "the deities of a thousand groves and a thousand streams" in his discussion of Roman polytheism (1:57 [1.2]).

175. Ibid., 1:471–72 (1.15).

176. Ibid., 1:479 (1.15).

177. Ibid., 1:476–77 (1.15). See also 1:483 (1.15).

178. Ibid., 1:38–39 (1.1).

179. Ibid., 1:478 (1.15).

180. Ibid., 1:478 (1.15).

181. See especially *DF*, 1:481–82 (1.15). "This indolent, or even criminal disregard to the public welfare," Gibbon writes, "exposed [the Christians] to the contempt and reproaches of the Pagans who very frequently asked, what must be the fate of the empire, attacked on every side by the barbarians, if all mankind should adopt the pusillanimous sentiments of the new sect" (1:482 [1.15]; compare 1:562 [1.16]).

182. *DF*, 1:447 (1.15).

183. Ibid., 1:497 (1.15).

184. Ibid., 1:496 (1.15). In the following chapter, Gibbon summarizes the advice of Maximin's ministers: "The Christians had been indebted for their victories to their regular discipline . . . the weakness of polytheism had principally flowed from a want of union and subordination among the ministers of religion" (1:575 [1.16]).

185. *DF*, 1:41 (1.15), 1:250 (1.9).

186. Ibid., 1:127 (1.5).

187. Ibid.

188. Ibid., 1:39 (1.1).

189. Ibid., 1:483 (1.15); compare 1:563 (1.16).

190. Gibbon comments on the incentives controlled by the Christian clergy: "They were destitute of any temporal force, and they were for a long time discouraged and oppressed, rather than assisted, by the civil magistrate; but they had acquired, and they employed within their own society, the two most efficacious instruments of government, rewards and punishments; the former derived from the pious liberality, the latter from the devout apprehensions, of the faithful" (*DF*, 1:490 [1.15]).

191. *DF*, 1:38 (1.1), 1:493 (1.15), emphasis added.

192. Ibid., 1:494–95 (1.15); compare 1:67–69 (1.2), 87 (1.3), 106–7 (1.3).

193. Ibid., 1:477, 479, etc. (1.15).

194. Womersley, *Watchmen*, notes that since Cyprian "was the Father upon whose teaching, above that of all others, the distinctive church government of the Church of England had been grounded," Gibbon's suggestion of avaricious or ambitious motives elicited defenses of the bishop (112–16). Athanasius dominates the twenty-first chapter of the *Decline and Fall*, which at times reads as an *aristeia*: "Amidst the storms of persecution, the archbishop of Alexandria was patient of labor, jealous of fame, careless of safety; and although his mind was tainted by the contagion of fanaticism, Athanasius displayed a superiority of character and abilities, which would have qualified him, far better than the degenerate sons of Constantine, for the government of a great monarchy" (*DF*, 1:796 [2.21]). Pocock notes that Gibbon "admired Athanasius more than either Arius or Julian" (Pocock, "Clergy and Commerce," 556, Pocock, *Barbarism and Religion*, 6:129–33; see also Womersley, *Watchmen*, 126–46). Ambrose resists an empress and receives an emperor's penance in the *Decline and Fall*'s third volume (*DF*, 2:40–60 [3.27]). For the more ambivalent case of John Chrysostom, see *DF*, 2:252–59 (3.32); Pocock rightly concludes that "Chrysostom is not quite a second Athanasius; he does not challenge heresy or established authority" (*Barbarism and Religion*, 6:376).

195. *DF*, 1:487–88 (1.15).

196. Ibid., 1:489 (1.15).

197. Ibid., 1:496 (1.15).

198. Ibid., 1:496–97 (1.15); compare 1:544 (1.16). Recall Gibbon's description of his Aunt Hester (Laws' "Miranda"): "She was surrounded by dependents, poor and abject as they were, who implored her bounty and imbibed her lessons" (*A*, F:23). We discuss this passage in chapter 2.

199. When Gibbon returns to "the zealous, the eloquent, the ambitious Cyprian" in the concluding chapter of the *Decline and Fall*'s first volume, the superiority of Christian to pagan glory is made even more explicit: "The honors which Rome or Athens bestowed on those citizens who had fallen in the cause of their country, were cold and unmeaning demonstrations of respect, when compared with the ardent gratitude and devotion which the primitive church expressed towards the victorious champions of the faith" (*DF*, 1:541–46 [1.16]).

200. *DF*, 1:486 (1.15).

201. Ibid.

202. Ibid., 1:487 (1.15).

203. Ibid., 1:490 (1.15).

204. Ibid., 1:497 (1.15).

205. Ibid., 1:498 (1.15).

206. Ibid.

207. Ibid., 1:571 (1.16). "The motives of [Constantine's] conversion . . . and the progress of the revolution, which, under his powerful influence, and that of his sons, rendered Christianity the reigning religions of the Roman empire, will form a very interesting and important chapter in the second volume of this history."

208. Ibid., 1:55 (1.1).

209. Ibid., 1:515 (1.16).

210. Ibid., 1:578–79 (1.16).

211. For Gibbon's hints, see his comment on the emperors' persecution of the Jews: "We are tempted to applaud the severe retaliation which was exercised by the arms of the legions against a race of fanatics, whose dire and credulous superstition seemed to render them the implacable enemies not only of the Roman government, but of humankind" (*DF*, 1:516 [1.16]). See also Gibbon's summary of the late adoption, by pagan advisors to Maximin, of Christian innovations in religious governance (*DF*, 1:575 [1.16]).

212. *DF*, 1:580 (1.16).

213. As we have noted (see above, note 6) this is one of the central arguments of Pocock's *Barbarism and Religion*.

CHAPTER 5

1. *DF*, 2:293 (3.33). Womersley notes that in this fable the "investigation of causality . . . now threatened historical judgment" ("Introduction to *The History of the Decline and Fall*," 1:lxiv; see also Womersley, *Transformation*, 182–83).

2. The fable ends with everyone rushing to the cave where they had slept, while the sleepers themselves "bestowed their benediction, related their story, and at the same instant peaceably expired" (*DF*, 1:292 [3.33]; see also *DF*, 1:528 [1.16]).

3. Compare *DF*, 3:1084 (6.71), where Gibbon writes that "the footsteps of heroes, the relics, not of superstition, but of empire, are devoutly visited by a new race of pilgrims from the remote, and once savage, countries of the North." Gibbon is perhaps too easily placed among these new pilgrims; his interest in the relation between the two sets of relics sets him apart.

4. *DF*, 2:511 (General Observations).

5. Craddock notes the disappointment readers have expressed in the "General Observations," starting with John Pinkerton who called the conclusion "pitiably unfortunate" (*Edward Gibbon*, 8, 370n20). Pocock calls the "General Observations" "puzzling and disappointing" (Pocock, "Gibbon's *Decline and Fall*"; compare Pocock, *Barbarism and Religion*, 2:392–96, 6:489–500); see too Baridon, *Edward Gibbon*, 656–58. Womersley agrees with Pocock's general assessment but finds the "incoherence" of the "General Observations" suggestive of Gibbon's emerging indifference about the regular patterns of historical causation that dominated the *Decline and Fall*'s first volume and a "growing interest in the immense tidal movements of history and their source in minute springs . . . his rising sensitivity to the marvelous" (*Transformation*, 189–91). Charlotte Roberts extends Womersley's analysis: The "General Observations," she writes, reflects the "insufficiency of interpretive narratives as intellectual tools" (*Edward Gibbon*, 50). Compare Ghosh, "Gibbon's Dark Ages," 18–19, and the more developed Ghosh, "Gibbon Observed," especially 153, which defends the "General Observations" against its critics.

6. *Memoirs* first appeared in Sheffield's 1796 edition of Gibbon's *Miscellaneous Works*; the "General Observations" was published with the second and third volumes of the *Decline and Fall* in 1781. Of course the "General Observations" was Gibbon's first foray into the history of Rome's decline only as the author of the *Decline and Fall*. As we have seen, prior to taking up the *Decline and Fall* Gibbon had devoted a substantial portion of the *Essai sur l'étude de la littérature* (1761) and a number of unpublished scholarly works to the history of Rome.

7. *A*, E:324.

8. *DF*, 2:513 (General Observations).

9. Roche, "Historian Gibbon," 467. Pocock, *Barbarism and Religion*, 2:78–79.

10. *A*, E:324n48.

11. In the third paragraph of the "General Observations," Gibbon speaks of "what this history has already shewn"; in the footnotes, he refers to earlier volumes of his own work, to the fifth voyage of discovery commanded by George III (James Cook's, which left England on July 12, 1776), and to the first volume of Joseph-Marie Amiot's *Memoires sur les Chinois*, which also dated from 1776 (*DF*, 2:512n6, 513, 513n7, 516n15 [General Observations]). Lacking the pre-1774 draft of "General Observations" to compare to what was published in 1781, we cannot know whether these minor revisions reflect a more significant refashioning of the text, but even these small changes suffice to show that the "General Observations" had not gone untouched since 1774. See Womersley, "From Polybianism to Perfectibilism," especially 53–54, "Introduction to *The History of the Decline and Fall*," 1:lxv, and Roche, "The Historian Gibbon," 468, which claims that "General Observations" was "last, not only in position, as they appear in the volume, but in composition." Ghosh acknowledges the revisions collected by Womersley, but holds that Gibbon's editing was not extensive and focused on footnotes rather than the main text, which was published in 1781 largely as it had been written in 1772 ("Gibbon Observed," 135–36).

12. Ghosh notes the "striking fact that the 'General Observations' was not criticized by contemporaries, nor was it considered worth separate mention by nineteenth-century writers such as Milman or Cotter Morison, which almost certainly indicates that modern criticism of it in isolation is in one sense unhistorical" ("Gibbon Observed," 153). On the dating of Gibbon's drafts of the *Memoirs*, see Bonnard, "Preface, *Memoirs*," xx–xxxi.

13. As, indeed, does Ghosh in "Gibbon Observed."

14. Gibbon refers here to Plutarch's "On the Fortune of the Romans," which he considers a "malicious declamation." Admirers of Plutarch need not despair, however. This is hardly Plutarch's last word on the causes of Roman greatness (see, e.g., the *Life of Romulus*, in Plutarch, *Lives*, 1:136–37 [16.5]), nor is it Gibbon's last word on Plutarch, whom he cites frequently, praises occasionally (e.g., *DF*, 1:377n65 [1.13], 941n89 [2.24], 1026n9 [2.26]), and places among the sages of the early Empire who "exalt the

dignity of human nature" while taking no notice of Christianity (1:510 [1.15]).

15. On Gibbon's notion of "philosophical history," see our discussion in chapter 3.

16. On Gibbon's admiration for Polybius, see especially Ghosh, "Gibbon Observed," 137. Pocock notes that among the ancients, Gibbon considered only Polybius and Tacitus "philosophical historians" (*Barbarism and Religion*, 1:269).

17. *DF*, 2:509 (General Observations); Ghosh notes that attributing Rome's fall to its excessive size was "an eighteenth-century commonplace" ("Gibbon's Dark Ages," 17n111); Pocock notes that Gibbon's emphasis on this cause was not meant to exclude others (*Barbarism and Religion*, 2:395, 6:491). Compare *DF*, 1:499 (1.15), where Gibbon says that having lost their faith in Rome's pantheon, the multitude were ready to accept new gods: "Those who are inclined to pursue this reflection, instead of viewing with astonishment the rapid progress of Christianity, will perhaps be surprised that its success was not still more rapid and still more universal."

18. Löwith's *Meaning in History* is still a very useful introduction to the contrast between cyclical and linear theories of history. Coetzee, *Waiting for the Barbarians*, 131, gives perhaps the most beautiful expression of the problem as it relates to our theme: "What has made it impossible for us to live in time like fish in water, like birds in air, like children? It is the fault of Empire! Empire has created the time of history. Empire has located its existence not in the smooth recurrent spinning time of the cycle of the seasons but in the jagged time of rise and fall, of beginning and end, of catastrophe. Empire dooms itself to live in history and plot against history."

19. Polybius, *Histories*, 3:438–41 (6.57).

20. Hume's initial response to the *Decline and Fall*'s first volume drew the same parallel between Britain and Rome. He worried that the conclusion of Gibbon's first volume might stir controversy because "among many other marks of decline, the prevalence of superstition in England prognosticates the fall of Philosophy, and decay of taste" (*A*, E:311–13n30).

21. Craddock, *Edward Gibbon*, 97. Gibbon confirms the chance encounter with Franklin in a letter to Holroyd from Paris on June 16, 1777 (*L*, 2:150), but does not mention Franklin's subsequent invitation or the final quip. Craddock traces these details to William Cobbett by way of Parton's *Life and Times of Benjamin Franklin* (2:209); Cobbett does not vouch for the truth of the anecdote but notes that "the expressions imputed to the two personages were strictly in character." The story of Henry Laurens, the US ambassador to Holland during the Revolutionary War, might be compared to Franklin. Having been captured by a British frigate and imprisoned in the Tower of London, Laurens consoled himself by copying out long passages of the text by hand, drawing parallels between the policy of Rome in its decline and England during the ongoing war, and circulating them among British "friends of America" (Wallace, *Life*, 381).

22. *The Decline and Fall of the British Empire* was the title of pamphlets published in 1884 (ostensibly from Auckland in 1984) and 1905 (ostensibly from Japan in 2005, ten years after the fall of Japan's "Western Ally," an event that the author says would not have happened had the British studied Gibbon more carefully). This is also the title of a number of more recent histories of the British Empire, including Piers Brendon's *The Decline and Fall of the British Empire: 1781–1997*, an invaluable resource for charting Gibbon's *nachleben* among the British. Brendon discusses the two pamphlets mentioned here (*Decline and Fall of the British Empire*, 176, 232), and documents Gibbon's influence on colonial revolutionaries (see especially his discussion of Gibbon's influence on Indian resistance to the Empire: *Decline and Fall of the British Empire*, xviii, 382–83). Along similar lines, Gaddis has recently shown that George Kennan's reading of Gibbon had a profound influence on the development of "containment." Having learned from Gibbon that empires control nations along their periphery only with great difficulty, Kennan was confident that the Soviet Empire would collapse internally if it were allowed to do so (Gaddis, *George F. Kennan*, 167, 195, 278, 322).

23. Perhaps the most vivid depiction of this approach to Gibbon can be found in Isaac Asimov's Foundation series. These novels feature a Gibbonesque "psycohistorian," Hari Seldon, who has anticipated the course of the declining Galactic Empire with such precision that the holograms he records prior to his death continue for a millennium to guide the founders of the Second Galactic Empire. Asimov has

commented on his deep and continuous reading of Gibbon and its influence on the series in a number of venues. See, for instance, Asimov, *In Memory Yet Green*, 311, 400; and Asimov, *I, Asimov*, 117 and 230, where Asimov remarks in a chapter on plagiarism: "I borrowed freely from Gibbon's *History of the Decline and Fall of the Roman Empire* in planning the Foundation series, and I believe that the motion picture *Star Wars* did not hesitate, in turn, to borrow from the Foundation series."

24. *A*, E:307.

25. For late-night sessions of Parliament, see *L*, 1:204, 257, 365; 2:8. On Gibbon's election to Parliament, see *L*, 2:31–32; Craddock, *Edward Gibbon*, 39–42.

26. *A*, E:310. Compare Gibbon's remark to Deyverdun in a letter of May 7, 1776: "A historian is always in a certain sense a politician; and each reader according to his particular opinions searches the most remote ages for clues of the writer's opinions on different men, kings, and governments" (*L*, 2:107).

27. Gibbon's reports of Parliamentary debates on American affairs are a constant presence in his correspondences with Holroyd and his stepmother. Gibbon does not discuss his relationship with Hutchinson in the *Memoirs*, but from Gibbon's correspondence we glean that it began in December 1774, not long after Hutchinson had arrived from the colonies (*L*, 2:51). Gibbon describes his first encounters with Lord North in letters to his stepmother on April 11 and May 2, 1775 (*L*, 2:64–66). A constant, though not uncritical, supporter of Lord North in Parliament, Gibbon remained loyal after leaving government, as the dedication of volumes four through six of the *Decline and Fall* attests (see *DF*, 2:520–21). Craddock discerns from Keynes's *Library* that between 1770 and 1775 Gibbon "was adding as many books dealing with America and Parliament as with Rome and her neighbors" (Craddock, *Edward Gibbon*, 50).

28. Womersley, *Transformation*, 67–68, collects instances of scholars attempting to link Gibbon's views of Rome and Britain, while cautioning against "such a facile use of history" (70n38). In the same vein Karen O'Brien holds that Gibbon "recognizes no moral or structural equivalence between the Roman and British empires" ("Gibbon's Prospects," 245–50), and Pocock insists on the difference between continental and commercial empires (*Barbarism and Religion*, 3:8, 4:5–6; see also 3:476, 6:370, 462). Black adds, correctly, that though Gibbon himself was reluctant to draw reductive parallels between quite different empires, he "benefitted from the popular interest that a sense of parallelism between Rome and Britain encouraged" ("Gibbon and International Relations," 244).

29. *A*, C:271–72, E:328; see also *L*, 1:254, 367. The line is from Horace, *Odes*, 212–13 (3.12): "the smoke, and wealth, and din of Rome." Gibbon frequently refers to members of Parliament as senators. See, for instance, *L*, 1:31, 2:31, 80; *A*, E:322, F:31. Gibbon's father is a "new Cincinnatus" at *A*, B:183, C:287, and D:412. Late in his life Gibbon would refer to the French revolutionaries as "the savages of Gaul," although in the wake of some military success they were "the new Romans" (*L*, 3:277, 283, 286). Compare Roberts, "*Memoirs*," 212–13.

30. *L*, 2:69; see also *L*, 2:64, 97. Gibbon wrote to Deyverdun on June 4, 1779: "About the man of letters and the statesman, it's enough for you to know that the decline of the two empires, the Roman and the British, advances at the same pace. However, I have contributed much more effectively to the former" (*L*, 2:218).

31. North's government asked Gibbon to write the *Mémoire* in July or August 1779 and it was published that October (*L*, 2:229). See *A*, E:319–20, and Craddock, *Edward Gibbon*, 134–36, for background and discussion of work's mixed reception.

32. *MW 1814*, 5:26. Gibbon himself compares the *Mémoire* to the work of a lawyer at *A*, E:320n42.

33. See, for instance, Swain, *Edward Gibbon*, 135–36, and Pocock, *Barbarism and Religion*, 2:257.

34. *DF*, 1:1073–76 (1.26).

35. Although Gibbon did not formally dedicate the early volumes of the *Decline and Fall* to his spirited, militarily efficient, politically ambitious, and eminently practical friend Holroyd (as he would dedicate the fourth, fifth, and sixth volumes to Lord North), it is sometimes helpful to imagine Holroyd as the author's interlocutor (for Gibbon's sketch of his friend's character, see *L*, 3:266–67). Several of Gibbon's letters to Holroyd support this line of approach to the great work. While working on the first volume, for instance, Gibbon says to his

friend: "In truth when I am writing a page, I not only think it a sufficient reason of delay, but even consider myself as writing to you, and that much more to the purpose than if I were sending you the tittle tattle of the town" (*L*, 2:14). A month later, Gibbon begins a letter by saying "I wrote three folio pages to you this morning and yet you complain" (*L*, 2:19). (Note, however, that Gibbon could joke in a similar way with his stepmother: a letter following on the heels of a gift copy of the second and third volumes begins, "As you have probably received my last letter of thirteen hundred pages, I shall be very concise" [*L*, 2:260].) We should also not forget that Gibbon could inhabit the mindset of a practical, political man because that persona was one he himself possessed. Recall Gibbon's claim to have attended a "school of civil prudence" as a Member of Parliament (*A*, E:310). Consider also Gibbon's narration of his service as an officer in the Hampshire militia and its memorable, half-ironic conclusion: "The discipline and evolutions of a modern battalion gave me a clearer notion of the Phalanx and the Legions, and the Captain of the Hampshire grenadiers (the reader may smile) has not been useless to the historian of the Roman Empire" (*A*, B:190, C:258, D:401–2, E:299).

36. Having explored the world's oceans and extended into central Asia, Europeans can surveille remaining nomads; their "forces may be almost numbered" (*DF*, 2:512 [General Observations]). Pocock notes a Voltairean precedent for Gibbon's argument (*Barbarism and Religion*, 2:117–18, 396).

37. *DF*, 2:514 (General Observations).

38. Ibid.

39. Womersley recounts John Whitaker's attack on Gibbon during the French Revolution for failing to recognize that "material refinement" might coincide with "moral barbarism" (*Watchmen*, 335–39). Black agrees: for Gibbon, "the threat to European civilization appeared remote precisely because there was no sense that it could come from within" ("Gibbon and International Relations," 236; Pocock, *Barbarism and Religion*, 6:498). As Woudhuysen notes, this sense was clearly in evidence by 1793 when Gibbon refers to the French revolutionaries as "the most dangerous fanatics that have ever invaded the peace of Europe . . . the new Barbarians" ("Gibbon among the Barbarians," 94; *L*, 3:321).

40. *DF*, 2:512 (General Observations).

41. Ibid., 1:84 (1.2).

42. Ibid., 2:513 (General Observations).

43. Ibid., 2:511 (General Observations). As a result, civilized nations that fade in relative power do not cease to enjoy the fruits of national emulation. Black, "Gibbon and International Relations," 224–27, offers valuable comments on this passage, which he attributes in part to the influence of William Robertson's *History of the Reign of the Emperor Charles V*.

44. *DF*, 2:513 (General Observations). This remark about multiplying ministerial talents leads to the line that got Gibbon intro trouble with Louis XVI.

45. Perhaps a more precise analogy would be the Athenians evacuating Athens in 480 (Herodotus, *Histories*, 570–71 [8.40–41]). Pocock links this line to Voltaire's claim that the Dutch could escape by boat to Indonesia, if necessary (*Barbarism and Religion*, 2:89).

46. *DF*, 2:513–14 (General Observations).

47. Ibid., 2:511 (General Observations).

48. Ibid., 1:31 (1.1), 83 (1.2), 93, 106–7 (1.3), 389 (1.13).

49. Ibid., 1:106 (1.3). For further elaboration of this theme in the second and third volumes, consider Gibbon's moving description of Honorius's Gallic confederacy: "If such an institution, which gave the people an interest in their own government, had been universally established by Trajan or the Antonines, the seeds of public wisdom and virtue might have been cherished and propagated in the empire of Rome. The privileges of the subject would have secured the throne of the monarch; the abuses of an arbitrary administration might have been prevented, in some degree, or corrected, by the interposition of these representative assemblies; and the country would have been defended against a foreign enemy by the arms of natives and freemen. Under the mild and generous influence of liberty, the Roman empire might have remained invincible and immortal; or if its excessive magnitude, and the instability of human affairs, had opposed such perpetual continuance, its vital and constituent members might have separately preserved their vigor and independence. But in the decline of the empire, when every principle of health and life had been

exhausted, the tardy application of this partial remedy was incapable of producing any important or salutary effects" (2:235–36 [3.31], compare 1:487 [1.15]).

50. *DF*, 1:56–61 (1.2), 497–99 (1.15).

51. Division figured prominently in Montesquieu's account of the Empire's fall in the seventeenth chapter of the *Considérations*. Machiavelli stressed Christianity's erosion of warlike manners; see for instance, *Discourses on Livy*, 36–39 (1.12), 129–33 (2.2). Gibbon allows that division and Christianity were new phenomena: the division is a "dangerous novelty"; Christianity introduces a "new species of tyranny" (*DF*, 2:510–11 [General Observations]). He denies, however, that these novelties contribute materially to the decline and fall. Compare Giarrizzo, *Edward Gibbon*, 384.

52. *DF*, 2:510 (General Observations).

53. Ibid., 2:510–11 (General Observations). As Pocock glosses this passage, "A simple causal connection between religion and decline is not to be offered, and since Christianity plays some part in civilizing the barbarians—the very thing for which a true *philosophe* could not forgive it—there is a counter-connection between religion and civil society itself" (*Barbarism and Religion*, 2:395, 6:493–95).

54. *DF*, 2:510 (General Observations).

55. Ibid., 2:511 (General Observations).

56. Ibid., 3:237 (3.32).

57. Womersley has suggested that even before he died, the French Revolution had destroyed the international order Gibbon meant to defend: "The 'Christian republic of nations' from within which, and on behalf of which, Gibbon had composed his great history was now being destroyed before his eyes" (*Watchmen*, 242). Pocock suggests that this order had indeed already passed as early as 1739, but Gibbon was "content in 1781, and again in 1788, to see the Utrecht order as still in effect, guiding his readers in understanding their own place in history" (*Barbarism and Religion*, 6:496). Compare Black, "Gibbon and International Relations," 234–35.

58. *DF*, 1:499 (1.15).

BIBLIOGRAPHY

Adams, Henry. *The Education of Henry Adams.* New York: Library of America, 1983.

Addison, Joseph. "A Letter from Italy." In *The Works of the Right Honorable Joseph Addison*, edited by Richard Hurd, 1:29–41. 6 vols. London: George Bell and Sons, 1881.

———. *Remarks on several parts of Italy, &c. in the years 1701, 1702, 1703*. London: J. Tonson, 1718 [1705].

Aldridge, Alfred Owen. "Shaftesbury and the Deist Manifesto." *Transactions of the American Philosophical Society* 41, no. 2 (1951): 297–382.

Amherst, W. J. *The History of Catholic Emancipation and The Progress of the Catholic Church in the British Isles (Chiefly in England) from 1771 to 1820*. 2 vols. London: Kegan Paul, Trench, 1886.

Asimov, Isaac. *I, Asimov*. New York: Doubleday, 1994.

———. *In Memory Yet Green: The Autobiography of Isaac Asimov, 1920–1954*. New York: Avon, 1979.

Aston, Nigel. "A 'Disorderly Squadron?': A Fresh Look at Clerical Responses to *The Decline and Fall*." In Womersley, *Edward Gibbon*, 253–77.

Augustine. *Confessions*. Translated by William Watts. 2 vols. Loeb Classical Library 26–27. Cambridge, MA: Harvard University Press, 2002 [1912].

Bacon, Francis. "A Copy of a Letter Conceived to be Written to the Late Duke of Buckingham [. . .]." In *The Letters and the Life of Francis Bacon*, edited by James Spedding, 6:27–56. 7 vols. London: Longmans, Green, Reader, and Dyer, 1872.

———. "On Travel." In *The Works of Francis Bacon*, edited by J. Spedding, R. L. Ellis, and D. D. Heath, 6:417–18. 7 vols. London: Longman, 1857–70.

Badian, Ernst. "Gibbon and War." In *Gibbon et Rome à la lumière de l'historiographie moderne: 10 exposés suivis de discussions*, edited by Pierre Ducrey, 103–29. Geneva: Droz, 1977.

Bann, Stephen. "Envisioning Rome: Granet and Gibbon in Dialogue." In Edwards, *Roman Presences*, 35–52.

Baridon, M. "Edward Gibbon en Italie." *Études Anglaises* 15, no. 2 (1962): 130–37.

———. *Edward Gibbon et le mythe de Rome: Histoire et idéologie au siècle des Lumières*. Paris: Edition Honoré Champion, 1977. First published 1975 by Service Reproduction des Thèses (Lille).

———. "Une lettre inédite d'Edward Gibbon à Jean-Baptiste-Antoine Suard." *Études Anglaises* 24, no. 1 (1971): 79–87.

Baxter, Richard. *Reliquiae Baxterianae, or, Mr. Richard Baxter's narrative of the most memorable passages of his life and times*. Edited by Matthew Sylvester. London, 1696.

Berkeley, George. *The Works of George Berkeley*. Edited by George Sampson. 3 vols. London: George Bell and Sons, 1897.

Bishop, Morris. *Pascal: The Life of Genius*. New York: Reynal and Hitchcock, 1936.

Bissons, Lillian M. *Chaucer and the Late Medieval World*. New York: St. Martin's Press, 1998.

Black, Jeremy. *The British Abroad: The Grand Tour in the Eighteenth Century*. Sparkford: J. H. Haynes, 2003 [1992].

———. "Gibbon and International Relations." In McKitterick and Quinalt, *Edward Gibbon and Empire*, 217–46.

———. *Italy and the Grand Tour*. New Haven: Yale University Press, 2003.

Bonazzi, M., and S. Schorn, eds. *Bios Philosophos: Philosophy in Ancient Greek Biography*. Turnhout, Belgium: Brepols, 2016.

Bonnard, G. A., ed. *Edward Gibbon: Memoirs of My Life*. New York: Funk and Wagnalls, 1966.

———. "Gibbon's '*Essai sur l'Étude de la Littérature*' as Judged by Contemporary Reviewers and by Gibbon Himself." *English Studies* 32 (1951): 145–53.

———. Preface to *Gibbon's Journey from Geneva to Rome: His Journal from 20 April to 2 October 1764*, edited by G. A. Bonnard, v–xviii. London: Thomas Nelson and Sons, 1961.

———. Preface to *Memoirs or My Life*, by Edward Gibbon. Edited by G. A. Bonnard, vii–xxxiii. New York: Funk and Wagnalls, 1966.

Bossy, John. *The English Catholic Community: 1570–1850*. New York: Oxford University Press, 1976.

Boswell, James. *Boswell for the Defence, 1769–1774*. Edited by William K. Wimsatt Jr. and Frederick A. Pottle. New York: McGraw-Hill, 1959.

———. *The Life of Samuel Johnson*. Edited by David Womersley. London: Penguin, 2008.

Bowersock, G. W. *From Gibbon to Auden: Essays on the Classical Tradition*. Oxford: Oxford University Press, 2009

———. "Gibbon and Julian." In *Gibbon et Rome à la lumiére de l'historiographie moderne*, 191–217. Publications de la Faculté des Lettres, XXII. Lausanne, Switzerland: Université de Lausanne, 1977..

———. "Gibbon on Civil War and Rebellion in the Decline of the Roman Empire." In Bowersock, *From Gibbon to Auden*, 20–32. Originally published in *Daedalus* 105, no. 3 (1976): 63–71. Reprinted in *Edward Gibbon and the Decline and Fall of the Roman Empire*, ed. G. W. Bowersock, J. Clive, and S. R. Graubard (Cambridge, MA: Harvard University Press, 1977), 27–35.

———. "Gibbon's Historical Imagination." In Bowersock, *From Gibbon to Auden*, 3–19. Originally published in *The American Scholar* 57 (Winter 1988): 33–47.

———. "Reflections on Gibbon's Library." In Bowersock, *From Gibbon to Auden*, 33–42. Originally published in *Gazette of the Grolier Club* 52 (2001): 49–59.

Bremmer, Jan N. *The Rise of Christianity Through the Eyes of Gibbon, Hamack, and Rodney Stark*. Groningen: Barkhuis, 2010.

Brendon, Piers. *The Decline and Fall of the British Empire, 1781–1997*. New York: Vintage, 2007.

Bromwich, David. *The Intellectual Life of Edmund Burke: From the Sublime and Beautiful to American Independence*. Cambridge, MA: Belknap Press of Harvard University Press, 2014.

Brownley, Martine. "'The Purest and Most Gentle Portion of the Human Species': Gibbon's Portrayals of Women in the *Decline and Fall*." *South Atlantic Quarterly* 77 (1978): 1–14.

Burke, Edmund. *Reflections on the Revolution in France*. In *Select Works of Edmund Burke*, foreword and biographical note by Francis Canavan. 4 vols. Indianapolis: Liberty Fund, 1999.

———. "Speech at Bristol Guildhall." In *On Empire, Liberty, and Reform: Speeches and Letters*, edited by David Bromwich, 210–57. New Haven: Yale University Press, 2000.

Burnet, Gilbert. *Some letters, : containing an account of what seem'd most remarkable in travelling thro' Switzerland, Italy, some parts of Germany, & c. in the years 1685. and 1686*. London, 1724.

Burrow, J. W. *Gibbon*. Oxford: Oxford University Press, 1985.

Burton, John Hill. *Life and Correspondence of David Hume*. 2 vols. Edinburgh: William Tate, 1846.

Carnochan, W. B. *Gibbon's Solitude: The Inward World of the Historian*. Stanford: Stanford University Press, 1978.

Cartledge, P. "The Enlightened Historiography of Edward Gibbon, Esq.: A Bicentennial Celebration." *Maynooth Review* 3, no. 2 (1977): 67–93.

———. "The 'Tacitism' of Edward Gibbon (Two Hundred Years On)." *Mediterranean Historical Review* 4, no. 2 (1989): 251–70.

Chaney, Edward. *The Grand Tour and the Great Rebellion: Richard Lassels and 'The Voyage of Italy' in the Seventeenth Century*. Geneva: Slatkine; Moncalieri, Italy: Centro interuniversitario di ricerche sul "Viaggio in Italia," 1985.

———. "Lassels [Lascelles], Richard (c. 1603–1668), Roman Catholic Priest and

Travel Writer." *Oxford Dictionary of National Biography*, September 23, 2004, https://www.oxforddnb.com/view/10.1093/ref:odnb/9780198614128.001.0001/odnb-9780198614128-e-16083.

Chard, Chloe. *Pleasure and Guilt on the Grand Tour: Travel Writing and Imaginative Geography, 1600–1830*. Manchester: Manchester University Press, 1999.

Chaucer, Geoffrey. *The Canterbury Tales*. Translated by Frank Ernest Hill. London: Longmans, Green, 1935.

———. *The Canterbury Tales*. In *The Riverside Chaucer*, edited by Larry D. Benson, 3–328. Boston: Houghton Mifflin, 1987.

Chelsum, James. "Remarks on the Two Last Chapters of Mr. Gibbon's History, of the Decline and Fall of the Roman Empire, in a Letter to a Friend." In Womersley, *Religious Scepticism*, 1–43.

Clark, Gillian. "Pilgrims and Foreigners: Augustine on Travelling Home." In *Travel, Communication, and Geography in Late Antiquity: Sacred and Profane*, edited by Linda Ellis and Frank Kidner, 149–56. Aldershot, UK: Ashgate, 2004.

Clark, J. C. D. *English Society, 1688–1832*. Cambridge: Cambridge University Press, 1985.

Coetzee, John. *Waiting for the Barbarians*. New York: Penguin, 1980.

Collins, Anthony. *A Discourse of Free-Thinking, Occasioned by the Rise and Growth of a Sect Called Free-Thinkers*. London, 1713.

———. *An Historical and Critical Essay, on the Thirty-Nine Articles of the Church of England*. London: R. Francklin, 1724.

———. *Priestcraft in Perfection: Or, a Detection of the Fraud of Inserting and Continuing this Clause* [. . .] *in the Twentieth Article of the Articles of the Church of England*. London, 1710.

Corp, Edward. *The Stuarts in Italy, 1719–1766: A Royal Court in Permanent Exile*. Cambridge: Cambridge University Press, 2011.

Craddock, Patricia B. *Edward Gibbon, Luminous Historian, 1772–1794*. Baltimore: Johns Hopkins University Press, 1989.

———, ed. *The English Essays of Edward Gibbon*. Oxford: Clarendon Press, 1972.

———. *Young Edward Gibbon: Gentleman of Letters*. Baltimore: Johns Hopkins University Press, 1982.

d'Alembert, Jean le Rond. *Discours préliminaire de l'encyclopédie*. In *Oeuvres complétes de D'Alembert*, by Jean le Rond d'Alembert, 1:17–99. 5 vols. Genève: Slatkine Reprints, 1967.

Davis, Henry Edwards. "An Examination of the Fifteenth and Sixteenth Chapters of Mr. Gibbon's History of the Decline and Fall of the Roman Empire." In Womersley, *Religious Scepticism*, 185–214.

de Smet, Ingrid A. R. *Thuanus: The Making of Jacques-Auguste de Thou (1553–1617)*. Geneva: Librairie Droz S. A., 2006.

de Thou, Jacques-Auguste. *Jacobi Augusti Thuani Historiarum sui temporis libri CXXXVIII*. Edited by Thomas Carte and Samuel Buckley. 7 vols. London: Samuel Buckley, 1733.

———. *La Vie de Jacques-Auguste de Thou*. Translated by Anne Teissier-Ensminger. Paris: Honoré Champion Éditeur, 2007.

Dihle, A. *Studien zur griechischen Biographie*. 2nd ed. Göttingen: Vandenhoeck and Ruprecht, 1970 [1956].

Edwards, Catharine. "Gibbon and the City of Rome." In O'Brien and Young, *Cambridge Companion*, 62–77.

———, ed. *Roman Presences: Receptions of Rome in European Culture, 1789–1945*. Cambridge: Cambridge University Press, 1999.

Field, Clive D. "Counting Religion in England and Wales: The Long Eighteenth Century, c. 1680–c. 1840." *Journal of Ecclesiastical History* 63, no. 4 (2012): 693–720.

———. "Measuring Religious Affiliation in Great Britain: The 2011 Census in Historical and Methodological Context." *Religion* 44, no. 3 (2014): 357–82.

Foucault, Michel. *The Order of Things: An Archaeology of the Human Sciences*. New York: Vintage, 1994. Originally published as *Les mots et les choses* (Paris: Editions Gallimard, 1966).

Fouqueray, Henri. *Histoire de la Compagnie de Jésus en France: Des Origines a la Suppression (1528–1762)*. 5 vols. Paris:

Librairie Alphonse Picard et Fils, 1910–25.

Foxcroft, H. C. *A Supplement to Burnet's History of My Own Time*. Oxford: Clarendon Press, 1902.

Gaddis, John Lewis. *George F. Kennan: An American Life*. New York: Penguin, 2011.

Gallus, Joannis Baptista [Jean de Machault]. *In Jacobi Augusti Historiarum libros notationes, auctore Joanne Baptisto Gallo*. In de Thou, *Jacobi Augusti Thuani Historiarum*, 7.3:32–70.

Gay, Peter. *Deism: An Anthology*. Princeton, NJ: D. Van Nostrand, 1968.

Ghosh, P. R. "Gibbon Observed." *Journal of Roman Studies* 81 (1991): 132–56.

———. "Gibbon's Dark Ages: Some Remarks on the Genesis of the Decline and Fall." *Journal of Roman Studies* 73 (1983): 1–23.

———. "Gibbon's First Thoughts: Rome, Christianity and the *Essai sur l'étude de la littérature*, 1758–1761." *Journal of Roman Studies* 85 (1995): 148–64.

———. "Gibbon's Timeless Verity: Nature and Neo-Classicism in the Late Enlightenment." In Womersley, *Edward Gibbon*, 121–62.

Giarrizzo, Giuseppe. *Edward Gibbon e la cultura europea del settecento*. Naples: Istituto per gli Studi Storici, 1954.

Gibbon, Edward. *The Autobiographies of Edward Gibbon*. Edited by J. Murray. London: John Murray, 1896.

———. *Edward Gibbon, "Essai sur l'étude de la littérature": A Critical Edition*. Edited by R. Mankin and P. Craddock. Oxford: Voltaire Foundation, 2010.

———. *The English Essays of Edward Gibbon*. Edited by Patricia Craddock. Oxford: Clarendon, 1972.

———. *Gibbon's Journal to January 28th, 1763: My Journal I, II, and III and Ephemerides*. Edited by D. M. Low. London: Chatto and Windus, 1929.

———. *Gibbon's Journey from Geneva to Rome: His Journal from 20 April to 2 October 1764*. Edited by G. A. Bonnard. London: Thomas Nelson and Sons, 1961.

———. *The History of the Decline and Fall of the Roman Empire*. Edited by D. J. Womersley. 3 vols. London: Allen Lane, 1994.

———. *Le Journal de Gibbon à Lausanne*. Edited by G. A. Bonnard. Lausanne: Librairie de l'Université, 1945.

———. *Journal de mon voyage dans quelques endroits de la Suisse*. Edited by G. R. de Beer and G. A. Bonnard. In *Miscellanea Gibboniana*, edited by G. R. de Beer, G. A. Bonnard, and Louis Junod, 5–84. Lausanne: Librairie de l'Université, 1952.

———. *The Letters of Edward Gibbon*. Edited by J. E. Norton. 3 vols. London: Cassell and Company, 1956.

———. *La lettre de Gibbon sur le gouvernement de Berne*. Edited by Louis Junod. In *Miscellanea Gibboniana*, edited by G. R. de Beer, G. A. Bonnard, and Louis Junod, 109–41. Lausanne: Librairie de l'Université, 1952 [1755].

———. *Miscellaneous Works*. Edited by Lord Sheffield. 2 vols. London: A. Strahan, T. Caddell Jun., and W. Davies, 1796.

———. *Miscellaneous Works*. Edited by Lord Sheffield. 5 vols. London: John Murray, 1814.

———. *Le séjour de Gibbon à Paris*. Edited by G. A. Bonnard. In *Miscellanea Gibboniana*, edited by G. R. de Beer, G. A. Bonnard, and Louis Junod, 85–107. Lausanne: Librairie de l'Université, 1952.

———. *Vindication*. In *The English Essays of Edward Gibbon*, edited by Patricia Craddock, 231–313. Oxford: Clarendon, 1972.

Grafton, Anthony. *The Footnote: A Curious History*. Cambridge, MA: Harvard University Press, 1997.

———. *Joseph Scaliger: A Study In The History Of Classical Scholarship*. 2 vols. Oxford: Clarendon Press, 1983.

Harris, James A. *Hume: An Intellectual Biography*. Cambridge: Cambridge University Press, 2015.

Haydon, Colin. *Anti-Catholicism in Eighteenth-Century England, c. 1714–80: A Political and Social Study*. Manchester: Manchester University Press, 1993.

Hempton, David. *Methodism: Empire of the Spirit*. New Haven: Yale University Press, 2005.

Herodotus. *The Histories*. Translated by David Grene. Chicago: University of Chicago Press, 1987.

Heyd, Michael. *"Be Sober and Reasonable": The Critique of Enthusiasm in the Seventeenth and Early Eighteenth Centuries*. Leiden: E. J. Brill, 1995.

Hobbes, Thomas. *Leviathan*. Edited by Edwin Curley. Indianapolis: Hackett, 1994.

Horace. *Odes*. In *Odes and Epodes*, translated by Niall Rudd, 22–261. Loeb Classical Library 33. Cambridge, MA: Harvard University Press, 2004.

Howell, James. *Instructions for forreine travell: shewing by what cours, and in what compaese of time, one may take an exact Survey of the Kingdomes and States of Christendome, and arrive to the practicall knowledg of the languages, to good purpose. With a new appendix for travelling into Turkey and the Levant parts*. London, 1642.

Hudson, Wayne. *The English Deists: Studies in Early Enlightenment*. New York: Routledge, 2016.

———. *Enlightenment and Modernity: The English Deists and Reform*. New York: Routledge, 2016.

Hume, David. "Hume's *My Own Life*." In Mossner, *Life of David Hume*, 611–15.

———. *The Letters of David Hume*. Edited by J. Y. T. Greig. 2 vols. Oxford: Clarendon Press, 1932.

———. *New Letters of David Hume*. Edited by Raymond Klibansky and Ernest Mossner. Oxford: Clarendon Press, 1954.

Hurd, Richard. *Dialogues on the Uses of Foreign Travel; Considered as a Part of an English Gentleman's Education; between Lord Shaftesbury and Mr. Locke*. London: W. B., 1764.

Ignatius of Loyola. *The Autobiography of St. Ignatius*. Edited by J. F. X. O'Connor. New York: Benziger Brothers, 1900.

Johnson, Oliver. *The Mind of David Hume*. Urbana: University of Illinois Press, 1995.

Jones, William. "The Difficulties of and the Resources of the Christian Ministry in the Present Time." In *Sermons on Various Subjects and Occasions*, edited by W. H. Walker, 2:382–97. 2 vols. London: C. J. G. and F. Rivington, 1830.

Jordan, David. *Gibbon and His Roman Empire*. Urbana: University of Illinois Press, 1971.

Junod, Louis. Preface to *La lettre de Gibbon sur le gouvernement de Berne*. Edited by Louis Junod. In *Miscellanea Gibboniana*, edited by G. R. de Beer, G. A. Bonnard, and Louis Junod, 111–21. Lausanne: Librairie de l'Université, 1952 [1755].

Juvenal. *Satires*. In *Juvenal and Perseus*, edited by and translated by Susanna Morton Braund, 127–532. Loeb Classical Library 91. Cambridge, MA: Harvard University Press, 2004.

Kapossy, Béla, and Richard Whatmore. "Gibbon and Republicanism." In O'Brien and Young, *Cambridge Companion*, 128–46.

Kaufman, Peter Iver. *On Agamben, Arendt, Christianity, and the Dark Arts of Civilization*. New York: Bloomsbury, 2019.

Kelly, Christopher. "A Grand Tour: Reading Gibbon's *Decline and Fall*." *Greece and Rome* 44, no. 1 (April 1997): 39–58.

Kennedy, Duncan F. "A Sense of Place: Rome, History, and Empire Revisited." In Edwards, *Roman Presences*, 19–34.

Keynes, Geoffrey. *The Library of Edward Gibbon*. Godalming, UK: St. Paul's Bibliographies, 1980.

Kinser, Samuel. *The Works of Jacques-Auguste de Thou*. The Hague: Martinus Nijhoff, 1966.

Kraus, Christina, and C. A. Stray. "Form and Content." In *Classical Commentaries: Explorations in a Scholarly Genre*, edited by Christina Kraus and C. A. Stray, 1–18. Oxford: Oxford University Press, 2016.

Lassels, Richard. *The voyage of Italy, or, A compleat journey through Italy in two parts: with the characters of the people, and the description of the chief towns [. . .] with instructions concerning travel*. Paris, 1670.

Law, William. *A Serious Call to a Devout and Holy Life*. London: J. M. Dent and Sons, 1940 [1729].

Leland, John. *A View of the Principal Deistical Writers That Have Appeared in England in the Last and Present Century, and Some Account of the Answers That Have Been Published Against Them. In Several Letters to a Friend*. 2 vols. London: B. Dod, 1755.

Lerner, Ralph. "Gibbon's 'Jewish Problem.'" In Lerner, *Naïve Readings*, 92–118.

———. *Naïve Readings: Reveilles Political and Philosophic*. Chicago: University of Chicago Press, 2016.

———. *Revolutions Revisited*. Chapel Hill: University of North Carolina Press, 1994.

———. "The Smile of a Philosophic Historian." In *Playing The Fool: Subversive Laughter in Troubled Times*, by Ralph Lerner, 109–32. Chicago: University of Chicago Press, 2009.

Lewis, Lesley. *Connoisseurs and Secret Agents in Eighteenth Century Rome*. London: Chatto and Windus, 1961.

Lock, F. P. *Edmund Burke*. 2 vols. Oxford: Clarendon Press, 2006.

Locke, John. *An Essay Concerning Human Understanding*. Oxford: Clarendon Press, 1979.

———. *The Reasonableness of Christianity, as Delivered in the Scriptures*. In vol. 6 of *The Works of John Locke in Nine Volumes*, by John Locke, 1–158. London: Rivington, 1824.

———. *Some Thoughts Concerning Education*. Edited by Ruth W. Grant and Nathan Tarcov. Indianapolis: Hackett, 1996.

Loftus, Smyth. "A Reply to the Reasonings of Mr. Gibbon, in his History of the Decline and Fall of the Roman Empire." In Womersley, *Religious Scepticism*, 116–84.

Losovsky, Natalia. *"The Earth Is Our Book": Geographical Knowledge in the Latin West, ca. 400–1000*. Ann Arbor: University of Michigan Press, 2000.

Low, D. M. *Edward Gibbon, 1737–1794*. New York: Random House, 1937.

———. Introduction to *Gibbon's Journal to January 28th, 1763: My Journal I, II, and III and Ephemerides*, by Edward Gibbon, xiii–cxvii. Edited by D. M. Low. London: Chatto and Windus, 1929.

Löwith, Karl. *Meaning in History*. Chicago: University of Chicago Press, 1949.

Luther, Martin. "Preface to the Complete Edition of Luther's Latin Writings, 1545." Translated by Lewis W. Spitz Sr. In vol. 34 of *Luther's Works: Career of the Reformer IV*, edited by Lewis W. Spitz, 323–38. Philadelphia: Fortress Press, 1960.

Machiavelli, Niccolò. *Discourses on Livy*. Translated by Harvey C. Mansfield and Nathan Tarcov. Chicago: University of Chicago Press, 1996.

———. *The Prince*. Translated by Harvey C. Mansfield. Chicago: University of Chicago Press, 1985.

Mallet, Paul Henri. *Northern Antiquities: Or, A Description of the Manners, Customs, Religion and Laws of the Ancient Danes* [...]. Translated by Thomas Percy. 2 vols. London, 1770. Originally published as *Introduction à L'histoire du Dannemarc où l'on traite de la religion, des moeurs, des lois, et des usages des anciens Danois* (Copenhagen, 1755).

Manent, Pierre. *Metamorphoses of the City: On the Western Dynamic*. Translated by M. LePain. Cambridge, MA: Harvard University Press, 2013. Originally published as *Les métamorphoses de la cité: Essai sur la dynamique de l'Occident* (Paris: Flammarion, 2010).

Mankin, Robert. "Gibbon's Mind and Libraries." In O'Brien and Young, *Cambridge Companion*, 184–202.

Mayhew, Robert. "Gibbon's Geographies." In O'Brien and Young, *Cambridge Companion*, 41–61.

McKitterick, Rosamond, and Roland Quinalt. *Edward Gibbon and Empire*. Cambridge: Cambridge University Press, 1997.

Mead, William Edward. *The Grand Tour in the Eighteenth Century*. New York: Benjamin Blom, 1972.

Middleton, Conyers. *A Free Inquiry into the Miraculous Powers, Which are Supposed to Have Subsisted in the Christian Church* [...]. Dublin: J. Smith, 1749.

———. *The Life and Letters of Marcus Tullius Cicero*. London: Edward Moxon, 1839 [1741].

Milner, Joseph. "Gibbon's Account of Christianity Considered." In Womersley, *Religious Scepticism*, 215–34.

Misch, Georg. *Geschichte der Autobiographie*. 2nd ed. 3 vols. Leipzig and Berlin: Teubner, 1931.

Misson, Francis Maximilian. *A New Voyage to Italy*. 2 vols. London, 1739 [1691]. English translation of *Nouveau voyage d'ltalie*, *avec un mémoire contenant des avis utiles à ceux qui voudront faire le mesme voyage.*

Momigliano, Arnaldo. *The Development of Greek Biography*. Cambridge, MA: Harvard University Press, 1993.

———. "Gibbon's Contribution to Historical Method." In *Studies in Historiography*, by Arnaldo Momigliano, 40–55. New York: Garland, 1985 [1966].

Montesquieu, Charles Louis de Secondat, Baron de. *Complete Works*. 4 vols. London, 1777.

———. *Spirit of the Laws*. Translated by and edited by Anne Cohler, Basia Miller, and Harold Stone. Cambridge: Cambridge University Press, 1989.

More, Henry. *Enthusiasmus Triumphatus; or, A Brief Discourse of the Nature, Causes, Kinds, and Cure of Enthusiasm*. London: James Flesher, 1662 [1656].

Mossner, E. C. *The Life of David Hume*. Austin: University of Texas Press, 1954.

Mulligan, Winifred Joy. "The British Constantine: an English Historical Myth." *Journal of Medieval and Renaissance Studies* 8, no. 2 (1978): 257–79.

Natoli, Charles. *Fire in the Dark: Essays on Pascal's* Pensées *and* Provinciales. Rochester: University of Rochester Press, 2005.

New, Melvyn. "Gibbon, Middleton, and the 'Barefooted Fryars.'" *Notes and Queries* 223 (February 1978): 51–52.

Nichols, Mary P. *Thucydides and the Pursuit of Freedom*. Ithaca: Cornell University Press, 2015.

Norton, Jane A. *A Bibliography of the Works of Edward Gibbon*. Oxford: Oxford University Press, 1940.

O'Brien, Karen. "Gibbon's Prospects: Rhetoric, Fame, and the Closing Chapters of *The Decline and Fall*." In Womersley, *Edward Gibbon*, 235–52.

O'Brien, Karen, and B. Young, eds. *The Cambridge Companion to Edward Gibbon*. Cambridge: Cambridge University Press, 2018.

Ogilvie, John. *An inquiry into the causes of the infidelity and skepticism of the times: with occasional observations on the writings of Herbert, Shaftesbury, Bolingbroke, Hume, Gibbon, Toulmin, &c. &c.* London, 1783.

Ostade, Ingrid Tieken-Boon van. "Kirkby, John (c. 1705–1754), Church of England Clergyman and Grammarian." *Oxford Dictionary of National Biography*, September 23, 2004, https://www.oxforddnb.com/view/10.1093/ref:odnb/9780198614128.001.0001/odnb-9780198614128-e-15657.

Paley, William. *Principles of Moral and Political Philosophy*. Boston: Richardson and Lord, 1825 [1785].

Parton, James. *Life and Times of Benjamin Franklin*. 2 vols. New York: Mason Brothers, 1865.

Pascal. *Pensées*. Translated by Honor Levi. Edited by Anthony Levi. Oxford: Oxford University Press, 1995.

Peacocke, Emma. *Romanticism and the Museum*. New York: Palgrave Macmillan, 2015.

Petrarch, Francesco. *Letters on Familiar Matters (Rerum Familiarum Libri)*. Translated by Aldo S. Bernardo. 3 vols. New York: Italica Press, 2005 [1975].

Phillipson, Nicholas. *Adam Smith: An Enlightened Life*. New Haven: Yale University Press, 2010.

———. *David Hume: The Philosopher as Historian*. New Haven: Yale University Press, 2011 [1989].

Pitts, Vincent J. *Henry IV of France: His Reign and Age*. Baltimore: Johns Hopkins University Press, 2009.

Pliny (the Elder). *Natural History*. Translated by W. H. S. Jones. 10 vols. Loeb Classical Library 330, 352–53, 370–71, 392–94, 418–19. Cambridge, MA: Harvard University Press, 1938–63.

Pliny (the Younger). *Letters*. Translated by William Melmoth. 2 vols. Loeb Classical Library 55 and 59. New York: Macmillan, 1915.

Plutarch. *Lives*. Translated by Bernadotte Perrin. 11 vols. Loeb Classical Library 46–47, 65, 80, 87, 98–103. Cambridge, MA: Harvard University Press, 1914–26.

———. "On Praising Oneself Inoffensively." Translated by Philip H. De Lacy and Benedict Einarson. In *Moralia, Volume VII: On Love of Wealth. On Compliancy. On Envy and Hate. On Praising Oneself Inoffensively. On the Delays of the Divine Vengeance. On Fate. On the Sign of*

Socrates. *On Exile. Consolation to His Wife*, 114–67. Loeb Classical Library 405. Cambridge, MA: Harvard University Press, 1959.

Pocock, J. G. A. *Barbarism and Religion*. 6 vols. Cambridge: Cambridge University Press, 1999–2015.

———. "Clergy and Commerce: The Conservative Enlightenment in England." In vol. 1 of *L'Età dei lumi: studi storici sul settecento europeo in onore di Franco Venturi*, edited by R. Ajello et al., 523–62. Napoli: Jovene, 1985.

———. "Enthusiasm: The Antiself of Enlightenment." *Huntington Library Quarterly* 60, no. 1/2 (1997): 7–28.

———. "Gibbon's *Decline and Fall* and the World View of the Late Enlightenment." *Eighteenth-Century Studies* 10, no. 3 (1977): 287–303. Reprinted in *Virtue, Commerce, and History* (Cambridge: Cambridge University Press, 1985), 143–56.

———. "Response and Commentary." *Journal of the History of Ideas* 77, no. 1 (2016): 157–71.

———. "Superstition and Enthusiasm in Gibbon's History of Religion." *Eighteenth-Century Life* 8, no. 1 (1982): 83–94.

Polybius. *The Histories*. Translated by W. R. Paton. 6 vols. Loeb Classical Library 128, 137–38, 159–61. Cambridge, MA: Harvard University Press, 2010–12.

Porson, Richard. *Letters To Archdeacon Travis, In Answer To His Defence Of The Three Heavenly Witnesses, I John V. 7*. London: T. and J. Egerton, 1790.

Prothero, Rowland E., ed. *Private Letters of Edward Gibbon (1753–1794)*. 2 vols. London: John Murray, 1896.

Quinalt, Roland. "Winston Churchill and Gibbon." In McKitterick and Quinalt, *Edward Gibbon and Empire*, 317–32.

Rawson, Claude. "Gibbon, Swift, and Irony." In Womersley, *Edward Gibbon*, 179–202.

———. "Musing on the Capitol: The Subject and Sources of Gibbon's 'Grave and Temperate Irony.'" Review of David Womersley's edition of *The Decline and Fall*. *Times Literary Supplement* 4185 (1995): 3–5.

Reames, Sherry L. *The Legenda Aurea: A Reexamination of Its Paradoxical History*. Madison: University of Wisconsin Press, 1985.

Reynolds, L. D., and N. G. Wilson. *Scribes and Scholars: A Guide to the Transmission of Greek and Latin Literature*. Oxford: Clarendon Press, 1991 [1968].

Rivers, Isabel. "Biographical Dictionaries and Their Uses from Bayle to Chalmers." In *Books and Their Readers in Eighteenth-Century England: New Essays*, edited by Isabel Rivers, 135–69. New York: Continuum, 2001.

Roberts, Charlotte. *Edward Gibbon and the Shape of History*. Oxford: Oxford University Press, 2014.

———. "The *Memoirs* and Character of the Historian." In O'Brien and Young, *Cambridge Companion*, 203–18.

Robertson, John M. *A Short History of Freethought Ancient and Modern*. 2 vols. London: Watts, 1915.

Roche, James [JR]. "The Historian Gibbon—His Autobiography." *Gentleman's Magazine*, n.s., 12 (November 1839): 465–82.

Rosenblatt, Helena. "On Context and Meaning in Pocock's *Barbarism and Religion*, and on Gibbon's 'Protestantism' in His Chapters on Religion." *Journal of the History of Ideas* 77, no. 1 (2016): 147–55.

Rosman, Doreen. *The Evolution of the English Churches, 1500–2000*. Cambridge: Cambridge University Press, 2003.

Ross, Ian Campbell. *Laurence Sterne: A Life*. Oxford: Oxford University Press, 2001.

Ross, Ian Simpson. *The Life of Adam Smith*. Oxford: Oxford University Press, 2010 [1995].

Rousseau, Jean-Jacques. "Emile and Sophie, or the Solitaires." In vol. 13 of *The Collected Writings of Rousseau*, edited by Roger D. Masters and Christopher Kelly, 685–721. Hanover: Dartmouth College Press, 1990.

———. "Discourse on the Origin and Foundations of Inequality Among Men or Second Discourse." In *The Discourses and Other Early Political Writings*, edited by Victor Gourevitch, 111–222.

Cambridge: Cambridge University Press, 1997.
———. "Observations by Jean-Jacques Rousseau of Geneva On the Answer Made to His Discourse." In *The Discourses and Other Early Political Writings*, edited by Victor Gourevitch, 32–51. Cambridge: Cambridge University Press, 1997.
———. *The Social Contract*. In *The Social Contract and Other Later Political Writings*, translated by Victor Gourevitch, 39–152. Cambridge: Cambridge University Press, 1997.
Shaftesbury, Third Earl of [Anthony Ashley-Cooper]. *Characteristicks of Men, Manners, Opinions, Times*. 3 vols. Indianapolis: Liberty Fund, 2001.
Shaw, Jane. *Miracles in Enlightenment England*. New Haven: Yale University Press, 2006.
Sher, Richard B. *Church and University in the Scottish Enlightenment*. Edinburgh: University Press, 1985.
Sismondi, J. C. L. Simonde. *De la vie et des écrits de P. H. Mallet*. Geneva: J. J. Paschoud, 1807.
Smith, Adam. *An Inquiry into the Nature and Causes of the Wealth of Nations*. Edited by R. H. Campbell, A. S. Skinner, and W. B. Todd. Indianapolis: Liberty Fund, 1981.
Smith, David Dillon. "Gibbon in Church." *Journal of Ecclesiastical History* 35, no. 3 (1984): 452–63.
Smithers, Peter. *The Life of Joseph Addison*. Oxford: Clarendon, 1968 [1954].
Smollett, Tobias. *Travels through France and Italy*. Oxford: Oxford University Press, 1919 [1766].
Spacks, Patricia Meyer. *Imagining a Self: Autobiography and Novel in Eighteenth-Century England*. Cambridge, MA: Harvard University Press, 1976.
Spinoza, Baruch. *Tractatus Theologico-Politicus*. Edited by Jonathan Israel. Cambridge: Cambridge University Press, 2007.
Stephen, Leslie. *History of English Thought in the Eighteenth Century*. 3rd ed. 2 vols. London: John Murray, 1902 [1876].
Sterne, Laurence. *The Florida Edition of the Works of Laurence Sterne*. Edited by Melvyn New. 8 vols. Gainesville: University Press of Florida, 1978–2008.
———. *A Sentimental Journey Through France and Italy*. In *A Sentimental Journey and Other Writings*, edited by Ian Jack and Tim Parnell, 3–104. Oxford: Oxford University Press, 2003 [1768].
Stuart-Buttle, Tim. "Gibbon and Enlightenment History." In O'Brien and Young, *Cambridge Companion*, 110–27.
[Suard], Jean-Baptiste. "Article III. *Essai sur l'étude de la littérature. Dernier Extrait.*" *Journal étranger* (October 1761): 65–85.
———. "Article VIII. *Essai sur l'étude de la littérature. A Londres, chez T. Becket & P. A. de Hondt, 1761.*" *Journal étranger* (August 1761): 175–88.
———. "Article VIII. *Essai sur l'étude de la littérature. Second Extrait.*" *Journal étranger* (September 1761): 201–17.
Suetonius. *Lives of the Caesars*. Translated by J. C. Rolfe. 2 vols. Loeb Classical Library 31 and 38. Cambridge, MA: Harvard University Press, 1997.
Swain, Joseph Ward. *Edward Gibbon the Historian*. London: Macmillan, 1966.
Swain, Simon. "Character Change in Plutarch." *Phoenix* 43, no. 1 (1989): 63–68.
Sweet, Rosemary. *Cities and the Grand Tour: The British in Italy, c. 1690–1820*. Cambridge: Cambridge University Press, 2012.
Syme, Ronald. *Tacitus*. Oxford: Clarendon Press, 1958.
Tacitus. *Annals*. Translated by John Jackson. 3 vols. Loeb Classical Library 249, 312, 322. Cambridge, MA: Harvard University Press, 1937.
———. *Germania*. In *Agricola. Germania. Dialogue on Oratory*, 119–218. 1:128–215. Translated by M. Hutton. Loeb Classical Library 35. Cambridge, MA: Harvard University Press, 1963.
———. *Histories*. Translated by Clifford H. Moore. 2 vols. Loeb Classical Library 111 and 249. Cambridge, MA: Harvard University Press, 1925–31.
Taylor, Charles. *A Secular Age*. Cambridge, MA: Belknap Press of Harvard University Press, 2007.
Teissier-Ensminger, Anne. Introduction to *La Vie de Jacques-Auguste de Thou*, by Jacques-Auguste de Thou. Translated by Anne Teissier-Ensminger. Paris: Honoré Champion Éditeur, 2007 .

Teresa of Ávila. *The Life of Teresa of Jesus.* Translated by E. Allison Peers. London: Sheed and Ward, 1950.

Tertullian. *De Spectaculis.* Translated by T. R. Glover. In *Apology: De Spectaculis. Minucius Felix: Octavius*, 230–301. Loeb Classical Library 250. Cambridge, MA: Harvard University Press, 1931.

Trevor-Roper, H. R. "Edward Gibbon after Two Hundred Years." *Listener* 72 (1964): 617–19, 657–59.

———. "Historiography I: The Other Gibbon." *American Scholar* 46, no. 1 (1977): 94–103.

———. *History and the Enlightenment.* New Haven: Yale University Press, 2010.

Turnbull, Paul. "'Buffeted for Ancestral Sins': Some Neglected Aspects of Gibbon's Roman Conversion." *Eighteenth Century Life* 11, no. 1 (1987): 18–35.

———. "Gibbon's Exchange with Joseph Priestly." *British Journal for Eighteenth-Century Studies* 14, no. 2 (1991): 139–58.

———. "Une Marionette Infidèle: The Fashioning of Edward Gibbon's Reputation as the English Voltaire." In Womersley, *Edward Gibbon*, 279–307.

———. "The 'Supposed Infidelity' of Edward Gibbon." *Historical Journal* 25, no. 1 (1982): 23–41.

Voltaire. *The Complete Works of Voltaire.* Edited by Theodore Besterman. 142 vols. Geneva: Institut et Musée Voltaire, 1968–.

Voragine, Jacobus de. *The Golden Legend: Readings on the Saints.* Translated by William Granger Ryan. Princeton: Princeton University Press, 2012 [1993].

Wallace, David Duncan. *The Life of Henry Laurens.* New York: G. P. Putnam's Sons, 1915.

Walpole, Horace. *The Letters of Horace Walpole, Fourth Earl of Oxford.* Edited by Paget Toynbee. 16 vols. Oxford: Clarendon Press, 1903–5.

Watson, Richard. "An Apology for Christianity, in a Series of Letters, Addressed to Edward Gibbon." In Womersley, *Religious Scepticism*, 44–115.

Wesley, John. *The Journal of the Rev. John Wesley, A.M.* Edited by Nehemiah Curnock. 9 vols. London: The Epworth Press, 1909.

Whitaker, Thomas D. *Gibbon's History of the Decline and Fall of the Roman Empire [...] reviewed.* London: John Murray, 1791.

———. "Review of *The Miscellaneous Works of Edward Gibbon* [...]." *Quarterly Review* 12 (January 1815): 368–91.

Wilson, Mona. "How It Began." In *Grand Tour: A Journey in the Tracks of Aristocracy*, edited by R. S. Lambert, 17–33. New York: E. P. Dutton, 1937.

Womersley, David, ed. *Edward Gibbon: Bicentenary Essays.* Oxford: Voltaire Foundation, 1997.

———. "From Polybianism to Perfectibilism: Gibbon and the Chevalier de Chastellux." *British Journal for Eighteenth-Century Studies* 13 (1990): 47–58.

———. *Gibbon and the 'Watchmen of the Holy City': The Historian and His Reputation, 1776–1815.* Oxford: Clarendon Press, 2002.

———. "Gibbon's Apostasy." *British Journal for Eighteenth-Century Studies* 11, no. 1 (1988): 51–70.

———. "Gibbon's Religious Characters." In *History, Religion, and Culture: British Intellectual History, 1750–1950*, edited by S. Collini, R. Whatmore, and B. Young, 69–88. Cambridge: Cambridge University Press, 2000.

———. "The Historical Writings of William Robertson." *Journal of the History of Ideas* 47, no. 3 (1986): 497–506.

———. Introduction to *Religious Scepticism: Contemporary Responses to Gibbon*, by David Womersley, vii–xxiii. Bristol: Thoemmes Press, 1997.

———. Introduction to *The History of the Decline and Fall of the Roman Empire*, by Edward Gibbon, 1:xi–cvi. 3 vols. London: Allen Lane, 1994.

———, ed. *Religious Scepticism: Contemporary Responses to Gibbon.* Bristol: Thoemmes Press, 1997.

———. *The Transformation of "The Decline and Fall of the Roman Empire."* Cambridge: Cambridge University Press, 1988.

Wood, Anthony. *Athenae Oxonienses: an exact history of all the writers and bishops who have had their education in the University of Oxford: to which are added the Fasti, or Annals of the said University*. Edited by Phillip Bliss. 5 vols. London, 1813–20 [1691–92].

Wootton, David. "Gibbon, Irony, and Faith in Gibbon's *Decline and Fall*." In Womersley, *Edward Gibbon*, 203–34.

Woudhuysen, George. "Gibbon among the Barbarians." In O'Brien and Young, *Cambridge Companion*, 93–109.

Wrigley, Edward A., and Roger Schofield. *The Population History of England, 1541–1871: A Reconstruction*. Cambridge, MA: Harvard University Press, 1981.

Young, Arthur. *The Autobiography of Arthur Young*. Edited by M. Betham-Edwards. London: Smith, Elder, 1898.

Young, B. W. "Gibbon and Catholicism." In O'Brien and Young, *Cambridge Companion*, 147–66.

———. "'Scepticism in Excess': Gibbon and Eighteenth-Century Christianity." *Historical Journal* 41, no. 1 (1998): 179–99.

Ziegler, Robert J. "Edward Gibbon and Julian the Apostate." *Papers on Language and Literature* 10, no. 2 (Spring 1974): 136–49.

Zimmerman, Doron. *The Jacobite Movement in Scotland and in Exile, 1746–1759*. New York. Palgrave Macmillan, 2003.

INDEX